EMERGING AFRICA
Potential and Challenges

ABOUT THE AUTHOR

Dr. Reji D. Nair is Asst. Professor in the Department of Economics, Arba Minch University, Ethiopia. He was formerly with the Kerala State Planning Board, Thiruvananthapuram and a member (2000-02) of the Natural Disaster Management Faculty constituted by Government of India in Kerala (Institute of Land Management, Thiruvananthapuram). Dr. Reji started his career as lecturer in the Sree Sankracharya University of Sanskrit, Kerala. He has published more than 50 research papers and articles in the field of economics, environment and development issues in both the national and international journals. His other major publications include *'Natural Resources Management and Agrarian Development,' 'Environmental Conservation in Twenty First Century'* (Malayalam), and *'Land Economics: Issues in Land Use'*, which got Dr. B.R. Ambedkar National Fellowship Award (2006) of the Bharathiya Dalit Sahitya Academy, New Delhi. Dr. Reji is member of several international and national professional organizations including the International Society for Ecological Economics (USA) and Rift Valley Environment Society (Ethiopia). Dr. Reji is reputed science fiction writer in Malayalam.

Email: rejidnair2000@rediffmail.com

EMERGING AFRICA
Potential and Challenges
Africa in the New Millennium

Dr. Reji D. Nair

CONCEPT PUBLISHING COMPANY, NEW DELHI-110059

Cataloging in Publication Data--DK
Courtesy: D.K. Agencies (P) Ltd. <docinfo@dkagencies.com>

Nair, Reji D.
Emerging Africa : potential and challenges : Africa in the new millennium / Reji D. Nair.
p. cm.
Includes bibliographical references (p.).
Includes index.
ISBN 13: 9788180695971
ISBN 10: 8180695972

1. Economic development--Africa. 2. Africa--Economic policy. 3. Agriculture--Economic aspects--Africa. 4. Food supply--Africa. 5. Sustainable development--Africa. 6. Africa--Social policy. I. Title.

DDC 338.96 22

ISBN: 13-978-81-8069-597-1
ISBN: 10-81-8069-597-2

First Published 2009

Published and Printed by
Ashok Kumar Mittal
Concept Publishing Company
A/15-16, Commercial Block, Mohan Garden
New Delhi-110059 (INDIA)
Phone : 25351460, 25351794
Fax : 091-11-25357109
Email : publishing@conceptpub.com

Preface

Sub-Saharan Africa (Africa) enters the 21st Century with many of the world's poorest countries; in many of these countries the average income per capita is lower than at the end of the 1960s. Incomes, assets, and access to essential services are unequally distributed and the region contains a growing share of the world's absolute poor, who have little power to influence the allocation of resources. Moreover, many development problems have become largely confined to Africa. They include lagging primary school enrollments, high child mortality, and endemic diseases—including malaria and HIV/AIDS—that impose costs on Africa at least twice those in any other developing region. One African in five lives in countries severely disrupted by conflict. Making matters worse, Africa's place in the global economy has been eroded, with declining export shares in traditional primary products, little diversification into new lines of business, and massive capital flight and loss of skills to other regions. Now the region stands in danger of being excluded from the information revolution.

Many countries have made important economic reforms, improving macroeconomic management, liberalizing markets and trade, and widening the space for private sector activity. Even as parts of the region are making headlines with wars and natural disasters, other parts are making headway with rising interest from domestic and foreign businesses and higher investment. But the response has not been sufficient to overcome years of falling income or to reverse other adverse legacies from the long period of economic decline—including deteriorated capacity, weakened institutions, and inadequate infrastructure. Major changes are needed if Africans—and their children—are to claim the 21st century. With the region's rapidly growing population, 5 per cent annual growth is needed simply to keep the number of poor from rising. Halving severe poverty by

2015 will require annual growth of more than 7 per cent, along with a more equitable distribution of income. Moreover, Africa will not be able to sustain rapid growth without investing in its people. Many lack the health, education, and access to inputs needed to contribute to—and benefit from—high growth. Women are one of Africa's hidden growth reserves, providing most of the region's labour, but their productivity is hampered by widespread inequality in education and access. Thus gender equality can be a potent force for accelerated poverty reduction. And HIV/AIDS looms as a new menace, threatening to cut life expectancy by 20 years and undermine savings, growth, and the social fabric in many countries.

Africa thus faces an immense, multifaceted development challenge. But the new Millennium offers a window of opportunity to reverse the marginalization of Africa's people—and of Africa's Governments, relative to donors, in the development agenda. Improving governance and resolving conflict is perhaps the most basic requirement for faster development. Widespread civil conflicts impose enormous costs, including on neighbouring countries. Africa's conflicts are driven by poverty, underdevelopment, and lack of economic diversification, as well as by political systems that marginalize large parts of the population. But conflicts perpetuate poverty, creating a vicious circle that can be reversed only through special development efforts—including long-run peace building and political reforms.

Investing in people is also essential for accelerated poverty reduction. Many countries are caught in a trap of high fertility and mortality, low education (especially of women—less than one-quarter of poor rural girls attend primary school), high dependency ratios, and low savings. In addition, greater political commitment is urgently needed to fight HIV/AIDS. Increasing competitiveness and diversifying economies must be a third area of focus if Africa is to claim the new Millennium. Job creation is slow not because of labour market rigidities (though there are exceptions) but because of the high perceived risks and costs of doing business in Africa. These need to be lowered by locking in reforms and delivering business services more efficiently—with less corruption, better infrastructure and financial services, and increased access to the information economy. Africa trails the world on every dimension of these essentials. Lowering these barriers requires new approaches, including more participation by the private sector and by local communities, a more regional approach to overcome the problems posed by small African economies, and a Central Government shift to regulating and facilitating services rather than providing them.

Though Africa's agriculture has responded to limited reforms, it remains backward and undercapitalized, the result of centuries of extractive policies. Recapitalizing the sector will require maintaining and improving price incentives, channeling more public spending and foreign aid to rural communities (including for local infrastructure), and tapping into the savings potential of farmers. These changes are also needed to create incentives to reverse severe environmental degradation. Public-private partnerships can make a contribution, including in agricultural research and extension, where a regional approach would also help. And wider access to Western markets for agricultural products would make a big difference ' at some $300 billion, subsidies to OECD agriculture are equal to Africa's GDP. Since the late 1960s Africa's loss of world trade has cost it almost $70 billion a year, reflecting a failure to diversify into new, dynamic products as well as a falling market share for traditional goods. Africa's trade reforms have mostly been negotiated with donors as part of adjustment programmes. Reforms still need to be embedded in a development strategy that is export-oriented, anchored on competitive and stable real exchange rates, and enables exporters to access imported inputs at world prices.

Reducing aid dependence and strengthening partnerships will have to be a fourth component of Africa's development strategy. Africa is the world's most aid-dependent and indebted region. Concessional assistance is essential if Africa is to grow rapidly while also increasing consumption to reduce poverty. Excluding private inflows, the savings gap for a typical country is about 17 per cent of GDP, and other regions show that private flows cannot be sustained at more than 5 per cent of GDP without risk of crisis. But aid, particularly when delivered in a weak institutional environment by large numbers of donors with fragmented projects and requirements, can weaken institutional capacity and undermine accountability.

The present book reviews the potential of Africa and the major challenges facing the continent while entering the New Millennium.

African nations dominate the lower reaches of the UN Human Development Index. Infant mortality is high, while life expectancy, literacy, and education are all low. The UN also lowers the ranking of African States because the continent sees greater inequality than any other region. Catastrophes caused deadly periods of great shortages. The most damaging are the famines that have regularly hit the continent, especially the Horn of Africa. These have been caused by disruptions due to warfare, years of drought, and plagues of locusts. Most African States saw inflation of around 10 per cent per year. The first chapter in this book analyses the nature and determinants of underdevelopment in Africa. It also reviews the impact of globalization including the debt crisis on the continent and major challenges of economic growth.

The second chapter reviews the major bottlenecks of the African agriculture in attaining a sustainable level of growth based on the on-farm activities. The economic and food problems characterizing underdevelopment in the continent is a product of both internal and external factors; which aggravated since the latter half of the twentieth century. The reflections of Policy Reform Agenda prescribed by the international agencies are also part of the discussion. Key influences on farm production and the need for mechanization in small-holder agriculture are all part of enquiry in this chapter.

Food security in Africa has substantially worsened since 1970. Although recent data show that the proportion of malnourished individuals in Sub-Saharan Africa fell slightly from 35 per cent in 1990-92 to 33 per cent in 1999-2001, a long-term perspective reveals that this share has remained within the 33-35 per cent range since around 1970. Even more discouraging, the absolute number of malnourished people in Africa has increased substantially with population growth, from around 88 million in 1970 to an estimate of over 200 million in 1999-2001 (FAO, 2004). This record is in stark contrast to that of other developing regions such as South and East Asia, which have made significant strides in combating malnutrition over the same time frame. The third chapter analyses the food security challenges in Africa with emphasis on required interventions. It also reviews the worsening food security situation in Africa and also makes forecasting based on important scenarios.

The fourth chapter reviews the prehistoric origins of agriculture as part of human civilizations with emphasis on Africa. The vast majority of human history was as hunter-gatherers; which extends back more than 4 million years. At the end of the Pleistocene some human groups began to produce food rather than collect it and to domesticate wild plants and animals. The most remarkable transition of our entire prehistory is almost simultaneous appearance of domesticated plants and animals in several parts of the world between 10,000 and 5,000 years ago.

In recent years, rainwater harvesting has been acquiring a higher social acceptance world-wide. Its main domestic form, roof-water harvesting (DRWH), has been aided by the rapid growth in the use of hard roofing (usually corrugated iron sheeting) in areas formerly dependent on grass-roofing. DRWH has thereby become feasible in most of Sub-Saharan Africa. It is a technique with the great attraction of delivering water to the very door of the user's house. The objective of fifth chapter was to evaluate the potential of rainwater harvesting, which currently provides less than 2 per cent of household water needs in Eastern Africa because it is largely restricted to expensive forms. The purpose of the chapter is to assess the feasibility of VLC DRWH, examining its performance and its affordability by the bulk of rural households.

Nech Sar National Park (NSNP) is one of the eight national parks in Ethiopia covering an area of 514 sq. kms. and is situated in one of the most scenic parts of the Ethiopian Rift valley; locating around 500 km south of the Ethiopian capital Addis Ababa. With the objective of insuring economic viability, African Parks (APs), a Company to protect the bio-diversity through community participation, took over the management of the Park for a specified period. APs envisioned NSNP to be one of the finest and most productive protected areas in Ethiopia that it delivers and demonstrates bio-diversity conservation and sustainable natural resources management for the benefit of the neighbouring communities. One of the most important objectives is the betterment of the socio-economic conditions of communities in and adjacent to the Park. Chapter six analyses the sustainability of NSNP through private participation on the one hand and environmental conservation and eco-tourism promotion on the other hand.

A number of commentators, journalists and analysts have recently focused on competition for natural resources, increasingly scarce due to global warming, as the trigger of the conflict in Western Sudan. The deadly carnage in Darfur, Sudan, which is almost always discussed in political and military terms, has roots in an ecological crisis directly arising from climate shocks. As the UN Secretary-General Ban Ki-moon remarked, "Amid the diverse social and political causes, the Darfur conflict began as an ecological crisis, arising at least in part from climate change". The UN Environment Programme (UNEP) Report says competition over oil, gas, water, timber and land use are behind the "instigation and perpetuation" of decades of fighting throughout Sudan. With more than five million internally displaced and international refugees, Sudan has the largest refugee population in the world today. There is the spread of deserts by an average of 100 km in the last 40 years, a loss of almost 12 per cent of forest cover in 15 years and overgrazing of fragile soil. Ignoring these environmental issues will ensure that some political and social problems remain unsolvable and even likely to worsen, as environmental degradation mounts at the same time as population increases. The seventh chapter reviews the environmental factors underlying the crisis in Sudan and also assesses the economic forces and vicious circles including poverty.

The global employment situation has not improved much in the beginning of the New Millennium despite a pick-up in economic growth world-wide. Unemployment grew slightly despite a world-wide growth in GDP of 3.2 per cent and a slight increase in trade from 2.5 per cent in 2002 to 3.0 per cent in 2003. Sub-Saharan Africa has slightly reduced its unemployment rate but not enough to improve its high incidence of working poverty. In addition, the region has to face the enormous pressure that the HIV/AIDS pandemic is placing on labour markets. This, together with the continuing 'brain-drain' is depriving the region of much needed human capital, making it unlikely to reach the Millennium Development Goals. The eighth chapter analyzes the trends, problems and prospects of employment situation in the Sub-Saharan region; which is trying for a take off in the New Millennium.

Decentralization is an instrument to give opportunities for people at the local level to be involved in determining their economic and political choices. Decentralization is directly and indirectly associated with many aspects of good governance, including consensual decision making, equity, representation, accountability and responsiveness of public institutions to community concerns. Countries world-wide have embraced the policy of decentralization as a means of advancing participatory development and governance. Democratic African countries are also not an exception in this political process at least at the national level. The ninth chapter reviews the decentralization process in the East African country of Ethiopia, and analyses the nature of self-rule and decision-making power of local government institutions.

Sub-Saharan Africa has been worst affected by the global AIDS epidemic and has caused vast amounts of human suffering. Nearly two-thirds of all HIV positive people live in this area, although it contains little more than 10 per cent of the world's population. The most obvious effect of this crisis has been illness and death, but the impact of the epidemic has certainly not been confined to the health sector; households, education, workplaces and economies have been significantly affected, along with other sections of society. During 2005 alone, an estimated 2 million adults and children died as a result of AIDS in Sub-Saharan Africa. Since the beginning of the epidemic more than 15 million Africans have died from AIDS. The tenth chapter discusses the social and economic impacts of the HIV/AIDS in Africa. It also gives special attention to the impacts on the health sector, education, labour force and also review the required interventions.

The eleventh chapter analyses the status, causes and consequences of mounting inflation in Zimbabwe. It also reviews the long-term impact of globalization and the structural adjustment programmes, including the land reforms on the socio-economic institutions. For untold numbers of Zimbabweans, toilet paper and bread, margarine, meat, even the once ubiquitous morning cup of tea had become unimaginable luxuries. Zimbabwe has been tormented this entire decade by both deep recession and high inflation, and in recent months the economy seems to have abandoned whatever moorings it had left. The national budgets are insufficient and Government services have crumbled.

Ethiopia is characterized by efforts of the Government to establish structural stability as per the Constitution of 1994 and the general principle of good governance; the legal and constitutional framework provides a federal system with democratic and decentralized decision making. However, the political and administrative culture is rooted and influenced by periods of strong centralization in feudalistic and socialistic system. New norms of cooperation and development of effective coordination platform at the interfaces between all levels (from national to local, state and civil society) have to be developed. Important success emerged in the form of inclusion of non-governmental or no party actors in political decision-making processes; unique dialogue between the Government and civil society. The Oromo Self-Help Organization is a non-profit, non-political, and non-religious humanitarian organization with the aim of contributing to relief, rehabilitation and development of Oromia Region in Ethiopia. It was implementing projects with different funding sources since 2003 in the field of integrated food security and rural infrastructure. The objective of twelfth chapter is to address and to analyze the socio-economic results of OSHO's Development Oriented Emergency Food Aid Project in the field of food security and to know its effectiveness in rural development in Ziway Dugda Woreda (Panchayat).

Last chapter is a quest for a Sub-Saharan African Model of development. The quest for an indigenous model of development in Africa should start from the historical influences during the colonial period. Western influence during the colonial period was concentrated in those areas brought into the international economy by Europeans. In ports and mineral or export crop areas European political, economic, social or cultural practices were dominant. Post-independence Africa under African, albeit often Westernized, leaders continued the spread of Western practices usually to the detriment of indigenous ways. The post-independence African elite attempted to protect Africa from the West in the Group of 77, NAM and OAU. Much of traditional African political, economics, culture and society have withstood the Western onslaught. African practices managed to survive by blocking out or else adapting to Western institutions. Many African countries have taken Western institutions and altered them to fit the African context.

The overall objective of this book is to give a broad understanding of African economies and its potentials in a competitive world. At the same time it will give special attention to the challenges facing the continent. In writing this book I got a lot of advice and assistance from many of my friends, colleagues and teachers; without their help I could not have completed this work. I wish to express my deep sense of gratitude to Dr. Radharamanan Pillai, Professor, Department of English Education, Arba Minch University, Ethiopia and Prof. Sivadasan Kottai, Associate Professor, Department of Electrical Engineering, Yanbu Industrial College, Saudi Arabia for their solid advices. I owe a deep sense of gratitude to all my colleagues in the Economics Department, Arba Minch University, especially Mr. Asrath Haile, Former Vice-Dean, Faculty of Business and Economics, Mr. Kumsa Dadene, Head, Department of Business and Education and Mr. Tesfay Falaha, Head, Department of Economics for their constant encouragement and co-operation. No less is the gratitude which owe to all my family members, without their visible and invisible support I could not have completed the present work.

I dedicate this book to the millions of Africans who are suffering due to poverty, health hazards such as HIV/AIDS and malaria, and various socio-political conflicts including the ethnic clashes.

Dr. Reji D. Nair

Contents

Preface v

List of Tables xxi

List of Figures and Boxes xxiii

1. Africa in the New Millennium: Potential and Challenges 1

1.1 Introduction 1

1.2 Economic Development in Africa: Regional Variation 2

1.3 Determinants of Underdevelopment in Africa 5

1.4 Historical Background of Development in Africa 11

1.5 Human Development Paradigm 12

1.6 Globalization and its Implications 15

1.7 Foreign Debt and the Crisis of African Economies 18

1.8 Challenges for Africa's Development 20

1.9 Attempts at Promoting Growth 23

1.10 Conclusion 25

2. African Agriculture in the New Millennium: Lessons from the Twentieth Century 31

2.1 Introduction 31

2.2 Africa's Economic and Food Problems 32

2.3 The Policy Reform Agenda 34

2.4 External Determinants of Africa's Agrarian Crisis 36

2.5 Nature of Farm Production and Key Influences 38

2.6 Mechanization and Small-holder Agriculture 39

2.7 Conclusion 41

3. Food Security in Africa: Challenges and Interventions 45

3.1 Introduction 45

3.2 Entitlements Approach to Food Security 46

3.3 Worsening Food Security in Africa 48
3.4 Three Scenarios for the Future: Business as Usual, Pessimistic and Vision 54
3.5 Challenges to Food Security in Africa 58
3.6 Food Security Interventions 62
3.7 Conclusion 65

4. Origins of Agriculture and African Roots: An Enquiry in the Prehistoric World 69

4.1 Introduction 69
4.2 Archaeological Perceptions 69
4.3 Mastering the Environment and Domestication 70
4.4 Primary Centres of Domestication 72
4.5 Theories Regarding Origins of Agriculture 74
4.6 Evidences 77
4.7 Origin of Agriculture: The African Roots 78
4.8 Spread of Agriculture 82
4.9 Success and Consequence of Food Production 82
4.10 Conclusion 84

5. Relevance of Rainwater Harvesting in Eastern Africa: A Case Study 88

5.1 Introduction 88
5.2 The VLC DRWH Technology 90
5.3 Water Needs in the Region and the Possible Contribution of VLC DRWH 92
5.4 Economics of DRWH 96
5.5 Theory of Combining RWH with Other Water Sources 100
5.6 Domestic Water Storage Facility 101
5.7 Regional Experience of Promoting DRWH 106
5.8 Conclusion 108

6. Sustainable Development of Rift Valley Bio-diversity: A Case of Nech Sar National Park in Ethiopia 111

6.1 Introduction 111
6.2 Bio-diversity 112
6.3 Local Community 113
6.4 Sustainable Development of the NSNP 113
6.5 Conclusion 115

7. Environmental Refugees: Lessons from the Horn of Africa: A Case of Sudan **117**

7.1 Introduction 117
7.2 Global Scenario 119
7.3 Sudan: A Victim of Environmental Destruction 120
7.4 Causes of the Present Crisis 123
7.5 Poverty Dimensions 126
7.6 Agrarian Structure and Poverty 128
7.7 Concerns for Environmental Security 129
7.8 Environmental Refugees and International Migration 130
7.9 Policy Actions 131
7.10 Conclusion 134

8. Employment Potential of Sub-Saharan Africa in the New Millennium: Problems and Prospects **138**

8.1 Introduction 138
8.2 Global Employment Scenario 139
8.3 Employment Scenario in Sub-Saharan Africa 141
8.4 Economic Performance 143
8.5 Reflection of Economic Performance on the Labour Market 145
8.6 Conclusion 148

9. Decentralized Governance in an African Federal System: Regionalization in Ethiopia **151**

9.1 Introduction 151
9.2 Nature of Decentralization 151
9.3 Organizational Structure 152
9.4 Features of Decentralization 153
9.5 Woreda Level Governance 155
9.6 Kebelewotch at the Grassroots Level Governance 156
9.7 Conclusion 156

10. Socio-Economic Impacts of HIV/AIDS Menace in Africa **162**

10.1 Introduction 162
10.2 Impact on the Health Sector 162
10.3 Social Impacts 164
10.4 Impact on the Education Sector 166

10.5 Impact on the Labour Force 168
10.6 Economic Impacts 169
10.7 Interventions 171
10.8 Conclusion 173

11. Zimbabwe's Mounting Inflation: A New History in the Economic Theory of Inflation 176

11.1 Introduction 176
11.2 Political Economy of the Zimbabwean Crisis 177
11.3 Socio-Economic Crisis 180
11.4 Road to the Crisis 183
11.5 Globalization and the Zimbabwean Crisis 185
11.6 Mounting Inflation 189
11.7 Anti-Inflation Campaigns: Chaos to Economy 191
11.8. Conclusion 192

12. Role of NGOs in Rural Development in Africa: A Case of Oromo Self-Help Organization (OSHO) in Ethiopia 196

12.1 Introduction 196
12.2 Role of NGOs in Ethiopia 197
12.3 Background of the Development Oriented Emergency Food Aid Project 199
12.4 Project Site and the Target Groups 200
12.5 Development Oriented Emergency Food Aid Project 202
12.6 Result-Based Monitoring and Evaluation 203
12.7 Applying RBME in Development Oriented Emergency Food Aid Project 206
12.8 Conclusion 209
Appendix 211

13. Non-Western Ideologies of Economic Development: Quest for an Indigenous Sub-Saharan African Model 213

13.1 Introduction 213
13.2 Space for Non-Western Models of Economic Development 214
13.3 Modernization Theory *Vs* Dependency Theory: A Non-Western View 215
13.4 Influence of the West in Africa 220

13.5 Africa's Rediscovery of its Traditions and Resistance to the West 222
13.6 Quest for a Sub-Saharan African Development Model 225
13.7 Conclusion 228

Bibliography 231

Index 245

List of Tables

1.1	Economic Indicators of Africa, 2003	13
3.1	Cereal Demand and Production in Africa	51
3.2	Projected Meat Demand and Production in Africa	52
3.3	Projected Per Capita Kilocalories Available in Africa under the Business as Usual Scenario	55
3.4	Projected Crop Production Growth Rates in Africa under the Business as Usual Scenario	56
3.5	Cereal Area, Production, and Yield in Africa (BAU)	57
5.1	Use of Different Water Sources in Mbarara District (Rwanda Nat Census, 2001)	93
5.2	Distribution of Roofing Types in Mbarara District (Rwanda Nat Census, 2001)	93
5.3	Analysis of Water Collection Distances/Times	94
5.4	Analysis of Survey Data	95
8.1	Unemployment in the World, 1993 and 2003 (Millions)	139
8.2	Regional Economic Growth in the New Millennium, 2000-03	141
8.3	Labour Market and Economic Indicators in Sub-Saharan Africa, 1993 and 2003	142
8.4	Youth Unemployment Rates in Sub-Saharan Africa, 1997–2003	143
9.1	Details of Regional State Governments and Autonomous Administrative Areas, 1998-99	153
9.2	Revenue Sharing between Federal and Regional State Governments in Ethiopia	154
11.1	Important Economic Indicators of Zimbabwe	182
11.2	Devaluation of Currency in Zimbabwe	184
11.3	Prices of Important Grocery Commodities in Zimbabwe	190

12.1 Infrastructure Created through FFW and CFW by OSHO 207
12.2 Micro Financing and Credit Provision by OSHO 208
12.3 Training and Capacity-Building 209
12.A.1 Projects/programmes implemented by OSHO in Ziway Dugda 211

List of Figures and Boxes

Figures

1.1	GDP Per Capita (US$)	3
1.2	Africa's Vulnerability to Climate Change	16
3.1	A Simplified Food System	47
3.2	Food Insecure Population in Africa	49
3.3	Cereal Demand and Production in Africa (MMT)	51
4.1	Appearance of Domesticated Plants and Animals in the Prehistoric Era	73
4.2	Population *Versus* Subsistence Strategies in the Prehistoric World	83
5.1	'Diminishing Returns' Output *Vs* Cost Curve	91
5.2	Value of Water	97
5.3	Cost Per Litre	101
8.1	Annual Growth Rate of Unemployment in the World (%)	140
8.2	SSA's Economic and Employment Scenario, 2003	144
8.3	Unemployment Trend: SSA *Vs* World	146
9.A.1	Organizational Structure of Decentralized Governance in Ethiopia: Federal Level	159
9.A.2	Grassroots Level Governance	160
9.A.3	Structure of Regional Level Government	161
13.1	Modernization Process (Modernization: I)	216
13.2	Dependency Argument	217
13.3	Modernization Process-II (Since 1987-88)	219
13.4	Colonial Influence in Africa	223
13.5	A SSA Development Model	226

Boxes

3.1	Declaration of the Abuja Food Security Summit (December 4-7, 2006, Abuja, Nigcria)	53
5.1	Children and Water Collection	90
5.2	Sickness and Water Collection	98
5.3	Rainwater and Water Security	103
7.1	Sudan Floods: A Show Case for Environmental Destruction	122
11.1	Witnesses of Mounting Inflation in Zimbabwe	179

1

Africa in the New Millennium

Potential and Challenges

1.1 INTRODUCTION

Africa's economic malaise is self-perpetuating, as it engenders more of the disease, warfare, misgovernance, and corruption that created it in the first place. Other effects of poverty have similar consequences. The most direct consequence of low GDP is Africa's low standard of living and quality of life. African nations dominate the lower reaches of the UN Human Development Index. Infant mortality is high, while life expectancy, literacy, and education are all low. The UN also lowers the ranking of African states because the continent sees greater inequality than any other region. Catastrophes caused deadly periods of great shortages. The most damaging are the famines that have regularly hit the continent, especially the Horn of Africa. These have been caused by disruptions due to warfare, years of drought, and plagues of locusts. Most African states saw inflation of around 10 per cent per year.

There are no reliable numbers for unemployment in most African nations, but it is an important problem. Environmental degradation occurs on many fronts. Farmers on the verge of starvation are unlikely to be concerned about the fate of the rainforest in their pursuit of new land, and starving people do not often consider the rarity of an animal before eating it. Along the length of the Sahel, deforestation and overgrazing has caused increased desertification as the Sahara spreads south.

Agricultural development is crucial to Africa's sustainable development. It is the sector that employs most of Africa's people and upon which the continent depends for food security. According to the World Trade Organization, rich countries now spend up to $1 billion per day subsidizing their agricultural sectors. Because of these subsidies, African producers find it very difficult to compete with rich country agribusinesses, whose production costs are much lower. The UN estimates that the total cost to poor countries of such trade barriers is more than $100 billion per year (1999). Trade liberalization may have increased the importance of international trade for Africa, but it has also increased the continent's marginalization in the global economy. Over the last decade, while world trade has expanded by 85 per cent, Sub-Saharan Africa's trade has only grown by 38 per cent (Chossudovsky, 1997). Africa's share of total world trade has declined to less than half of what it was in 1980, and now rests at only 1 per cent. African countries remain over-dependent on primary commodities and are extremely vulnerable to swings in market prices.

The present chapter analyses the nature and determinants of underdevelopment in Africa. It also reviews the impact of globalization including the debt crisis on the continent and major challenges of economic growth.

1.2 ECONOMIC DEVELOPMENT IN AFRICA: REGIONAL VARIATION

The temperate northern and southern ends of the continent are wealthier than tropical Sub-Saharan Africa (See, Figure 1.1). Within the tropics, East Africa, with its long pre-colonial history of trade and development, has tended to be wealthier and more stable than elsewhere. Island nations such as the Seychelles, Cape Verde, and Mauritius, have remained wealthier than the continental nations, although the unstable Comoros remain poor. Arab North Africa has long been closely linked to the economies of Europe and the Middle East. South Africa is by far the continent's wealthiest state, both in GDP per capita and in total GDP, and its neighbours have shared in this wealth. The small but oil-rich such as Gabon and Equatorial Guinea round out the list of the ten wealthiest states in Africa.

The poorest states are those engaged in or just emerging from civil wars. These include the Democratic Republic of the Congo, Sierra Leone, Burundi, and Somalia. In recent times the poorest region has been the Horn of Africa, although it had historically been one of the wealthiest regions of Sub-Saharan Africa (Kayizzi Mugerwa, 1999). Ethiopia in particular had a long and successful history. The current poverty of the region, and the associated famines and wars, have been a problem for decades. There is considerable internal variation within countries. Urban areas, especially capital cities, are generally wealthier than rural zones.

Figure 1.1: GDP Per Capita (US$)

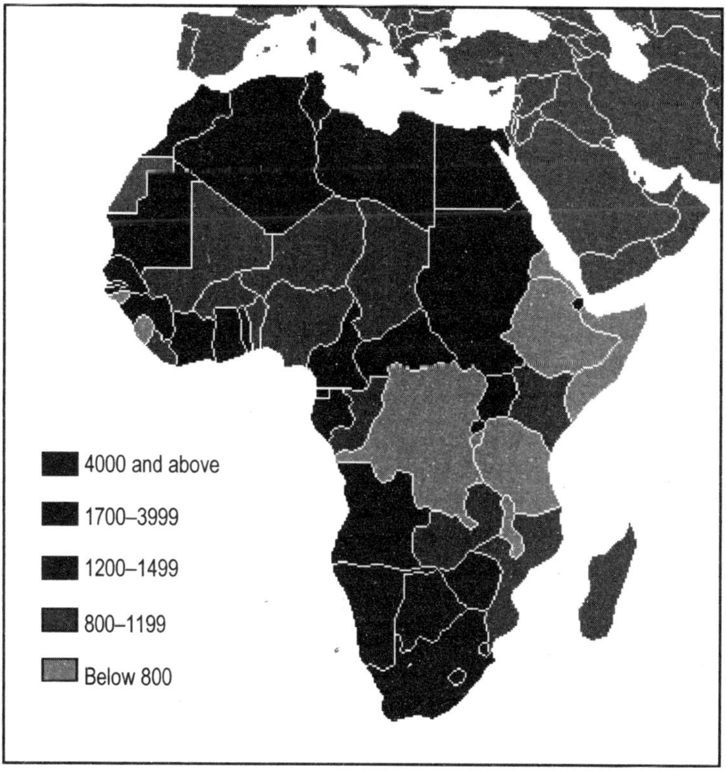

Note: National GDP per capita ranges from wealthier states in the north and south to poorer states in the east.

Development of different sectors shows that some regions are well endowed with natural resources including climate and are able to gain comfortable growths, whereas the regions which are facing drought and famines are not lucky enough to have the same level of progress.

(i) Agriculture

Around sixty per cent of African workers are employed in the agricultural sector with about three-fifths of African farmers being subsistence farmers. Subsistence farms provide a source of food and a relatively small income for the family, but generally fail to produce enough to make re-investment possible. Larger farms tend to grow cash crops such as coffee, cotton, cocoa, and rubber. These farms, normally operated by large corporations, cover tens of square kilometres and employ large numbers of labourers. The situation whereby African nations export crops to the West while millions on the continent starve has been blamed on Western countries like the European Union and the United States. Due to these market forces, in Africa excess capacity is devoted to growing crops for export. Thus, when civil unrest or a bad harvest occurs, there is often very little food saved and many starve.

(ii) Mining and Drilling

Africa's most valuable exports are minerals and petroleum. A few countries possess and export the vast majority of these resources. The southern nations have large reserves of gold, diamonds, and copper. Petroleum is concentrated in Nigeria, its neighbours, and Libya. While mining and drilling produce most of Africa's revenues each year, these industries only employ about two million people, a tiny fraction of the continent's population. Profits normally go either to large corporations or to the governments. Both have been known to squander this money on luxuries for the elite or on megaprojects that return little value[1].

(iii) Manufacturing

Africa is the least industrialized continent; only South Africa, Egypt and North Africa have substantial manufacturing sectors. Despite readily available cheap labour, nearly all of the continent's natural resources are exported for secondary refining and manufacturing. About 15 per cent of workers are employed in the industrial sector (Oyejide, 1998). The multi-national corporations that control most of the world's major industries and their financiers require political stability before erecting an expensive factory. An educated populace, good infrastructure and a stable source of electricity are essential to investments. These factors are rare in Africa. Other developing regions such as India and China have been more attractive to companies looking to build a new factory or invest in a local enterprise. Many African states used to limit foreign investment to ensure local majority ownership. Close governmental control over industry further discouraged international investment. Attempts to foster local industry have been hampered by insufficient technology, training, and investment. The paucity of local markets and the difficulty of transporting goods from major African centres to world markets contribute to the lack of manufacturing outside of South Africa and Egypt.

(iv) Investment and Banking

Banking in Africa has long been problematic. Since local banks are often unstable and corrupt, governments and industry rely on international banks. South Africa alone has a thriving banking sector, aided by the international sanctions of the apartheid era, which forced out the once-dominant British banks. In the years after independence, African governments heavily regulated the banking sector and placed strict limits on international competition. In recent decades, banking reform has been a priority of the IMF and World Bank. One important reform was obtaining permission for increased penetration by foreign banks. South Africa has been the most successful in attracting local operation of foreign banks. Encouraging foreign investment in Africa has been difficult. Even Africans are reluctant to invest locally; about forty per cent of Sub-Saharan African savings are invested in other markets (Sache and Warner, 1995). Foreign governments who invest may have ulterior motives not in the best interest of the African economies. Even the IMF and World Bank lend money only after imposing stringent conditions such as austerity policies.

1.3 DETERMINANTS OF UNDERDEVELOPMENT IN AFRICA

The intractable nature of Africa's poverty runs counter to modern economic theory, leading to debate concerning its root causes.

Endemic warfare and unrest, widespread corruption, and despotic regimes are both causes and effects of the continued economic problems. The most important causes of underdevelopment are the following.

(i) Geography

Majority of the world's population and wealth is found in the temperate zone. There are no tropical countries in the OECD, apart from Mexico and Australia which have significant tropical sections, and only a handful have a GDP per capita above the world average, again apart from Singapore, Brunei, Malaysia and Thailand (Mule, H., 2000). Tropical latitude is not a guarantee of poverty, but globally there is a definite correlation between wealth and climate, and the African tropical climate is a real obstacle to its overall development.

Africa is well-endowed with natural resources, including gold, diamonds, and oil reserves, but due to several factors including poor governance and global trade policies which place tariffs on finished goods from Africa, few African countries have materially benefited from their mineral wealth (Moshomba, 2000). Africa has the largest hot desert and the second largest tropical forest in the world that hinder building transcontinental means of transportations, hampering its economy. Although Africa has great river systems such as the Nile, Niger, Congo, and Zambezi, they do not link the continent into trade routes effectively as happens in Europe and China. Rapids and cataracts block African rivers, requiring development projects to allow navigation. The wet terrain of the interior complicates transport. Few roads are paved and during the wet season unpaved tracks become impassable mud.

Countries in Africa are also cut off from the sea more than those on other continents. Africa has more landlocked nations than any other continent, which support a high population density compared to the steppes or plains of North America and Asia. The ridge running from Zimbabwe to Ethiopia has superb volcanic soils and the higher altitude produces a more temperate climate. These enable more interior settlement, but the lack of access to the sea makes international trade harder.

(ii) Health Hazards

The tropics are more hospitable to disease than the colder climates. The most significant illness has long been malaria. A new problem of vast magnitude is the rise of HIV/AIDS in Sub-Saharan Africa. AIDS, whose spread correlates with poverty, has nevertheless hit hardest in some of the wealthiest African countries, including Botswana, Swaziland, and South Africa. AIDS has decimated or will decimate the working-age population of many states (Thorbecke, E., 1997). The healthcare cost, including those of importing anti-retroviral AIDS drugs from the West, is a new burden on many African states. Disease not only reduces the work force and creates a burden on health care, but also harms agriculture and transportation, as most forms of livestock cannot survive the diseases of the region. The cost of vaccines and medical supplies compounds the economic cost of the labour force becoming medical dependents. As parents die or become unable to work, their children must find care elsewhere, adding to the burden of already struggling families and states.

(iii) Impact of Colonialism

By 1913, European powers had divided the African continent into a patchwork that showed little regard for ethnic or linguistic boundaries. The economic impact of the colonization of Africa has been debated (For a detailed discussion refer, Rodney, 1982). It is a surprise to see that Africa acquired its greatest relative wealth in the 1960s, just prior to decolonization. African countries have yet to return to those levels of wealth. Some see this as evidence that colonialism helped local economies by creating a cyclical economic link with the ruling colonial power, and with independence this link was broken. To achieve wealth during the colonial period, imperial overseers geared the economies of Africa towards exporting raw materials. Egypt produced cotton, Ruanda-Urundi was almost completely dedicated to growing coffee, and Upper Volta specialized in palm oil. Basing an entire nation's wealth on one commodity in this way would have debilitating effects later. These monocultures left national economies extremely vulnerable to price swings, making economic planning difficult (Akindele, S.T., 1990). European culture in the late

19th century brought racism and social Darwinism. The elevation of the white race above blacks had lasting repercussions in lands with significant European immigration, notably South Africa and Rhodesia.

(iv) Cultural and Linguistic Diversity

In the Scramble for Africa, national boundaries in Sub-Saharan Africa were established by Europeans using latitude and longitude rather than natural borders. This separated population centres from their supplies of food and natural resources[2]. The artificial borders of modern African states cut across cultural, tribal, linguistic and religious boundaries, creating ethnic and religious cleavages which impede national unity and induce internal violence. The African peoples speak over 2,000 languages (Fage, J.D., 2001). Africa is a much divided continent with many small countries. Successful economic growth requires regional cooperation, which political tensions make difficult.

(v) Governance

The political situation in Africa perpetuates the intractable nature of African poverty. Democracy in Africa has not been historically successful, almost always supplanted by centralized authoritarian rule such as military dictatorships[3]. According to international measures, the economies of Africa generally rank among the most corrupt. Bribery and graft abound, due to poverty and poorly handled de-colonization, and the superpowers' (Soviet Union and United States) practice during the Cold War by supporting any ruler with the desired political alignment, regardless of their managerial practices or human rights records (Kayizzi-Mugerwa, 1999). Corruption in Africa consists primarily of extracting economic rent and moving the resulting financial capital overseas instead of investing at home; the stereotype of African dictators with Swiss bank accounts is often accurate. It is estimated that from 1970 to 1996, capital flight from 30 Sub-Saharan African countries totalled $187 billion, exceeding those nations' external debts (Mule, H., 2000). Because governments were politically unstable and new governments often confiscated their predecessors' assets, officials would stash their wealth abroad, out of reach of any future expropriation. Corruption encouraged social inequality, because the wealthy elite not only avoided investing at home, but also imported most of its consumption. Desirable luxury goods were generally not locally available. This hindered the development of national markets. Historically, economic development is closely linked to the creation of a middle class with enough income to save and invest but limited influence on governance. In countries without such a middle class, development is all but impossible, except the illusory and destructive development based on extracting resources like oil.

(vi) Civil Wars and Militancy

Since independence, Africa has seen dozens of wars, both civil and international. This has contributed to poverty because states have spent their scarce resources on military equipment and supplies. Development has suffered, since warfare has scared off foreign investors, destroyed infrastructure, and created lasting animosities (Ake, C., 1996). Much conflict was instigated by the Cold War. The countries of the Western and Eastern blocs leveraged foreign aid money to coax countries into their camp. Aid was tied to the purchase of military weapons, and donor countries ignored misappropriation of the funds. Corruption became endemic, hampering economic development. Proxy conflicts erupted in Africa when each bloc would fund and assisted rebel or sectarian groups under the control of the opposing bloc.

In the decade from 1990 to 2000, Sub-Saharan Africa experienced more than twice the number of casualties from conflict of any other region in the world. While important progress has been made towards ending some of the continent's most deadly conflicts, continued insecurity affects millions of people. The social and economic disruption wrought by ongoing conflicts remains a real source of instability in Africa, with implications for global security. It is important to note that most of Africa is not at war. However, where conflicts do exist, they affect not only the stability of the countries involved, but also their neighbours, and entire sub-regions. For each of the major conflicts ongoing in Africa there exists a peace process, often a settlement plan, and an African body to guide a peace process.

What is crucially missing, in many cases, is the international support needed to ensure peace and stability[4] (Fage, J.D., 2001). Violence in Africa has increased following the Cold War, despite the slashing of foreign aid spending in developed countries. Civil wars have raged throughout the Great Lakes region, Somalia, Sudan, Mozambique, Liberia, Sierra Leone, Ivory Coast, and Guinea-Bissau. International wars include the First and Second Congo Wars between the Democratic Republic of the Congo and its neighbours, and conflict between Ethiopia and its former province Eritrea.

(vii) Democracy and Human Rights

Democracy and respect for human rights are the foundations for political and social stability and economic progress. They are also intrinsic to the goal of human development. Today, the struggle of Africa's people for democracy and human rights continues, and, as in the past, international support can play an important role. African victories in recent decades in overcoming colonial rule, apartheid, and other forms of dictatorship, have marked important progress, empowering Africa's people and unleashing their own vision (Wohicke, M., 1993). While democratic advances have been made across the continent, serious challenges still remain. As is the case everywhere, democracy in Africa is a work in progress. Constitutional reform movements now seek to advance the democratic process in many countries. African civil society organizations continue to struggle for women's rights, and for government accountability to the needs of Africa's poor majority (Obadina, T., 1998). Press freedom is also an important aspect of a vibrant democracy. The growing number of independent media across the African continent is an indicator of democratic progress. At the same time, however, media repression and persecution persist in many countries. In all instances where press freedom is curtailed international condemnation should be consistent and forceful.

The New Partnership for Africa's Development (NEPAD), the initial development plan adopted by the African Union (AU), lays out a commitment to democratic principles and good governance in Africa. This commitment is intended to be the cornerstone for attracting increased foreign investment. NEPAD is an ambitious new plan for African development, originally defined by a small group of

African leaders. However, the absence of civil society participation in the evolution of this plan makes it, as yet, incomplete. A true vision and agenda for Africa's future must be more inclusive, and should it be more democratic.

1.4 HISTORICAL BACKGROUND OF DEVELOPMENT IN AFRICA

Before the Roman Empire, Ancient Egypt was one of the world's most prosperous and advanced civilizations. The port of Alexandria, founded by Alexander the Great in 334 BC, was a hub for Mediterranean trade for centuries (Fage, J.D, 2001). Well into the 19th century, Egypt remained one of the most developed regions outside Europe. However, south of the Sahara conditions were different. Internal trade within the continent, hindered by thick forests and massive deserts, was always difficult. Prosperity in Sub-Saharan Africa was rare, excepting Nubia, Ethiopia, Mali and Ghana, which had trade routes north to the Mediterranean world and Middle East.

For most of the first millennium AD, the Axumite Kingdom had a prosperous trade empire on the eastern horn, where the modern states of Ethiopia and Eritrea lie. Axum had a powerful navy and traded as far as the Byzantine Empire, India, and possibly China (Ashton-Jones Nick, *et al.*, 1998). The introduction of the camel by North African Arab conquerors in the 10th century opened trade across the Sahara for the first time. The profits from the gold and salt trades created powerful empires in the western Sahel including the Kingdom of Ghana and the Mali and Kanem-Bornu Empires, where travellers reported vast wealth. Arabs helped build a maritime trade along Africa's east coast, which prospered as Swahili traders exported ivory and slaves across the Indian Ocean (Fage J.D., 2001). Further south empires were less common, with the notable exception of Great Zimbabwe. In the Great Lakes region, states such as Rwanda, Burundi, and Buganda became strongly centralized, due to its high population and agricultural surplus.

In the 15th century, Portuguese traders circumvented the Saharan trade route and began to trade directly with Guinea. Other European traders followed, rapidly boosting prosperity in Western Africa. States flourished, including the Kingdom of Benin, Dahomey, and the Ashanti Confederacy (Rodney, Walter, 1982). Loose federations of city states such as those of the Yoruba and Hausa were common. However, this wealth was principally based on the slave trade, which collapsed following the abolition of slavery and later European colonization.

Although Europeans were ostensibly committed to developing their colonies, colonial rulers employed a *laissez-faire* strategy during the first decades. It was hoped that European companies would prosper if given a secure operating environment. This only occurred in a few areas with rich resources; the colonial economies hardly grew from the 1890s through the 1920s (Rodney, Walter, 1982). The colonies had to pay their own way, receiving little or no development money from Europe. Only in the 1930s, with the rise of Keynesian economics, did the colonial administrations seriously encourage development. However, new projects could not transpire until after the Great Depression and the Second World War.

African economies boomed during the 1950s as growth and international trade multiplied beyond their pre-war levels. The insatiable demand for raw materials in the rebuilding economies of Asia and Europe and the strong growth in North America inflated the price of raw materials. By the end of the colonial era in the 1960s, there was great hope for African self-sufficience and prosperity. However, sporadic growth continued as the newly independent nations borrowed heavily from abroad.

The world economic decline of the 1970s, rising oil prices, corruption, and political instability hit Africa hard. In subsequent decades Africa has steadily become poorer compared to the rest of the world; South America experienced solid growth, and East Asia spectacular growth, during that same period. According to the World Economic Forum, ten per cent of the world's poor were African in 1970; by 2000, that figure had risen to fifty per cent (OECD, 2007). Between 1974 and 2000 the average income declined by $ 200. Beginning in 1976, the Lomé agreements and Cotonou agreement between the EU and ACP countries, including Sub-Saharan Africa, have structured economic relations between the two regions.

1.5 HUMAN DEVELOPMENT PARADIGM

Africa's human development challenges are immense. This is not surprising, given the continent's history and geography, and its place in the global political economy today. African struggles to meet these challenges can be successful, and international support in this area can make a real difference to the continent's future. Across much of Africa, human conditions are deteriorating, driven by the health crisis and by persistent poverty. More than 300 million people in Sub-Saharan Africa survive on under $1 per day (OECD, 2007). Almost half of the continent does not have access to safe water sources. Life expectancy in sub-Saharan Africa is the lowest of any region in the world, and is falling dramatically as a result of the HIV/AIDS crisis. Infant and child mortality rates remain high, and access to health care and education is shrinking in many countries. Food insecurity is growing, most seriously in southern Africa and in the Horn of Africa. Important economic indicators of Africa are given in Table 1.1.

Addressing these human development challenges must be a priority of donor nations and international cooperation with Africa, as these are Africa's priorities. The success of development efforts should be measured not by impersonal economic growth indicators but by poverty reduction and social progress. The achievement of sustainable development depends on Africa's greatest resource her people. It is this resource that is currently being devastated.

Table 1.1: Economic Indicators of Africa, 2003

	Indicators	*Values*
1.	Population	922 million (14%)
2.	GDP (PPP)	US$ 1.635 trillion US$ 2.572 trillion (2007)
3.	GDP (Currency)	$558 billion $1,150 billion (2007)
4.	GDP/capita (PPP)	$1,968 $2,975 (2007) IMF
5.	GDP/capita (Currency)	$671
6.	Annual growth in per capita GDP	5.16% (2004-2006)
7.	Income of top 10%	44.7%
8.	Millionaires	0.1 million (0.01 %)
9.	Population-living-on under $1 per day	36.2%
10.	External-debt-as-a % of GDP	60.7% (1998) 25.5% (2007) IMF
11.	External-debt-payments-as a % of GDP	4.2% [3.0% (2007) IMF]
12.	Foreign-aid-revenue-as-a % of GDP	3.2%(2001)
13.	Female-income	51.8% of male

The achievement of good health and education, and the attainment of a decent standard of living and well-being for Africa's people, are essential for the continent's future. Greater investment in people is proven to reduce poverty and promote economic growth. The efforts of African Governments to meet the basic needs of their people and to ensure access to essential services are hindered by lack of adequate resources. The heavy indebtedness of African Governments to rich country creditors drains money away from basic social services, such as health care and education. Economic policies imposed on African countries by these creditors, and by the World Bank and IMF in particular, have not only undermined African sovereignty, but have worsened poverty and decreased access to basic services for Africa's people (Thorbeke, E, 1997). The result has been a decline in human development indicators over the past two decades.

The Millennium Development Goals adopted in September 2000 by most governments provide the framework for mutually reinforcing steps to achieve global human development. These goals have been established as the benchmarks for monitoring and measuring development progress. They seek to improve health, education and the environment across the world, with the overarching aim of reducing by half the number of people living in extreme poverty by 2015. Achieving this ambitious target will require a new global partnership committed to human development. It will also require a massive increase in resources. The UN estimates that meeting the Millennium Development Goals will require a doubling of official development assistance worldwide, to at least $100 billion annually.

However, levels of development assistance have fallen in a consistent downward trend in the past decade. Despite repeated promises from rich countries to provide 0.7 per cent of their Gross National Product (GNP) for official development assistance for poorer countries, none of the G-7 richest countries reaches even half that figure (Gootu, S, 1993). The U.S ranks at the bottom of all donor countries, with only 0.1 per cent of GNP, or just over $10 billion, going to foreign aid worldwide[5]. Only 1/100th of 1 per cent of the U.S. budget around $1 billion is currently spent on aid to Sub-Saharan Africa, although Africa's need for such support is currently greater than ever (Krugman, *et al.,* 1995). There has been a nearly 50 per cent drop in official development assistance to Africa during the past decade from all donors combined. Aid to Sub-Saharan Africa over the past four years has been lower than any year since 1984.

1.6 GLOBALIZATION AND ITS IMPLICATIONS

In terms of commercial linkages with the global economy, Africa still has a long way to go and the move towards creating bigger markets through regionalism and increased intra-African trade is moving slowly. Countries remain fragmented and inward looking, with limited progress towards the harmonization of operating requirements across borders. African countries have been urged to do more to add value to their resources. In turn, western nations need to address the tariff and non-tariff barriers to Africa's exports in developed country markets.

Countries in Africa today, rarely define the rules and regulations of their economy, production, credits and exchanges of goods and services due to the rampaging menace of globalisation. They are hardly now capable of volitionally managing their political, economic and socio-cultural development. Globalization has imposed heavy constraints on the internal management dynamics of most if not all the polities in Africa (e.g., Nigeria) where the government now finds it difficulty in most cases to meet the genuine demands of the governed on many issues of national urgency (Ohuabunwa, 1999). Globalization has made it immensely difficult for governments to provide social insurance—one of their central functions and one that has helped many developed nations to maintain social cohesion and domestic political support. Trends like this have been largely dictated by the asymmetry of powers that accompany globalization.

The result of globalization in Africa, is basically a competition between the palatial centres (Developed World) and the slums (Africa) of the village where a preponderant majority of the people daily sink deeper into poverty and misery. Consequently, its ideology of free-market liberalism and property-based democracy remains a continuous licence for cultural imperialism and, the institutionalisation of both political and economic domination and exploitation of the weaker partners through their internal agents (Diagne and Ossebi, 1996).

It is apparent that, the globalization process is more symmetrical to the "origin and development of the neo-colonial states (in Africa)" which were "determined by the nature and structures of the colonising countries" rather than according to a concretely established philosophy or determination to get Africa out of lingering crises. Thus, globalization is a form of entrapment for Africa. Apart from its evocation of powerlessness already analysed, it creates a process through which the "poor countries in Africa are dominated and exploited by the rich countries and, a vicious circle of vulnerability of African governments" to outside parasitic economic manoeuvring as does the lack of capacity for independence of socio-political, cultural and psychological thinking relative to concrete actions.

The continent remains particularly exposed to global risks for various reasons, including its continuing dependence on raw materials and related vulnerability to price shocks, poverty, weak democratic processes, corruption, the slow movement towards creating regional efficiencies and a serious lack of skills and capacity.

Figure 1.2: Africa's Vulnerability to Climate Change

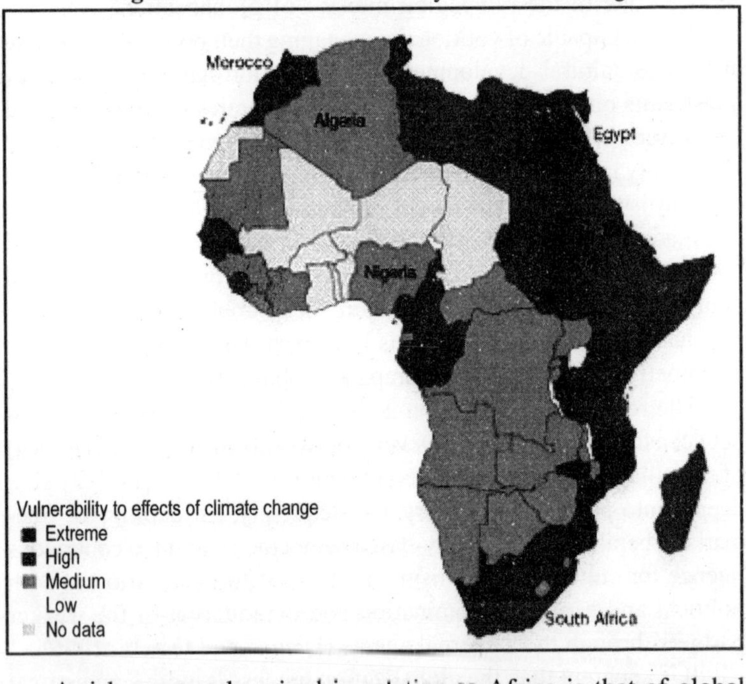

A risk commonly raised in relation to Africa is that of global warming and climate change. Although Africa's generally low levels of industrialization mean it is not a key contributor to changing climate patterns, the continent is likely to be the worst affected by the phenomenon. African governments do not appear to be prepared for the challenge, either in terms of mitigating the risks emanating from it, such as food and water scarcity, or in terms of taking advantage of the opportunities the situation presents. These include the development of biofuels on Africa's vast tracts of unused agricultural land, and carbon trading (Tussie, D., 1994). There are concerns that the continent's reaction to climate change will eventually be one of crisis management, particularly in addressing new frontiers of conflict in the battle over ever-reducing resources.

Without any gainsaying, Africa is the hardest hit continent by the rapaciousness of globalisation. Ironically, the African Growth and Opportunity Act (AGOA) put before the American Senate by President Bill Clinton in 1998 which was passed into law in May, 2000 and, the Multilateral Agreement on Investment (MAI) of the Organisation for Economic Co-operation and Developments (OECDs) are part of the instruments put in place by the West to further deplete whatever is left of Africa's resources. These are devices to "roll-back whatever gains the third world counties were able to make at the economic level during the cold war years" (Tandon, 1998). In fact, both the AGOA and MAI are traps aimed at foisting-without much conscious resistance by the victims of the so-called "global constitution"—a "global economy" on Africa and other developing economies. This constitution allows the powerful international corporations unfettered freedom to operate anywhere around the globe without any limitation by the policies of host nations irrespective of the consequences of their operation to the interests of the host nations.

This has promoted the argument that, globalization has damaged Africa's natural environment and, on balance of costs and benefits, it has been a disaster for Africa both in human and material resources. Twenty countries in Africa have per capita income lower than 20 years ago. Two-thirds of the Least Developed Countries (LDCs) are in Africa (Rodrik, 1994). A food-surplus continent twenty years ago, Africa is now food-deficit. This is especially disturbing in Africa, which is the only developing region where poverty is increasing, considering the fact that: African Governments seem to have lost control of the policy-making process, and are under pressure to accept dictation from creditor nations and financial institutions. African Governments now tend to discuss development issues less with their own nationals, and more with donors and creditors, about debt repayment, debt relief and rescheduling, and paradoxically about more development assistance.

However, Africa's global profile has been significantly enhanced in recent years by the keen interest taken in the continent, primarily in its raw materials, by China and India. The emerging South-South partnership has caused concern among the continent's traditional trading partners in Europe and America, who have done business on the continent on their own terms, unchallenged, for many years. These relationships are under scrutiny in light of both the new South-South trading relations and of a new assertiveness by Africans themselves in setting their own development agenda. Countries such as China and India have approached business with Africa differently from the West, seeking partnerships and cooperation rather than the neo-colonial and paternalistic relations many African countries believe they have with Western nations. China's voracious appetite for raw materials has changed global trading patterns, and Africa has been a major beneficiary. The quest for raw materials has been accompanied by increasing aid and trade with African countries as well as the financing and implementation of large infrastructure projects.

There is the need for an appropriate response to emerge from Africa with a view to understanding the dynamics that will hopefully help to evolve measures that will reduce the devastating effects of globalisation. One possible way out is the subordination of external relations to the logic of internal development. Through this, African revolutionary and activist classes (could be) actively engaged in building alternative (new) structures of power for organising production based on new values of humanity and care for the environment.

1.7 FOREIGN DEBT AND THE CRISIS OF AFRICAN ECONOMIES

Closely attached to the menace of globalization is the issue of foreign debt crisis. Sub-Saharan Africa's massive external debt is the single largest obstacle to the continent's economic development. Each year,

African countries are required to pay almost $15 billion to the international financial institutions and to foreign creditor governments, including the U.S (Toyo, 2000). This represents a crippling and unsustainable burden that fundamentally undermines economic growth. Over the past two decades, African Governments have paid out more in debt service than they have received in development assistance or in new loans.

Debt repayments divert money directly from spending on basic social needs, including the response to the HIV/AIDS crisis. They trap African countries in a cycle of underdevelopment and dependency. Moreover, much of Africa's foreign debt is illegitimate in nature, having been incurred by unrepresentative and despotic regimes during the era of Cold War patronage.

The cancellation of Africa's illegitimate debt is essential to the continent's economic development. It is also crucial to African efforts to fight HIV/AIDS and to address poverty (OECD, 2006-07). While the U.S. is a relatively minor bilateral creditor of African countries, it is the single largest shareholder in the World Bank and the IMF, to whom most of Africa's debt is owed. As such, it holds major influence over the international response to Africa's debt crisis.

Advocacy for debt relief has become widespread. Debt relief is not a panacea, but relieving some of the burden, especially of debts that were run up by regimes for their own benefit, may help the economies of Africa grow and prosper. However, arguments against full and unconditional debt relief exist. First, debt relief punishes nations which have managed borrowing well and do not need debt relief. Second, unconditional debt relief will not necessarily cause nations to spend more in social programmes and services, on the one hand, or to solve their financial problems without stifling the economy with the need for more taxes, on the other hand. Finally, debt relief may make it more difficult for nations to receive credit in the future. It has been suggested that any debt relief policy be conditional upon a commensurate reduction in aid.

The current international debt relief framework, the Heavily Indebted Poor Countries (HIPC) Initiative, has failed to provide a solution to the debt crisis. Designed by creditors, it seeks to extract the maximum in debt repayments from poor countries. It has failed to reduce Africa's debt burden to a sustainable level, which is its stated objective (Sahn, D.E. *et al.*, 1997). Recent World Bank and IMF reports concede that the HIPC Initiative is not working. Meanwhile, an independent audit of these two institutions by two British accounting firms has revealed that they can afford to write off Africa's debt completely, without negatively impacting their lending ability or their credit rating.

The developed countries should support immediate and complete debt cancellation for African countries. This should not be tied to structural adjustment programmes or other such policies imposed by the World Bank and IMF. These policies have led to a decline in average incomes, and worsening conditions of poverty and underdevelopment. They have also fueled the spread of the HIV/AIDS pandemic. Promoting economic development and poverty reduction in Africa requires a paradigm shift away from rich country creditors dictating economic policies to poor countries. The U.S. should support the economic policies and priorities defined by African countries. A more equitable economic relationship is essential to tackling the roots of Africa's economic crisis.

The New Partnership for Africa's Development (NPAD) is a new African initiative to help boost the continent's economic growth by encouraging greater foreign investment. However, for investment to generate sustainable growth, it must support African initiatives and increase employment opportunities for African workers.

1.8 CHALLENGES FOR AFRICA'S DEVELOPMENT

The challenges for Africa's development is multifaceted and in the post-colonial era its development tempo was highly vibrant and in most occasions depressing. Six countries in the continent have more than tripled their per capita incomes between 1960 and 2005, nine countries have per capita incomes equal to or less than where they started in 1960 and the rest have seen some net improvement, but not enough to make a real dent in poverty levels. Many countries seen as fast growers in 1970, such as Côte d'Ivoire, flamed out and have found themselves stagnating or declining during the past 30 years. Steady progress and consistent performance, in good times as in bad, are the watchwords (Kayizzi-Mugerwa, 1999). Many African countries made policy choices in 1974 that continue to haunt them today, whereas a few are experiencing the blessings of different choices made at the same time. The following are the important challenges of African growth.

(i) Extremely Varied and Episodic Growth

From a regional strategic perspective, addressing the challenges of the slow growth of large countries and the extreme instability of growth across large number of African countries are the key to success. Countries with large populations, such as the Sudan, the Democratic Republic of Congo, Nigeria, and Ethiopia, will have to grow more rapidly and on a more sustained basis to improve the livelihood of a "typical" African and to generate regional traction through positive spillover effects, similar to the experiences in Southern Africa and East Asia (Moshomba, 2000). Another cross-cutting challenge in the region is how to best manage responses to shocks, particularly in the resource-rich countries, in which their fortunes are currently closely tied to the fortunes of key minerals in the world market.

(ii) Slower Productivity Growth

Investment in Africa yields less than half the return measured in growth terms than in other developing regions. This situation clearly calls for looking beyond creating conditions for attracting new investors to more explicitly pursuing measures that help to raise productivity of existing and new investment. These include reducing transactions costs for private enterprise, particularly indirect costs; supporting innovation to take advantage of new technological opportunities; and improving skills and institutional capacity to support productivity growth and competitiveness (Krugman, *et al.*, 1995). African countries and populations are still highly dependent on agriculture for food, exports, and income earning more broadly. Productivity in this sector lags far behind the phenomenal progress made in Asia and Latin America, and should be a key target for raising overall productivity of African economies.

(iii) Inefficient Policies and Governance

Taking post-colonial years of African growth experience as a whole and controlling for differences in the composition of opportunities, the impacts of poor policy have been shown to typically account for between one-quarter and one-half of the difference in predicted growth between African and non-African developing countries. However, the evidence also suggests that the importance of policy in explaining the growth differential between African countries and others may have waned since the 1990s as a result of major reforms implemented in the region, which have moved policy performance in African countries much closer to the global average (Wohike, 1993). Thus, whereas it is imperative for countries to identify and address other binding constraints, sustaining these gains in the improvement of the policy environment will have to be a permanent feature of any growth strategy adopted by a country. In particular, it means maintaining durable macro-economic stability and continued propping up of efficient market functioning.

(iv) Geographic Isolation and Fragmentation

Estimates show that taking actions to compensate for these disadvantages may facilitate closing up to one-third of the growth gap with other developing countries. With much higher proportions of countries and populations in Africa being landlocked and resource rich, it is necessary to compensate for these disadvantages, primarily by closing the infrastructure gap and better managing and using resource rents.

(v) Influence of Trading Partner Countries

The key transmission mechanisms are trade and capital flows, strengthening capabilities for taking advantage of the rapid growth in the global markets, and improving the investment climate to make African countries better destinations for global capital than in the past. On the side of trade, evidence shows that integration with global markets is associated with higher growth, underpinning the need for growth strategies to emphasize scaling up and diversifying exports (Tussie, 1994). It is important to note that although concerns with border trade policies and facilities (for example, port capacity and efficiency) are still crucial, increasingly, constraints such as infrastructure, standards, and access to information have become much more binding. A core part of any growth strategy, therefore, will need to target reducing the costs of transacting trade—particularly reducing supply chain costs, as well as the cost of trade processes.

(vi) Delayed Demographic Transition

In all the empirical studies of the sources of growth differences, the demographic variables consistently predict two-thirds of the observed difference between average growth in Sub-Saharan Africa and other developing regions. Two types of consequences from this delayed transition are particularly important. The first, and probably the biggest, challenge is the uncharacteristically high level of age dependency, with its implications on fiscal and household/parental pressure for taking care of the overwhelming number of the young (Kayizzi-Mugerwa, 1999). The second relates to the rapid growth of the labour force, potentially a positive driver of growth but also possibly a negative force if employment opportunities do not keep pace. The latter concern relates to the growing potential instability from rapidly rising youth unemployment. Whereas the strategy needs to address the fundamentals of the slow demographic transition such as how to speed up a reduction in fertility, appropriate actions are also needed to increase employability of youth and expand opportunities to engage in a growing private sector at home.

1.9 ATTEMPTS AT PROMOTING GROWTH

The relative economic failure of Africa has long been an important issue both in Africa and abroad. Many attempts at solving Africa's poverty have been attempted, but few have had any great degree of success. The following are the important attempts at the promotion of economic growth in Africa having different ideologies.

(i) Socialism

In the years immediately after independence many nations saw the rapid industrialisations of the Soviet Union and China under communism as models to follow. This led to command economies and major investment in heavy industries such as coal and steel production to stimulate growth, but this approach had little success.

Only a handful of states formally adopted socialism and even fewer turned to outright Marxism. Everywhere Government intervention in the economy was seen as necessary for growth, especially since private companies and investors were unlikely to invest in the region. Often the approach of Governments in Africa was to borrow heavily from abroad and use this aid to grow the economy to a level that the loans could be paid off (Ake, C., 1996). Sporadic growth during the years after independence continued. The countries focused on exports to pay for these development efforts. The 1973 energy crisis hit Sub-Saharan Africa as hard as anywhere in the world. While some nations were net exporters, most were heavily reliant on imported fuels. Economies quickly began to falter and events such as famines hit Africa in the 1980s. The collapse of the Soviet Union, which had supported socialist and collectivist projects throughout the continent, undermined the legitimacy of such an approach, while it also meant that there were no longer any sources of international aid to help pursue this approach.

(ii) Liberalism

Thus in the 1980s, socialist ideas were discarded throughout almost the entire continent as "capitalism" became seen as the route to salvation in what became known as the Washington consensus. By 1990, forty of the nations of Sub-Saharan Africa had agreed to follow rigorous IMF restructuring plans. IMF recommendations saw the continent's currencies drop by an average of 50 per cent, the selling off of Government-owned industries, and the slashing of Government spending (Chossudovsky, 1997). After twenty years, however, these methods have seen as little success as the socialist approaches of the previous era. Average growth increased from 2.3 per cent per annum to 2.8 per cent. Only a handful of African states reached new levels of wealth, and many others became poorer over the course of the 1990s[6].

(iii) Autarky

The pursuit of self-sufficiency as advocated by dependency theory has been given limited trials in several African countries. In the 1980s, Nigeria banned the importation of many foodstuffs to stimulate domestic production (Adobo, A, *et al.*, 1997). The Lagos Plan of Action of 1982 called for Africa as a whole to block imports from the rest of the world, but few countries followed through on the idea. Eventually even Nigeria agreed to limited liberalization.

(iv) Foreign Aid

Since independence there has been a constant flow of foreign aid into Africa. The benefits of this aid have been mixed. In many cases much of this aid was misappropriated by unscrupulous leaders[7]. For many decades the leading notion of development was Government supervised mega-projects; today many believe that small grants to local businesses would be more effective (Moshomba, R.E., 2000). One example of foreign aid which has come under considerable criticism is food aid. In some circles, it is believed that food aid does not solve any fundamental problems and can also lead to a dependency on outside assistance, as well as hindering the development of indigenous industries. Food shipments in case of dire local shortage are generally uncontroversial; but as Amartya Sen has shown, most famines involve local lack of income rather than of food. In such situations, food aid—as opposed to financial aid—has the effect of destroying local agriculture and serves mainly to benefit Western agribusiness, which are vastly overproducing food as a result of agricultural subsidies. Historically, food aid is more highly correlated with excess supply in Western countries than with the needs of developing countries.

1.10 CONCLUSION

The persistent underdevelopment of Africa's economies demands a new approach to economic development. The chronic poverty and vulnerability of the continent is related to complex dynamics of the global economy. From the forgone discussion in this chapter we can see that there are mainly fours pillars, where attention is needed to accelerate the pace of overall development. The first pillar is improving the investment climate, mainly focused on reducing indirect costs to firms (which are generally infrastructure related), with energy and transportation topping the list of major impediments; and reducing and mitigating risk, particularly those relating to security of property, such as poor adjudication of disputes, crime, political instability, and macro-economic instability. Although effort in individual countries is the focal point of action, it is also advisable to pool efforts to develop cohesive investment areas by coordinating investment promotion, coordinating policy, improving security, and increasing connectivity.

The second pillar is infrastructure, mainly targeting transactions costs in production of goods and services. Transportation and energy make up the largest proportion of indirect costs for businesses, weighing heavily on the competitiveness of firms in most African countries in which investment climate surveys were conducted. Particular focus would be on how to reduce the high costs associated with the remoteness of landlocked countries to facilitate trade with neighbours, as well as with the rest of the world. It is clear that there will be a need to look beyond individual country borders and adopt a regional approach to coordinate cross-border infrastructure investment, maintenance, operational management, and use (for example, power pooling) to lower costs.

The third pillar is innovation, primarily emphasizing investment in information technology and skill formation (higher education) for enhanced productivity and competitiveness. The potential comparative advantage of low wages in Africa can be nullified by low productivity. Surveys of investors show that labour is not cheap where productivity is low. Information and Communication Technology (ICT) is now the main driver for productivity growth. There is strong empirical evidence that shows that investment in ICT and in higher education boosts competitiveness, making both key parts of the growth agenda. African countries can make a huge leap forward and over antiquated technology by exploiting the ICT technological advantages as late starters.

The fourth pillar is institutional capacity. The results from the investment climate assessment surveys and analysis of the World Development Report (2005) identify costs associated with contract enforcement difficulties, crime, corruption, and regulation as being among those weighing most heavily on the profitability of enterprises. The main focus of action here would be partly to strengthen the capacity of relevant public institutions for protecting property rights, and partly to strengthen scrutiny of, and accountability for, public actions. Building institutional capacity entails strengthening individual competencies, organizational effectiveness, and rules of the game. Under this pillar, particular attention should be paid to capacity and space for scrutiny of public action—mainly within a framework of a strong domestic accountability system and capacity to clarify and protect property rights to spur private enterprise. The key strategic areas of action, therefore, include enforcement of contracts (for example, commercial courts); exercise of voice as an agency of restraint—with enhanced involvement of civil society, media, and parliament; enhanced revenue transparency in resource-rich countries; and prevention of corruption as a country-driven agenda—including checks and balances.

Each country has to work within its own historical and geographical resources and constraints. The ideas and approaches raised here will enable analysts and policy-makers at the country level to approach their particular challenges with a more informed sense of what may be important, and of what has worked in the past in other situations.

NOTES

1. In some cases, these resources have turned out to be a curse. Although Congo is rich in minerals, the country remains one of the poorest countries in the world. This is historically due to ownership fights over these minerals, tracing back to the early 1900s. After Congo's independence from Belgium, the colonial government hesitated to leave behind these resources. Congo solicited UN help against Belgium, but that turned out to be a bad idea. In an attempt to get out of the quagmire, Congo sought Soviet assistance. This led the country into deeper trouble, as the country separated into two and a long proxy war between the West and East began.
2. However, those states that preserved pre-colonial boundaries have been no more successful. Few countries in Africa have more troubled recent histories than Rwanda and Burundi, although their borders are almost identical to those of the prosperous kingdoms from which they are descended. The ancient and only briefly occupied state of Ethiopia is one of the poorest on the continent, and ethnically unified Somalia has failed so completely that it no longer exists in any real sense.
3. Alhough some rulers worked to improve the lot of their nation's citizens, others used power purely for their own benefit. Among

the most notorious was Mobuto Sese Seko of Zaire, whose regime has been called a kleptocracy due to its looting of the nation's wealth.

4. The U.S has a particular historic responsibility for many of Africa's current conflicts. During the Cold War, the U.S. provided more than $1.5 billion worth of arms to African countries that were considered geo-strategic allies. The U.S. also bankrolled dictators in African states, such as Mobuto Sese Seko in the former Zaire, and Siad Barre in Somalia, to name but a few. It is many of these African countries that had "special" Cold War relationships with the U.S. that fell into political turmoil and violence in the 1990s and are often referred to as "failed states" (e.g. Liberia and Somalia). The U.S. must now take responsibility for the destabilizing effect of its intervention in these countries.
5. The U.S. has consistently failed to devote bilateral aid that is commensurate either with its interests and obligations or with poor countries' needs. For the U.S. to reach the target of 0.7 per cent of GNP, it must increase its development assistance to $70 billion per year. At least half of this, or $35 billion per year, should be committed to African countries. At present, however, the lion's share $5 billion of the foreign aid provided by the U.S. goes to two strategic allies in the Middle East (Egypt and Israel), not to fight poverty or to promote development.
6. Today there is a great deal of controversy on why this failed. One school of thought is that the reforms failed because they were only economic in nature and without democracy and the rule of law development cannot occur. Yet another school of thought attributes some of Africa's problems to insufficient liberalization. It has been pointed out that while the developed world has insisted that Africa open its markets and eliminate public subsidies, this has been one-sided as the developed world has not opened its markets to agricultural goods from Africa nor has it eliminated agricultural subsidies.
7. During the Cold War the main goal of much of the aid money was to win the allegiance of these rulers, and so their misappropriation of the aid was at the very least overlooked. Since the end of the Cold War almost all developed countries have slashed foreign aid spending. Many also allege that the aid that was not stolen was long misdirected.

REFERENCES

Adebo, A. and Akindele S.T. (1990). "The Political Economy of Neo-colonial state and under-development in Nigeria" in Bamisaye, O.A. and Egbuwalo, M.O. (Eds), *Readings on the Political Economy of Nigeria since Independence*, Venture Ltd, Lagos.

Ake, C. (1996). *Democracy and Development in Africa*, Brookings Institution, New York.

Akindele, S.T. (1990). "Colonialism and Economic Dependence: The case of Nigeria" in Bamisaye, O.A. and Egbuwalo, M.O. (Eds), (1990). *Readings on the Political Economy of Nigeria since Independence*, Venture Ltd, Lagos.

Ashton-Jones Nick; Arnott, Susi and Douglas Oronto, (1998). *The Human Ecosystems of the Niger Delta: An Era Handbook*, Environmental Rights Action, London.

Chossudovsky, Michel (1997). *The Globalization of Poverty: Impacts of IMF and World Bank Reforms*, 2nd Edition Book Ltd, London.

Diagne, S.B. and Ossebi (1996). "The Cultural Question in Africa: Issues, Politics and Research Prospects", *Codestria Working Paper Series* 3/98.

Fage, J.D. (2001). *A History of Africa*, 4th edition, Routledge.

Gootu, S. (1993). "Portfolio Investment flows to Emerging Markets" in: Claossens and Gooptu (eds.) *Portfolio Investment in Developing Countries,* World Bank Discussion Paper 228, Washington D.C.

Kayizzi-Mugerwa, Steve (1999). *The African Economy: Policy, Institutions and the Future*, Routledge.

Moshomba, Richard E. (2000). *Africa in the Global Economy*, Lynne Rienner.

Krugman, P. and Verables, A.J. (1995). "Globalization and the Inequality of Nations" *Quarterly Journal of Economics*, Volume 110.

Madunagu, E. (1999). "Globalization and its Victims," *Guardian,* July 26.

Mule, H. (2000). "Challenges to African Governance and Civil Society", *Africa Notes*, May.

Obadina, T. (1998). "Globalisation, Human Rights and Development", *Africa Today*, October.

Ohuabunwa, Mazi S.I. (1999). "The Challenges of Globalization to the Nigerian Industrial Sector", *Nigerian Tribune*, December 14.

OECD, (2007). *African Economic Outlook 2006-2007.*

Oyejide, T.A. (1998). "African Trade Prospects in a Globlizaing Era", *Cooperation South*, No. 2.

Rodney, Walter (1982). *How Europe Underdeveloped Africa,* Howard UP, Washington.

Rodrik, Dani (1994). "The rush to free trade in the developing world: Why so late? Why now? Will it last? in S. Haggard and S. Webb (eds), *Voting for Reform*, Oxford University Press and the World Bank, New York.

Sachs, Jeffrey and Andrew, Warner (1995). *Economic Reform and the Process of Global Integration,* Brookings Papers on Economic Activity, Vol. 1.

Sahn, David E., Paul A. Dorosh, and Stephen D. (1997). *Younger Structural Adjustment Reconsidered: Economic Policy and Poverty in Africa*, Cambridge University Press.

Tandon, Y. (1998). "Globalization and Africa Options", *AAPS Newsletter*, African Association of Political Science, Vol. 3, No. 1 January—April, Harare.

Thorbecke, E. (1997). "Whither Africa?" *Africa Notes*, April.

Toyo, Eskor (2000). *Background to Globalisation*, A Mimeograph Published by the Academic Staff Union of Universities (ASUU), Nigeria.

Tussie, D. (1994). "Globalization and Word Trade from Multilateralism to Regionalism" *Oxford Development Studies* 26 (1): 32-46.

Wohicke, M. (1993). "The Causes of Continuing Underdevelopment", *Law and the State*, (Vol. 47) Institute for Scientific Co-operation, Tubingen.

2

African Agriculture in the New Millennium

Lessons from the Twentieth Century

2.1 INTRODUCTION

The developing Africa is facing serious economic and in particular agricultural problems. What some scholars have characterized as economic malaise by severe emergencies are still prevailing in most of the countries in the region. Although the food emergencies are often triggered by short-term factors like drought or conflict, Africa's food emergencies are not a set of anomalies, but the very logical consequences of structural economic and agricultural problems (Henmer, *et al.*, 1996). A sustained decline in per capita food production and a corresponding decline in per capita food availability have severely reduced the slack available for coping with both physical and economic shocks in an environment in which both types of shocks have become prevalent. The precarious economic and agricultural situation makes increased food and agricultural production imperative.

In recent years the food security issue in drought prone Sub-Saharan Africa has received less attention than it did in the last century, as favourable climate conditions have resulted in satisfactory harvests in some countries. However, climate conditions are still variable, incomes are low, the population is increasing rapidly and production systems are unsustainable. The survival of the urban and rural poor depends on opportunities for their household members to find ways to diversify their incomes from the already underdeveloped farm sector. For instance, a close look at expenditure patterns of rural households show that production for self-sufficiency is still a major source of food consumption (Thorbecke, E., 1992). Crop failures make these households food insecure if they lack a sufficient cash income to purchase the additional foodgains they need. Moreover, food shortages inflate prices during the lean season, which lowers household's purchasing power.

The present chapter reviews the major bottlenecks of the African countries in attaining a sustainable level of growth based on the on-farm activities. The economic and food problems characterizing underdevelopment in the continent is a product of both internal and external factors; which aggravated since the latter half of the twentieth century. The reflections of Policy Reform Agenda prescribed by the international agencies are also part of the discussion. Key influences on farm production and the need for mechanization in small-holder agriculture are all part of the enquiry in this chapter.

2.2 AFRICA'S ECONOMIC AND FOOD PROBLEMS

Inadequate domestic food production has seriously weakened Africa's capacity for coping with both short-term food emergencies and the long-term nutritional needs of its population. The percentage of farming households unable to produce enough food to last from one harvest to the next varies with time and place, but is often surprisingly high according to empirical findings. In Mali during the later decades of 20th Century even one half of the farm households unable to produce enough to meet their consumption requirements (Sijm, J., 1997). Corresponding figures for Malawi and Tanzania reach as high as 80 per cent (*Ibid*)! For Zimbabwe it was 40 per cent (Tagwiregi, J., 1991). Per capita food production has fallen steadily since 1970 in most of the countries. As a result per capita calorie availability is now below the recommended levels for adequate nutrition in most countries of Africa. The implications of Africa's food production trends are stark.

Governments' food production policies, and often more generally agricultural policies, have contributed to the poor performance of food and agricultural production, although they are certainly not the only reason for faltering production. One important consequence of such policies and the attendant decline in per capita production has been to seriously weaken the ability of African countries to deal with natural shocks, such as drought, which frequently create sharp drops in production in systems where most agriculture is rain-fed. Inadequate aggregate production also exacerbates distributional inequities, making severe deprivation (or starvation) more likely[1]. This occurs for two main reasons.

(i) As aggregate supplies fall, and prices rise, the wealthier portion of the population will adjust its consumption relatively little. This forces a greater burden of adjustment on the poor.

(ii) Most rural food emergencies arise directly from production short-falls. Although, the urban areas in many African countries have structural food-aid requirements, which are regularly reflected in Government's request for aid, most rural areas are not regular recipients of imported foodstuffs.[2]

The market mechanism is inefficient when famines occur. Speculation and hoarding then tend to inflate prices and reduce the purchasing power of existing exchange entitlements. At the same time, production short-falls reduce the degree of self-sufficiency, which is a major food entitlement for rural and urban poor (Dreze, J. and Sen, A., 1989). Moreover, the loss of jobs due to economic decline after harvest failures implies a further loss of entitlements for many people. Consequently, a strong reduction in food production renders most of the poor food insecure. This is a case of transitional (rather than chronic) food insecurity. The market can't solve the problem as purchasing power is insufficient. Moreover, social relationships will not provide a solution for most households, as food insecurity will become a general phenomenon. Government action will be necessary to provide a safety net to cope with transiting food insecurity and possibly widespread famine. The action programme has to offer much more than just the channeling of food aid received from abroad. With regard to food accessibility the policies regarding income transfers and public works for vulnerable groups, and credit facilities for credit-worthy households need special attention (Zeller, M.G., *et al.*, 1997).

These trends in food production coincide with decades of economic problems for many of the African countries. International economic shocks are responsible for a significant portion of the downturn in Africa's economic performance. Low income African countries were affected more severely due to the recessions; for instance the recession of 1973-79 and 1980-83. Alongwith low saving rates and manufactured exports the African countries also characterized deterioration of public finance. However, a few countries with relatively open economies and policies that supported an export orientation were able to somewhat better.

2.3 THE POLICY REFORM AGENDA

In most of the countries of Africa there is a general recognition that the situation that prevailed in agriculture for the last few decades not only did unsustainable but must be changed. The International Financial Institutions (IMF and World Bank) responsible for the design of 'Structural Adjustment Programmes', and other donors involved in Africa's development, have reached the conclusion that African Governments, through their interventions in the agriculture and food sector, have failed to secure reliable food supplies of stable and affordable prices for their populations. Consequently 'Structural Adjustment' called for limiting Government involvement in the pricing and marketing of agricultural produce (Jayne, T. and S. Jones, 1997). Although there is a growing consensus that changes must be made, there remain disputes about what form these changes should take. The general diagnosis of the IMF/World Bank involves the notion that macro-imbalances and domestic supply constraints are at the root of Africa's ongoing crisis. The range of policy reforms suggested include changes in food and agricultural policies, changes in macro-economic policies, and changes in institutions and structures.

(i) Food and Agricultural Policy

Virtually all policy reform programmes focus on the need to increase food and agricultural production. Policy changes, therefore, focus heavily on ways to create greater incentives to domestic agricultural production. The initial phase of the policy reform concentrated heavily on changes in agricultural price policy. Non price factors include the availability of desired consumer goods, as well the institutional support required to evoke a large supply response to improved prices, such as effective marketing system, transportation, and financing.

Food policy is broader than agricultural policy as it also focuses on consumption and nutritional issues. A major concern in policy reform dialogue has been the reduction or elimination of consumer subsidies, which have frequently reflected an urban bias. Key elements of the discussion have focused on the need to reduce consumer subsidies in the process ending systems that were frequently unable to provide guaranteed supplies of low cost food.

(ii) Macro-economic Policy Agenda

The second policy reform agenda focuses on macro-economic policies, which are important not only for their impact on agriculture, but for their wider economic impact. The macro-economic policy dialogue has emphasized the need for changes in the exchange rate, generally to end the overvaluation of African currencies.

(iii) Institutional/Structural Policy Agenda

The institutional policy agenda has focused heavily on the state's role in the economy in general as well as the inefficiency and cost of the institutions created to support this role. The state plays a larger role in the economy in Africa than in any other developing region. There are a variety of historical reasons for this. Consensus on the need for institutional changes has emerged more slowly than in some other areas. Nevertheless, a variety of countries, generally in the context of financial stabilization programmes, have begun to address the public rationalized public sector enterprises.

The agriculture sector and small farmers in particular, are expected to benefit from these reforms on following grounds:

(a) Devaluation combined with internal decontrolling of price formation is assumed to enhance agricultural output;
(b) Replacement of inefficient parastatal marketing boards by private traders tends to lead to substantially lower operating costs of marketing activities (Gould, J. and A.Von Oppen, 1994). Gains resulting from more efficiency in the marketing system are assumed to translate into higher producer prices, and finally

(c) Liberalization of import/export regulations, in the form of reduced tariffs, quotas and subsidies are expected to clear the way for increased export trade and production in the agricultural sector.

However, these policy reform agendas and in particular the Structural Adjustment Programmes neglected the explicit goal of improving the food security conditions of the African population[3]. A substantial proportion of the food producing households in Africa are also food buyers on the market, when household stocks are depleted.

2.4 EXTERNAL DETERMINANTS OF AFRICA'S AGRARIAN CRISIS

Africa's agrarian crisis is well known and the continent is increasingly unable to feed its people; domestic food production in many countries is now woefully inadequate. The gap between production levels and national needs throughout the continent has greatly increased in the last century and is still persisting, requiring massive grain imports (See, USDA, 1981). And in certain of the most seriously affected countries, such as Ethiopia, Sudan, Mozambique, and Chad, even extraordinary efforts to provide food assistance have not prevented starvation. Refugee camps and starving children symbolize a continent-wide agrarian malaise for the last few decades. Although the people of Sub-Saharan Africa constitute only about 10 per cent of the World's population, about 25 per cent of the World's refugees reside there (World Bank, 1981). These figures include only those who cross international boundaries, ignoring the many who remain within their own countries.

An enduring, visible symptom of declining per capita food production is the skyrocketing demand for food imports. Studies conducted in many of the African countries show that prices of the domestic agricultural commodities exceeded import partly, reflecting not only African countries' low agricultural productivity and high transport and marketing costs, but also the highly subsidized nature of European Union and American exports which are prevailing[4]. Export oriented agriculture has also stagnated, resulting in foreign exchange shortages for most African countries. As most African countries depend upon agriculture to generate the earnings necessary not only for food purchase but to acquire other vital imports—including medical and educational supplies, petroleum products, transportation equipment, and consumer goods—the stagnant trend in agricultural exports is at least as alarming as that for food production. Stagnation in export performance thus contributes directly to the inadequate industrial performance of many African countries. As much of the Africa's industrial sector is built on the foreign exchange earning capacity of other economic spheres particularly agriculture, to finance the import of critically important inputs—capital goods, raw-materials and spare parts. For this reason, the extremely low rates of capacity utilization that now characterize many of Africa's industries are directly attributable to the disappointing performance of export agriculture.

The overemphasis on the export sector can be directly related to Africa's current food crisis (Seppala, P., 1998). Colonial governments vigorously promoted agricultural exports, but neglected food production. Consequently, by the eve of independence in the early 1960s and 1970s, numerous African countries had already become net food importers. They exhibited a weakness that would manifest itself as the severe Sahelian famine of the early 1970s and the equally critical food shortage in Ethiopia and Tanzania during that period. Out of the colonial bias favouring export agriculture emerged a market discrepancy between the pattern of production characteristics of export-oriented agriculture and that which prevailed in the production of food staples for domestic consumption[5].

The working of the international marketplace also contradicts the expectations. For the production of tropical export crops is now enormously competitive; new suppliers regularly enter the already overcrowded market, sometimes responding to minute and temporary upward shifts in commodities' prices (Singh, Shamsher, 1983). Coffee, cotton, and sugar, thus oversupplied, sell at prices at or barely above the cost of production. Kenya, Ethiopia, Uganda, Tanzania, and Ivory Cost not only compete with one another for a share of the international coffee market, they also compete with Brazil, Colombia, and Peru. If Africa is to recover economically, World demand for such pivotally important commodities as coffee, cocoa, tea, sugar and cotton would have to improve substantially over the coming decades.

2.5 NATURE OF FARM PRODUCTION AND KEY INFLUENCES

Numerous interrelated choices have to be made in planning the development of subsistence agriculture in Africa. It includes the following:

(i) Choices regarding promotion of profitable crop with an assured export market or development of the overall farming system.
(ii) Choices with regard to factor mix; that is capital intensive or labour intensive production process are to be promoted.
(iii) Choices of circumstances regarding development of farming necessitate settlement of populations on new land as distinct from intensification of already cultivated land.
(iv) Choices of conditions regarding development of farming that are brought about by concentration of financial and administrative resources in regions, as was attempted in the integrated rural development programmes.
(v) Choices regarding equitable allocation of resources between regions.

Studies show that, compared to Asia and Latin America, labour availability in Africa is frequently a grater constraint to increasing productivity than is the availability of land (Lele, Uma, 1975). As a result, technological innovations, which require intense labour input, often may no result in the full realization of potential production increases. At the same time, however, there is some *prima facie* evidence of surplus labour in African agriculture. On an average, African small holders devote only about 1000 man hours per adult per year to agricultural activities, compared upto 3000 man hours in several Asian and Latin American countries (John H. Cleave, 1974). Thus, there is the seeming paradox of a farm labour shortage compared with an apparent labour surplus. The explanation for this contradiction lies in the way the labour time is allocated in African agriculture; such as seasonality of labor usage, allotment of time between farm work, non-farm activities, and leisure, and division of labour between the sexes[6].

These factors influence the amount of labour allocated to agricultural work at any given point in time; they frequently pose a constraint to increasing productivity, limiting the effectiveness of interventions introduced through programmes.

The labour availability in smallholder agriculture is also closely related to the desire of subsistence producers to ensure domestic food needs. The food constraints can be attributed to the following two factors that are frequently noted in the traditional African agriculture:

(i) The generally high risk and low profitability of food technology, which ties up a substantial amount of labour in food crop production; and
(ii) The fragmented market systems for food crops which necessitate priority on food production to ensure supply for domestic consumption.

The neglect of food crop production may, apart from its adverse effect on allocative efficiency, also have adverse effects on nutrition of the rural population. The problem of ensuring food supplies in rural areas is frequently exacerbated by the pricing and marketing policies followed by Governments towards food crops. Food crop pricing is particularly susceptible to socio-political influences that are often not conducive to domestic food production.

The concentration of administrative and financial resources on a single export crop may have been justified in many of the past programmes, given the limited resources available for investment, the often low level of technology available for food production, and the frequent lack of price incentives necessary to increase cereal production. However, past experiences indicate that in the long-run such concentration may be detrimental to equity as well as to allocative efficiency. Rural development projects need to devote increasing attention to diversified farming and especially to food crop production.

2.6 MECHANIZATION AND SMALL-HOLDER AGRICULTURE

One of the solutions to the food-labour constraint has been the introduction of mechanical implements to increase the output per unit of labour. These implements vary from simple hand-powered devices to sophisticated engine machinery. Tractors have often been viewed as a symbol of modern agriculture in Africa and, consequently have been promoted through many rural development programmes. Though tractors have generally proven well adapted to large-scale western-style commercial farming, their role in development of smallholder agriculture has been less clear for a variety of reasons (Hans Ruthenberg, 1971). Since the labour bottleneck in peasant farming is largely seasonal, tractor services are needed at only the few critical periods of peak labour demand. Tractors are most useful in field preparation but often are of little utility in weeding or harvesting[7].

Tractors may therefore only postpone rather than break the labour bottleneck while doing little to alleviate the problem of underutilization of farm labour at periods of slack agricultural activity. Under some circumstances tractorization has aggravated labour bottleneck rather than relieving them. For example, mid-season weeding tends to be a highly labor-demanding activity in much of peasant agriculture, when tractors are used for land preparation but not for weeding, as frequently tends to be the case, tractorization increases weeding requirements. This is because tractorization allows expansion of cultivated area and hence the area to be weeded. Since the mid-season weeding period is already a time of peak labour demand, an even tighter labour bottleneck may be created. Therefore tractorization can be successful only if the necessary complementary innovations are introduced to alleviate the labour constraint.

It is estimated that tractors may require 1200 revenue earning hours per year to break even (John H. Cleave, 1974). However, tractors are frequently used only half as many hours. Several other problems are frequently encountered in the use of machines in small-holder farming. It include, the high capital costs of the equipment and herbicides, the high overhead involved in maintaining and servicing the underutilized machinery, the administrative problems in sharing a limited number of machines among a large number of diverse users, and the technical difficulties of employing tractors under certain topographical and soil conditions.

The Tanzanian experience indicates that careful attention has to be paid to ensure that in practice the increases in production resulting from the introduction of mechanization (especially tractorization) will justify their high cost[8]. Where labour is inexpensive, tractorization may only mean substituting high cost capital for low cost labour. Though there often is scope for mechanized input to farming, the introduction of manual or animal powered equipment may be a more feasible alternative than tractors.

The recognition of this fact is reflected in Tanzania's 'Ujamaa Policy', which emphasizes self-reliance among small-holders and less spectacular forms of mechanization that are consistent with local resources.

The availability of labour in small-holder agriculture is also strongly influenced by demographic patterns and intra-rural migration, which in turn are related to the relative return to investment in agriculture in various regions. Surplus and underemployed labour may be attracted to areas with profitable agriculture and obvious labour bottlenecks. An influx of population to such areas may lead to a rapid increase in production and employment. Conversely, areas with unattractive income and employment opportunities may suffer a net outflow of population, creating labour shortages and economic stagnation. Migration may be temporary or permanent and, in either case, may frequently add substantially to the income of the migrants. On the other hand, a rapid population influx may also lead to a decline in wages and aggravate servitude, rural poverty, and social tensions in the regions of immigration.

2.7 CONCLUSION

The forgone discussion in this chapter illustrates that hunger exists in Africa inspite of global improvements in economic growth and sustained increase in world output of agricultural products since the latter half of the 20th century. The fundamental cause of hunger in the continent is the poverty of specific groups of people and not a general shortage of food. In simple terms, what distinguishes the poor from the rest of the World's people is that they do not have sufficient purchasing power or what Sen has pointed out the entitlement to enable them to acquire enough to eat. The problem is in the relationship of particular groups of people to food, not food itself.

Important international linkages are also at work in the Sub-Saharan region. The ideology of free enterprise, free trade, and free movement of capital has shaped the international order and has been recommended wherever possible to developing countries. However, the real underdeveloped world society is entirely different from the western societies. Technology as well as western ideas can not obviate the need for social and institutional changes that is prevalently needed in most of the African countries if poverty and hunger are to be reduced significantly. Appropriate technology in situation specific and hardly ever succeeds as a direct plant from a western country.

Organizing to export agricultural commodities has left Africa vulnerable to adverse trends in the international economy. Despite hopes voiced by rent-for-surplus and comparative advantage advocates, little benefit has spilled from export agriculture to other sectors. The international donor countries have failed to develop policies and programmes that can effectively arrest the process of long-term structural decline. Despite the generations of neglect, Africa's small-holder farmers continue to demonstrate enormous social resiliency, market responsiveness, and productive capacity.

NOTES

1. Analysis of the US Department of Agriculture's Economic Research Service (USDA/ERS) indicates that if the upper 30 per cent of the population were able to avoid adjusting consumption during a food emergency, a shortfall of only 5 per cent in aggregate would translate into a 20 per cent decline is already low availability in the lower 30 per cent of the income distribution.
2. For instance in Tanzania the market-led policies under Structural Adjustment Programme have fundamentally altered the national policy balance, introducing an anti-rural bias, which is most dramatically led to the widespread rural famines.
3. Nevertheless, market and related price reforms have consequences for the food security of different socio-economic groups. In particular changes in producer and consumer prices and food availability in urban and rural markets.
4. See for example, Deborah Fahy Bryceson, *et al.,* 'Maize Marketing Policies in Tanzania, 1938-1998,' *Agricultural Marketing in Tropical Africa*, African Studies Centre, Leiden. 1999.
5. This discrepancy is sometimes referred to as agrarian dualism and is characterized firstly by an export enclave, which in turn characterized

by the production of a few raw-materials for export and processing in the factories of the developed countries. The expansion of this enclave is primarily determined by the growth of effective demand for agricultural raw-materials in the developed countries. Secondly, a hinterland in which the majority of population lives and works in the traditional agrarian economy. The main contribution of this hinterland to the export enclave is a flow of cheap, unskilled migrant labour.

6. In traditional African agriculture these frequently tends to be a market distinction in the roles of sexes, although this division is bewilderingly variable in various parts of Africa. Cash crops and heavy work such as ploughing have tended to be a male responsibility. Food crops and lighter work like weeding are more often the women's charge. Women are also responsible for the bulk of the domestic work—such as food preparation, wood and water gathering, and child rearing. The total amount of labour input by sexes is often quite disproportionate. UN Economic Council's studies show that women provide 60-80 per cent of the agricultural labour used in parts of Africa.
7. Studies conducted in the *Zaria* area of Northern Nigeria show that 26 per cent of total agricultural labour time devoted to weeding, the bulk of which occurs during June and July (Norman, D.W., 1974).
8. In 1960s the Tanzanian Government introduced a cotton block scheme in the *Sukumaland* region, which was hinged on the use of centralized tractor facilities. However, the scheme never achieved the scale envisaged. Rather then the proposed ratio of 121.5 hectares per tractor, each tractor worked an average of only 27.1 hectares. Yields were similar to those achieved by farmers non-participatory in the programme. The cost per hectare was approximately six times as high as the cost of production of non-participants.

REFERENCES

Deborah Fahy Bryceson, *et al.* (1999). 'Maize Marketing Policies in Tanzania, 1938-1998,' *Agricultural Marketing in Tropical Africa*, African Studies Centre, Leiden.

Dreze, J and A., Sen (1989). *Hunger and Public Action*, Clarendon Press, Oxford.

Gould, J. and A., Von Oppen (1994). 'Of Rhetoric and Market: The Liberalization of Food Trade in East Africa,' *Socilogia Ruralis*, Vol. 34, No. 1.

Hanmer, L. *et al.* (1996). *Poverty in Sub-Saharan Africa—What Can We Learn from the World Bank's Poverty Assessments?* Institute of Social Studies, The Hague.

Hans, Ruthenberg (1971). *Farming Systems in the Tropics*, Clarendon Press, Oxford.

Jayne, T. and S., Jones (1997). 'Food Marketing and Pricing Policy in Eastern and Southern Africa,' *World Development*, Vol. 25, No. 9.

John, H. Cleave (1974). *African Farmers: Labour Use in the Development of Small-Holder Agriculture*, Praeger, New York.

Lele, Uma (1975). *The Design of Rural Development: Lessons from Africa*, World Bank Research Publication, The Johns Hopkins University Press, Baltimore and London.

Norman, D.W. (1974). *The Organizational Consequences of Social and Economic Constraints and Policies in Dry Land Areas*, Paper Presented to the Second International Seminar on Change in Agriculture, September 9-19, Reading UK.

Seppala, P. (1998). 'Liberalized and Neglected? Food Marketing in Eastern Africa', *World Development Studies No. 12*, WIDER, United Nations University.

Sijm, J. (1997). *Food Security and Policy Interventions in Sub-Saharan Africa: Lessons from the Past Two Decades*, Erasmus University, Rotterdam.

Singh, Shamsher (1983). 'Sub-Saharan Agriculture: Synthesis and Trade Prospects,' *World Bank Staff Working Paper No. 608*, Washington D.C.

Tagwiregi, J. (1991). 'Zimbabwe: Food Access and Nutrition Linkages,' in M. Rukuni and J. Wyckoff (eds), *Market Reform Research Policies and SADCC Food Security*, UZ/MSU Food Security Research in Southern Africa Project, Harare.

Thorbecke, E. (1992). *The Anatomy of Agricultural Product Markets and Transactions in Developing Countries*, Institute for Policy Reform, Washington DC.

USDA, (1981). 'Food Problems and Prospects in Sub-Saharan Africa: The Decade of the 1980s,' *Foreign Agricultural Research Report*, No. 166, Washington.

World Bank, (1981). Accelerated Development in Sub-Saharan Africa: An Agenda for Action, Washington, D.C.

Zeller, M.G., *et al.* (1997). 'Rural Financing for Food Security for the Poor: Implications for Research and Policy,' *Food Policy Review*, No. 4, IF PRI, Washington.

3

Food Security in Africa
Challenges and Interventions

3.1 INTRODUCTION

Food security; a situation in which all people, at all times, have physical and economic access to sufficient, safe and nutritious food to meet their dietary needs and food preferences for an active healthy life. Achieving food security in its totality continues to be a challenge not only for the developing nations, but also for the developed world. The difference lies in the magnitude of the problem in terms of its severity and proportion of the population affected. The root cause of food insecurity in developing countries is the inability of people to gain access to food due to poverty. While the rest of the world has made significant progress towards poverty alleviation, Africa, in particular Sub-Saharan Africa, continues to lag behind.

While the definition of food security has evolved over time, a food-secure household is generally described as one that can reliably obtain food of adequate quality and quantity to support a healthy and active life for all members of the household. Food security is influenced by many factors, including poverty, consistent access to food, nutrition, food production, the availability of resources, and coping strategies. Food security in Africa has substantially worsened since 1970. Although recent data show that the proportion of malnourished individuals in Sub Saharan Africa fell slightly from 35 per cent in 1990-92 to 33 per cent in 1999-2001, a long-term perspective reveals that this share has remained within the

33-35 per cent range since around 1970. Even more discouraging, the absolute number of malnourished people in Africa has increased substantially with population growth, from around 88 million in 1970 to an estimate of over 200 million in 1999–2001 (FAO, 2004). This record is in stark contrast to that of other developing regions such as South and East Asia, which have made significant strides in combating malnutrition over the same time frame. The aggregate numbers, however, conceal considerable variation across the African continent. During the 1990s the proportion of malnourished people declined in all African regions except Central Africa, where it increased from 35 per cent in 1990-92 to 58 per cent in 1999-01.

The present chapter analyses the food security challenges in Africa with emphasis on required interventions. It also reviews the worsening food security situation in Africa and also makes forecasting based on important scenarios.

3.2 ENTITLEMENTS APPROACH TO FOOD SECURITY

The food entitlement concept was introduced by Prof. Sen by highlighting the demand side of the food security concept as contradictory to the conventional supply side bias[1]. Thus the modern definition of food security contains three crucial elements: the accessibility of food resulting from exchange entitlements[2], the availability of food through market channels and the certainty of both accessibility and availability, at every moment and in the places where required (Dreze, J. and A., Sen, 1989). This paradigm shift from inadequate food supplies to lack of purchasing power and its combined impact on the food security helped to distinguish between chronic food insecurity and transitory food insecurity. Chronic food insecurity is a continuously inadequate diet caused by the inability to acquire food. It affects households that persistently lack the ability either to buy food or to produce their own. Transitory food insecurity is a temporary decline in a household's access to enough food. It results from a major shortfall in food production or household income—and in its worst form it ends in hunger. Frequent famines in some Sub-Saharan African countries are the worst form of transitory food insecurity on a large scale.

Figure 3.1: A Simplified Food System

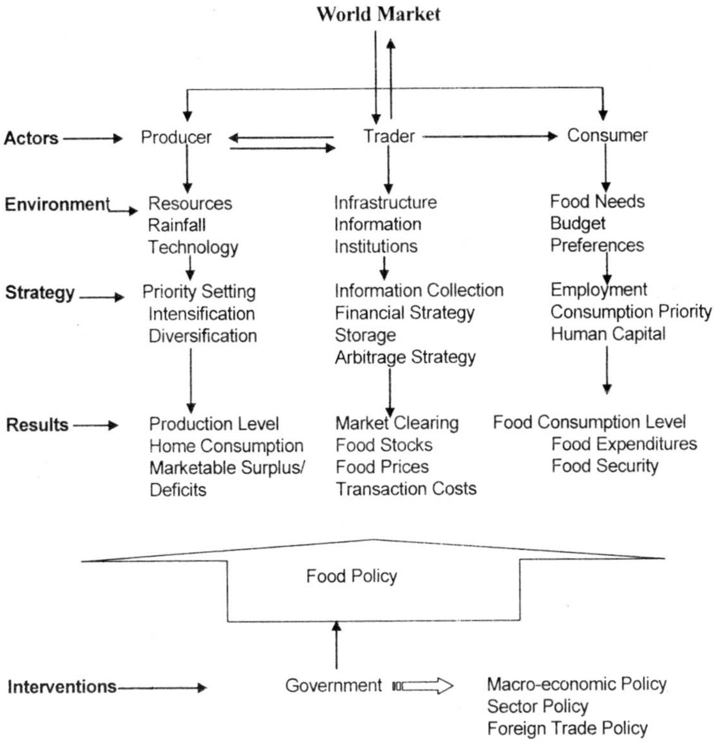

The distinction between chronic hunger and famines point towards important differences between policy instruments[3]. In the context of famine prevention Africa need emphasis on timely intervention and reliance on existing distributional mechanisms, supplemented by the logistic capability of relief agencies. On the other hand combating hunger requires quite different actions, like institution-building, entitlements protection, asset redistribution and provisioning in kind.

The food system of a country is characterized by a complex series of relationships between producers, traders and consumers (Figure 3.1). The model discussed here is a simplified agro-food system, based on three types of actors who transfer the surplus offered by the producers *via* the trader to the consumer. The food system encompasses all interactions and the underlying strategies of each of the actors involved in the food chain. Properly functioning food markets serve both the producers at the one end and the consumers at the other end; market failures or missing markets reduce opportunities for producers, as well as food availability for consumers.

In the present model, even though the Government is not an actor in the food system, it can intervene at the level of each of the three types of actor. The intervention may consist of measures to encourage producers to increase food production; to improve the functioning of the food markets; or to improve the accessibility of food producers to consumers. Other Government policies may indirectly affect the private decision-making of any of the actors (Maxwell, S, 1996). These actions include various macro-economic policies such as external trade policy, exchange rate policies, wage and tax policies or interest rate policies.

In the semi-arid areas of Sub-Saharan Africa the time patterns of food production and consumption do not coincide; there is only one harvest a year, while consumption is continuous (Weber, M.T, *et al.*, 1988). At the same time spatial arbitrage is crucial for the food system. Normally, the food chain goes from the rural producer towards the urban food consumer. In most of the African countries the situation is more complex. Many foodgrain producers are constrained by variable seasonal agro-ecological conditions and appear to be net food buyers, particularly in structural deficit regions. This feature implies specific requirements for the functioning of trade within the food system.

3.3 WORSENING FOOD SECURITY IN AFRICA

Food security on the continent has worsened since 1970 and the proportion of the malnourished population has remained within the 33 to 35 per cent range in Sub-Saharan Africa. The prevalence of malnutrition within the continent varies by region. It is lowest in Northern Africa (4%) and highest in Central Africa (40%). Over seventy per cent of the food insecure population in Africa lives in the rural areas. Ironically, small-holder farmers, the producers of over 90 per cent of the continent's food supply, make up the majority (50%) of this population. The rest of the food insecure population consists of the landless poor in rural areas (25%) and the urban poor (Figure 3.2). In countries where more than 34 per cent of the population is undernourished, agriculture represents 30 per cent of GDP and nearly 70 per cent of the population relies on agriculture for their livelihood. This fact has in the past been used in support of the argument as to why developing countries should move away from agriculture and invest in technology. Because over 70 per cent of the poor live in rural areas, where also the largest proportion of the food insecure live, it is evident that we cannot significantly and sustainably reduce food insecurity without transforming the living conditions in these areas (Rosegrant, *et al.*, 2005). The key lies in increasing the agricultural profitability of small-holder farmers and creating rural off-farm employment opportunities.

Figure 3.2: Food Insecure Population in Africa

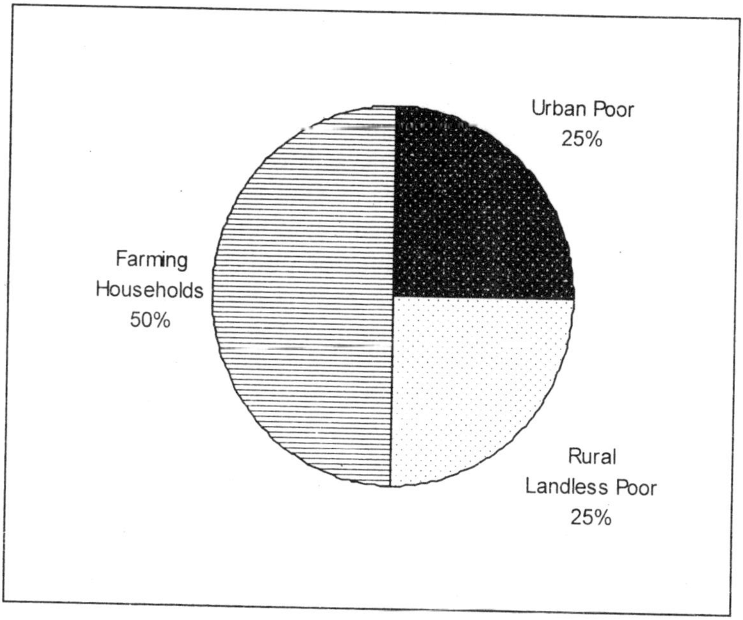

Ultimately food security should translate to an active healthy life for every individual. For this to take place the nutritionally adequate diet should be biologically utilized so that adequate performance is maintained in growth, resistance or recovery from disease, pregnancy, lactation and or physical work. Hence adequate health and care must be provided in addition to adequate food. Herein lies the problem facing poor households today. Food insecurity has the potential to influence food intake and ultimately the health and nutritional status of households. In developing countries over 85 per cent of the food consumed by poor households in rural setting is obtained from the farm. The importance of foods purchased from markets in meeting household food security depends on household food income and market price. The seasonality of foodgrains available at the household level may highly influence food availability in places where little to no food preservation is practiced. This is the case with fruits and vegetables, which are highly perishable.

Many studies show that the food crisis in Africa is continuing to worsen. The United Nations Food and Agricultural Organisation's (FAO) Freedom from Hunger Campaign aimed at reducing food insecurity and has failed miserably in Africa. The average "developing world" figure for under-nourishment is 17 per cent, in Sub-Saharan Africa the figure is 33 per cent. For Central Africa it is 55 per cent. On average the number of African food emergencies per year since the mid 1980s has tripled (Benson, T, 2004). The commitment to halve hunger by 2015, as part of the Millennium Development Goals, will not be met by in Africa at current rate of progress.

The food security of a region is mainly related to the discrepancy between cereal production and demand. In the region as a whole, cereal demand increases 5.7 per cent, while cereal production increases 8.0 per cent. The effect is greater in the Sub-Saharan region alone, where cereal demand increases 7.3 per cent and cereal production 9.7 per cent (See Table 3.1 and Figure 3.3). Cereal production and demand also increase in Egypt, by 6.8 per cent and 3.6 per cent, respectively, while production in other WANA increases by 4.6 per cent and demand by 4.2 per cent. The impact is even stronger for meat commodities, with an increase of 9.3 per cent in African meat demand and 9.8 per cent in meat production. As in the case of cereals, the effects on meat commodities are even greater in Sub-Saharan Africa, where meat demand increases by 12.6 per cent and meat production by 11.5 per cent (Table 3.2). North Africa also experiences an increase in meat production and demand, with a 7.8 per cent increase in production and a 5.7 per cent increase in demand.

Figure 3.3: Cereal Demand and Production in Africa (MMT)

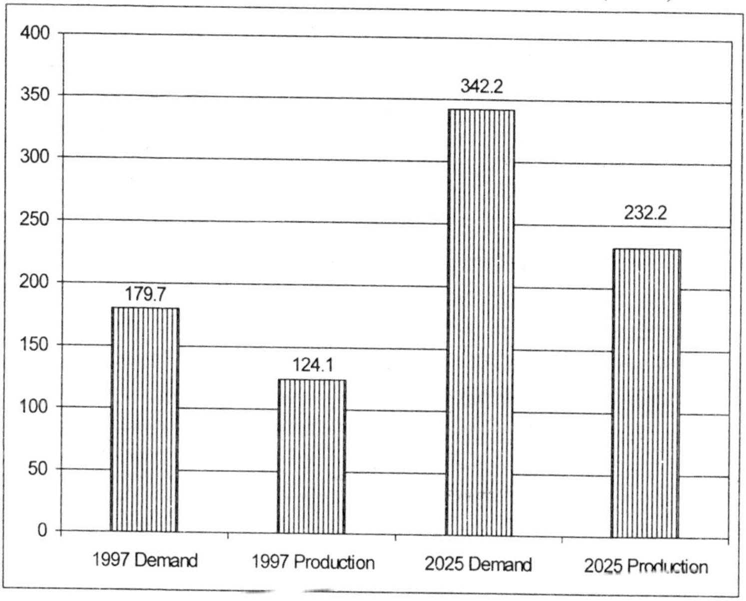

Table 3.1: Cereal Demand and Production in Africa

Region/Country	*Cereal Demand (million metric tons)*		*Cereal Production (million metric tons)*	
	1997	*2025*	*1997*	*2025*
1. Northern Sub-Saharan Africa	22.7	48.3	20.5	42.3
2. Central and Western Sub-Saharan Africa	13.9	32.3	9.4	22.7
3. Southern Sub-Saharan Africa	12.3	24.6	9.8	20.0
4. Eastern Sub-Saharan Africa	10.8	21.9	9.0	18.7
5. Nigeria	22.8	47.6	20.6	41.4
6. All Sub-Saharan Africa	82.5	174.6	69.3	145.1
7. Egypt	23.7	37.8	15.9	24.3
8. Other West Asia/North Africa	73.5	129.7	38.9	62.7
9. All Africa	179.7	342.2	124.1	232.2

Source: IFPRI IMPACT Projections, 2004.

The central reason why the situation has not improved is the major powers' failure to respond speedily and appropriately to the emergency food situations. It is a regular occurrence that emergency financial appeals by bodies such as the United Nations get a slow and partial response. Most UN emergency appeals receive only 30 per cent of the requested funds in their first month[4]. The UN estimates that 16 million people are at immediate risk in ten neglected and under-funded emergencies in Africa, which include the prolonged tragedies of Northern Uganda and the Democratic Republic of Congo (UNU-INRA and World Bank, 1999). Most of the aid provided to Africa is given as food, and related non-food needs are generally not met. It can take four to five months for food to be delivered. While purchasing food locally would be a cheaper and more efficient method of giving aid, the Governments of donor countries have their own agendas for shipping food instead.

Table 3.2: Projected Meat Demand and Production in Africa

Region/Country	*Meat Demand (million metric tons)*		*Meat Production (million metric tons)*	
	1997	*2025*	*1997*	*2025*
1. Northern Sub-Saharan Africa	1.6	3.9	1.6	3.8
2. Central and Western Sub-Saharan Africa	1.0	2.5	0.8	2.3
3. Southern Sub-Saharan Africa	0.9	2.0	0.9	2.1
4. Egypt	1.0	2.4	0.9	1.9
5. Eastern Sub-Saharan Africa	0.9	2.2	0.9	2.1
6. Nigeria	1.1	2.7	1.1	2.4
7. All Sub-Saharan Africa	5.5	13.3	5.4	12.7
8. Other West Asia/North Africa	4.9	9.9	4.3	8.6
9. All Africa	11.4	25.6	10.6	23.2

Source: IFPRI IMPACT Projections, 2004.

Increasing poverty is a key factor in the hunger crisis—in some food crises food may be available but is simply unaffordable. Since 1981 the number of those living on less than a $1 a day in Sub-Saharan Africa has increased twofold to over 310 million people. Over the last two decades Sub-Saharan Africa has had "inadequate debt cancellation, declining and poor quality development aid, flawed advice from donors, conditions attached to aid that forced countries to adopt damaging agricultural policies, and unfair trade rules. The root cause of Africa's ongoing food insecurity is the lack of investment in agricultural production. Sub-Saharan Africa has a predominantly rural economy, with 70 per cent of the population living in rural areas and providing the livelihoods of two-thirds of the population. Whilst immediate food aid from the West has been increasing, aid for agricultural production in Sub-Saharan Africa dropped by 43 per cent in the 1990s.

According to the New Partnership for African Development (NEPAD, 2002), it would require an investment of $18 billion a year into the rural infrastructure to achieve the World Food Summit goal to cut hunger by 50 per cent (See Box 3.1). Much of African agriculture remains rain-fed only, and those irrigation schemes that do exist are concentrated in large commercial agri-business estates.

Box 3.1: Declaration of the Abuja Food Security Summit (December 4-7, 2006, Abuja, Nigeria)

1. Increase Intra African trade by promoting and protecting rice, maize, legumes, cotton, oil palm, beef, dairy, poultry and fisheries products as strategic commodities at the continental level, and cassava, sorghum and millet at sub-regional level without prejudice to focused attention being given also to products of particular national importance;
2. Take urgent measures to accelerate the development of the strategic commodities by fast tracking the implementation of trade arrangements adopted in the Regional Economic Communities (RECs) through lowering tariff barriers and elimination of non-tariff barriers both technical and non-technical by 2010;
3. Ratify and implement harmonized standards and grades including sanitary and phytosanitary standards within and across RECs by 2010;
4. Construct and maintain critical infrastructure to facilitate the movement of strategic agricultural products across national boundaries at minimal cost;
5. Develop continental and regional market information systems and support the development of the same at national level by 2008;
6. Promote public sector investment in agriculture related infrastructure, particularly regarding water, irrigation, electricity and roads through public-private partnership;
7. Reduce risks of both natural and commercial origins, including through marketing arrangements and insurance schemes.
8. Call upon Africa based development banks and financial institutions to improve access to soft loans, small loans and grants;
9. Expand the implementation of the NEPAD Home-Grown School feeding initiative to reach 20 per cent of member states by 2008 through a financing and delivery partnership between Government and development partners with benefits to reach 25 per cent of the needy children by 2015;

(Contd.)

10. Initiate the implementation of the African Regional Nutrition Strategy, the NEPAD African Nutrition Initiative, and the NEPAD 10-year strategy for combating Vitamin and Mineral Deficiency by 2008 with focus on long-term household food security and ending child hunger and under-nutrition;
11. Establish a technical assistance programme for agriculture and food security based on African resources and expertise and in collaboration with development partners and develop regional centres of excellence;
12. Establish, in consultation with the African Development Bank (ADB) and the International Fund for Agricultural Development (IFAD) a funding mechanism or adapt existing ones to mobilize additional resources for purposes of up-scaling agricultural successes within and across countries in Africa;
13. Establish a system for selecting and prioritizing key AUC and NEPAD CAADP related summit commitments by undertaking a review and prioritization of past commitments for implementation to meet the objectives of food and nutrition security;
14. Take ownership of important commitments by way of formalizing and institutionalizing them, including making adequate resources available;
15. Call upon the African Union Commission to follow up with member states, RECs and other relevant stakeholders on the implementation of the above declarations and report to the Assembly of Heads of State and Government annually on progress and challenges.

3.4 THREE SCENARIOS FOR THE FUTURE: BUSINESS AS USUAL, PESSIMISTIC AND VISION

The business as usual scenario (henceforth BAU) assumes a continuation of current trends and existing plans in food policy, management, and investment. Investments by international donors and national governments in the agricultural sector continue to decline and this sluggish investment trend, combined with sporadic policy reform, leads to slow progress in meeting the major challenges facing African agriculture. Under this scenario, per capita kilocalorie consumption in Sub-Saharan Africa is projected to increase from 2,231 kilocalories per capita per day in 1997 to 2,526 kilocalories in 2025, lagging behind the rest of the world (Table 3.3). Despite increasing kilocalorie consumption, the number of malnourished children under the age of five increases from 32.7 million in 1997 to

38.3 million in 2025, although this absolute increase represents a decline in percentage terms from 32.8 per cent in 1997 to 28.2 per cent in 2025.

Table 3.3: Projected Per Capita Kilocalories Available in Africa under the Business as Usual Scenario

Region/Country	*Available kilocalories per capita per day*			
	Baseline	*Projected*		
	1997	*2015*	*2020*	*2025*
1. Northern Sub-Saharan Africa	2,175	2,253	2,293	2,346
2. Central and Western Sub-Saharan Africa	2,175	2,309	2,378	2,458
3. Southern Sub-Saharan Africa	2,022	2,162	2,225	2,305
4. Eastern Sub-Saharan Africa	1,999	2,110	2,167	2,233
5. Nigeria	2,759	3,073	3,203	3,356
6. All Sub-Saharan Africa	2,231	2,377	2,444	2,526
7. West Asia/North Africa	3,059	3,175	3,209	3,238
8. Developing countries	2,668	2,935	3,001	3,058

Source: IFPRI IMPACT Projections, 2004.

Contributing factor to ongoing food insecurity under this scenario is the expected modest growth in agricultural production by historical standards to 2025. Between 1997 and 2025, BAU projects annual African cereal production growth of 1.9 per cent for wheat, 2.3 per cent for maize, 2.4 per cent for other coarse grains, 2.5 per cent for rice, and 2.7 per cent for roots and tubers (Table 3.4). The projected 2.7 per cent cereal production growth in Sub-Saharan Africa is slightly less than the 3.6 per cent actual annual increase in production achieved during 1982–97; projected annual root and tuber production growth rates of 2.7 per cent per year also represent a decline from actual 1982–97 rates, which averaged 4.3 per cent per year (Leipziger, D, *et al.*, 2003). Under BAU, crop production in Africa continues to expand onto unused land. Area under cereal and root and tuber cultivation increases in Sub-Saharan Africa at rates ranging from 27 per cent in Nigeria to 40 per cent in Central and Western Sub-Saharan Africa, although this expansion is slow by historic equivalents.

Even with the relatively strong agricultural productivity growth projected under BAU, the food security implications for Africa are disappointing. Alternatively, Africa's future could be even bleaker with agricultural stagnation, drastically deepening poverty, and worsening social indicators. Many countries in the region have struggled with the transition to private sector input and output markets, and uncertain input availability and producer prices remain major factors limiting the ability of small-holders to plan investments with long time horizons (Breman, H, *et al.,* 2003). While BAU projects that area expansion will slow over the next two decades, even these projections may be optimistic given the extent of the ongoing degradation of the existing land base. Severe soil fertility depletion and erosion affect both marginal and high-quality rainfed lands, frequently characterized by inappropriate nutrient replacement or conservationist practices, pest problems, overdependence on maize mono-culture, and high water variability.

Table 3.4: Projected Crop Production Growth Rates in Africa under the Business as Usual Scenario

Region/Country	Production Growth Rates (% per year)				
	Wheat	Maize	Other Course Grains	Rice	All Roots and Tubers
1. Nigeria	3.3	2.1	2.6	2.9	2.7
2. Northern Sub-Saharan Africa	2.6	2.1	2.7	2.9	2.7
3. Central and Western Sub-Saharan Africa	3.0	3.0	3.4	3.4	2.9
4. Southern Sub-Saharan Africa	2.8	2.4	3.4	2.8	2.4
5. Eastern Sub-Saharan Africa	3.7	2.4	3.0	2.6	2.8
6. All Sub-Saharan Africa	2.9	2.4	2.8	3.0	2.7
7. Egypt	1.6	1.6	0.7	1.5	2.3
8. Other West Asia/North Africa	1.9	2.0	1.2	1.7	2.2
9. All Africa	1.9	2.3	2.4	2.5	2.7

Source: IFPRI IMPACT Projections, 2004.

The pessimistic scenario (PES) is quantified by subtracting 0.50 per cent from crop yield growth rates and 0.50 per cent from livestock growth (number of head) beginning in 2005. Additionally, because of the importance of agricultural production to African economies, BAU GDP growth rate assumptions are cut by 25 per cent under PES. Lastly, a variety of social indicators are also projected to worsen, with female access to secondary schooling and access to clean water falling by 15 per cent and the female-to-male life expectancy ratio falling by 1.5 per cent compared with BAU levels. Population growth is also expected to increase in Africa under PES, so the UN medium variant population growth projections used for BAU are replaced with the high variant for PES.

The third scenario, the vision scenario (henceforth VIS), attempts to answer this question by providing a sense of the magnitude of the region's challenges and the necessity of concerted attention by national Governments and international organizations. VIS models the interventions necessary to cut child malnutrition in Africa sufficiently to reach the MDG target of cutting the proportion of people suffering from hunger in half by 2015 (Fishbein, R., 2003). It provides a glimpse into a positive vision of substantial improvements in African agriculture, nutrition, and food security. A substantial increase in crop production is required to reach the malnutrition goals for Africa conceived under VIS. Annual cereal production growth rates are projected to be 3 per cent per year for all of Africa, and 3.5 per cent per year in Sub-Saharan Africa alone between 1997 and 2025 under VIS. Rice yields are projected to have the largest percentage growth over the period, with a 3.4 per cent annual growth in Africa and a 4 per cent growth rate in Sub-Saharan Africa alone. While both area and yield increases contribute to the increase in production, yield growth rates are higher over the time frame. Growth between 1997 and 2025 across Sub-Saharan Africa is 2.5 per cent for all cereals, compared with the BAU level of 1.7 per cent. Area, production and yield of cereals under BAU is given in Table 3.5.

Table 3.5: Cereal Area, Production, and Yield in Africa (BAU)

Indicators	*Baseline 1995*			*Projected 2025*		
	Irrigated	*Rainfed*	*Total*	*Irrigated*	*Rainfed*	*Total*
1. Cereal Area (million hectares)	12.8	90.1	102.9	15.4	119.9	135.3
2. Cereal Production (million metric tons)	40.8	79.8	120.6	67.0	150.8	217.8
3. Cereal Yield (metric tons per hectare)	3.19	0.89	1.17	2.43	1.26	1.48

Source: Rosegrant, Cai, and Cline, 2002.

3.5 CHALLENGES TO FOOD SECURITY IN AFRICA

Some progress has been made in Sub-Saharan regions, particularly in West Africa, where the rate of malnutrition fell from 21 per cent in 1990–92 to 15 per cent in 1999–2001. In Benin, Ghana, and Nigeria, in particular, both the percentage and the number of malnourished people have consistently declined over the past 20 years (Inter-Academy Council, 2004). Both East and Southern Africa have made some progress in reducing the percentage of undernourished people; nevertheless, around 40 per cent of the populations of both these regions are still malnourished. Not surprisingly, North Africa has a much lower proportion of malnourished people than the rest of the continent, at 4 per cent in 1999–2001. The following are the important issues facing Africa in the food security front, which are to be tackled through proper policy interventions.

(*i*) Poverty

According to a traditional measure of poverty (the number of people living on less than US$1 per day), 163.6 million people in Sub-Saharan Africa lived below the poverty line in 1981, and the number increased to 226.8 million in 1990 and 315.8 million in 2001. The poverty estimates also increased in percentage terms, with 41.6 per cent below the poverty line in 1981, 44.6 per cent in 1990, and 46.9 per cent in 2001 (World Bank, 2003). The history of poverty in Africa is punctuated by systematic marginalization by colonial powers, chronically poor resource endowments at both household and regional levels, and the vagaries of climate and geography, from massive droughts and floods to extreme remoteness. Instability due to continuing political, ethnic, and armed conflicts further entrenches parts of Africa in a cycle of chronic poverty and food insecurity. Poverty in Africa has also been affected historically by unfavourable trade policies and the external debt burdens held by many African nations. Lack of Government investments in social services and infrastructure has hindered economic development, thus adding to mounting poverty levels. Poverty has serious effects on food and nutrition security. It contributes to poor agricultural productivity, as many African farmers cannot afford to purchase inputs such as fertilizer, pesticides, and improved seeds, which would help to increase productivity. Additionally, poverty reduces the ability of poor consumers to purchase the food required to maintain a healthy and productive life.

(*ii*) Underdeveloped Agricultural Sector

The major challenge to food security in Africa is its underdeveloped agricultural sector that is characterized by over-reliance on primary agriculture, low fertility soils, minimal use of external farm inputs, environmental degradation, significant food crop loss both pre and post-harvest, minimal value addition and product differentiation, and inadequate food storage and preservation that result in significant commodity price fluctuation. Ninety five per cent of the food in Sub Saharan Africa is grown under rainfed agriculture (Benson, T., 2004). Hence food production is vulnerable to adverse weather conditions. There is an overall decline in farm input investment including fertilizers, seeds, and technology adoption. The soils continue to degrade leading to a reduction in the productivity of the farms. Poor handling and storage further increase the post harvest losses. Management of the African agricultural system is further complicated by the existence of diverse heterogeneous systems.

Moreover, lack of adequate infrastructure in much of Sub-Saharan Africa impedes more productive agriculture. Some experts argue that the full potential of irrigation in Africa has not yet been completely exhausted, claiming that of the 42.5 million hectares (ha) of potential irrigated land, only 30 per cent (12.7 million ha) is being irrigated (Inter-Academy Council, 2004). FAO (1996) points out that this prospective irrigated area is not being exploited because more than 60 per cent of the area is located in humid regions, with almost 25 per cent in the Congo Basin alone. These areas have excessive rainfall, and as a result irrigation is only supplementary. Unlike in Asia, investment costs in Africa are substantial, ranging from US$ 5,000 to US$ 25,000 per ha (Inter-Academy Council, 2004).

Analysis of global public agricultural research expenditures showed a declining annual growth rate in both developed and developing countries from 1976 to 1996. The poorest performance is in Sub-Saharan Africa, where public agricultural investment grew at only 1.5 per cent per year and actually declined in the first half of the

1990s (Beintema, N, *et al.*, 2004). As a result of this slow growth, annual expenditures on agricultural research were only 25 per cent higher in Sub-Saharan Africa in 1995 than in 1976, while they nearly tripled in other developing countries as a whole. All regions of the world showed an increasing share except for Sub-Saharan Africa, where public research expenditure as a share of agricultural GDP is declining, implying a reduction of Government support to agricultural R&D.

(*iii*) Disease and Infection

Disease and infection continue to plague the African continent. Diseases such as malaria, tuberculosis and HIV/AIDS not only reduce the man-hours available to agriculture and household food acquisition, but also increase the burden of household in acquiring food. In Sub-Saharan Africa, AIDS is the leading cause of adult mortality and morbidity. The FAO estimates that by 2020 the epidemic will claim the lives of 20 per cent or more of the population working in agriculture in many Southern African countries (FAO, 1996). Lack of resources also makes it more difficult for HIV-affected households to supplement their diet through the purchase of more nutritious and varied foods. The effect of malnutrition on food security is further exacerbated by the fact that individuals affected by disease and infection, have greater nutritional requirements. And also women in Southern Africa are a major source of agricultural labour, food production can be reduced by up to 60 per cent in HIV-infected households when women's time and energy are diverted to care for family members infected with HIV (Oxfam International and Save the Children, 2002). Households must often switch from the production of more nutritious, labour-intensive crops, such as maize, to less labour-intensive root crops that provide poor nutrition.

(*iv*) Lack of Sound Governance

Poor governance is a major issue in many African countries, and one that has serious repercussions for long-term food security. Problems such as corruption, collusion, and nepotism can significantly inhibit the capacity of Governments to promote development efforts[6]. Corruption and other governance problems are also often correlated with conflict, and governance-related conflicts are often linked with hunger and food security, both as a cause and as an effect (Messer and Cohen, 2004). Further, the political and legal frameworks that enable development through strong institutions, community participation and empowerment, social equity and justice, and Government accountability are preconditions for the success of agricultural development strategies. Poor policies have greatly affected the food security in Africa. When policies are not inclusive in their design they tend to handicap the exempted lot by providing barriers.

(*v*) Effects of Globalization

Globalization is a concept that allows countries to benefit from capital flows, technology transfer, cheaper imports and larger export markets in the long-term. However, the effect of globalization on any country depends on that country's level of economic development, structures in place during the implementation stage and flexibility of its economy. With globalization comes liberalization of markets. The food security threat caused by liberalization is due to dumping of heavily subsidized produce in developing countries and premature exposure of upcoming industries to genuine competition from producers in developing and developed countries. In addition, most profits are repatriated by transnational companies reducing the potential for poverty reduction to direct employment alone.

Economic liberalization in Africa has had mixed results. The economic crisis of the 1980s induced most African countries to accept long-run structural adjustment programmes representing a wide range of market liberalization and public sector reforms, including major agricultural sector reforms. Reforms focused on liberalizing input and output prices, eliminating regulatory controls on input and output markets, and restructuring public enterprises (including removing the regulatory functions of marketing boards) (Kherallah, *et al.*, 2000). These reforms were implemented with the idea that introducing market forces to the agricultural sector would immediately lead to economic growth. Reforms to food crop markets were more comprehensive than reforms to export crop markets in Central and Western Africa, and actual reforms in Southern and Eastern Africa have been limited, with state trading and price bands remaining in effect in a number of countries, including Kenya, Malawi, and Zimbabwe.

3.6 FOOD SECURITY INTERVENTIONS

The solution to food security lies in increasing food availability, food access and food adequacy for all. Because the food insecurity in Africa is directly correlated with poverty, it is necessary not only to alleviate poverty but also create wealth for the target population. The key lies in mutual honest intention from multi-stakeholders to ensure that all is done with the sole purpose of benefiting them. The following strategies are important as far as the food security in Africa is concerned.

(*i*) Nutritional Interventions

In addition to investing in short-term interventions, which are vital, African countries should increase their investment in long-term interventions such as dietary diversification, food sufficiency and biofortification. These have lower maintenance costs, a higher probability of reaching the poor who are vulnerable to food insecurity, and produce sustainable results. Dietary diversification still remains the best way to provide nutritious diets to the sustainability of any population. It is possible to obtain the right mix of food to alleviate malnutrition from that which is locally produced. The probability of so doing is increased with increase in locally produced foods. Africa needs to increase its production of animal products, fruits, pulses and vegetables. Increased production would in part make these foods affordable to the poor and increase their protein, vitamin and mineral intake. One sure way is to revisit the cultivation of traditional fruits and vegetables that are adapted to prevailing environmental conditions (Reardon, T, *et al.,* 1995). Once produced, there is need for more constringent post harvest loss prevention measures. In addition, East and Central Africa should increase their roots and tuber production so as to reduce their dependency on cereals. This reduces the risk of crop failure during droughts since tubers like cassava are relatively more drought tolerant. If Africa is to be food sufficient it must produce more food not only in quantity but also in variety.

(*ii*) Facilitating Market Access

There is need to remove the barriers to trade. The focus by most African Governments has been to open up markets in the hope that their people will benefit. Studies show that the projected gains of world trade liberalization tend to be minimal in Sub-Saharan Africa and that the income gains from trade liberalization will go to countries with a competitive advantage in the markets concerned (Kherallah, M, *et al.*, 2000). Perhaps it is time that Africans produced for Africans both within the continent and diaspora, increased their south to south trading, and consolidated their efforts on their comparative advantage for mutual benefit.

(*iii*) Rural Off-farm Opportunities

Rural off-farm opportunities will enhance the livelihood of both the landless rural poor and the group of non-adopters that fallout of business when the agricultural sector becomes more efficient. In addition, provision of off- farm opportunities will curb rural to urban migration and possibly induce some urban to rural migration. Some of the opportunities that African countries can look into include cottage industries that process food crops by value addition and/or enhancing shelf life through preservation techniques; production of small scale processing machinery; provision of credit; contract processing facilities; and market facilitation (Rosegrant, *et al.*, 2005). Specific activities may include the production of items with enhanced shelf life that would allow for marketing in distant markets. These products may range from dairy products such as butter, cheese and ghee, to pre-processed and packaged cut vegetables such as carrots and shelled garden peas for the urban population; to dried fruits and vegetables. More sophisticated, yet relatively technically easy to produce products, such as starch and vegetable oils, may also be produced. For this to be achievable there is need for collaboration amongst the multi-stakeholders.

(*iv*) Capacity-Building

Africa should focus on education, research and development, access to capital and infrastructure development. As an intervention to food security, education must go beyond the level of reading and writing to that of transfer of knowledge. In addition, education will open avenues to off-farm employment, thus acting as a safety net. It is time that Africans played an active role in research and development on matters that affect them. This includes food preservation at the village level, alternative medicine to make health more affordable to its people, creating more efficient agricultural extension, options for improving soil fertility, best approach to manage the different agricultural systems, and marketing strategies that would work best for a given group of farmers (Leipziger, D, *et al.,* 2003). Care should be taken to modify available technology to suit community setting and not the other way round. For benefits to be realized in all areas, infrastructure development must be high priority.

(*v*) Gender Sensitive Development

Women are important as food producers, managers of natural resources, income earners and caretakers of household food security. Agricultural productivity has been said to increase by as much as 20 per cent when women are given the same inputs as men. If women are to be fully effective in contributing to food and nutrition security, discrimination against them must be eliminated and the value of their role promoted (Brown, L.R, *et al.,* 2001). If both men and women had more equal schooling, incomes, and therefore the economy, would grow faster. When only half of the labour force is able to read and write, obtain credit, develop a work skill and obtain work, it is hardly surprising that there will be losses in output. There is, without question, a need to address issues related to women's low status that is evident in their minimal access to resources like inputs, land, and credit and the fact that they have low income and low literacy.

(*vi*) Building on Coping Strategies

While we all agree that poor societies need help to alleviate food insecurity and poverty, we must give them credit for surviving on meagre resources for so long. At the very least, they have an idea as to what strategies and implementation tactics would work, given their socio-cultural framework. Let us learn from them and build on strategies that have worked for them as we intervene to alleviate their food insecurity and poverty. They have strong family bonds that allow them to "pool resources". Everyone in the family participates. Even the elderly chip in by being caretakers of the little ones during working hours. To be successful in this setting, one would do well to have key informant interviews with these leaders.

(*vii*) Good Governance

While it could be argued that all the above interventions are part of good governance, special emphasis on the need for good governance is prudent. All the above strategies can only work in a peaceful, corruption free environment. Part of good governance is the provision of safety nets to vulnerable groups. It should also provide for the minority and be totally inclusive in its decision-making (Paarlberg R.L., 2002). There is need to delink political interests from the basic needs of a nation. More often than not sustainable food security measures are long-term strategies, which need to be protected from volatile political interests of leaders. In addition, it is in everyone's best interest to have only the best handling the issues at hand without political interference from Governments and donors alike.

3.7 CONCLUSION

Many of the challenges facing food security in Africa stem from a few root causes. One of the major factors leading to failures in this sector is poor political and economic governance in many African countries including ineffective institutions. Inadequate funding for the agricultural sector, including the weak role played by the private sector, has also hindered agricultural development. Water resources management has been at issue in many African countries, with poor infrastructure and lack of attention paid to climatic conditions, such as major droughts. In addition, the neglect of research and development and its funding has hindered the growth of the agricultural sector. The strategies for addressing these challenges should take into account local, natural, and human resources, as well as the political and economic agenda of each country.

In 2000 the world community adopted eight Millennium Development Goals that aimed to promote human development and reduce poverty, hunger, and disease, even in the poorest countries.

Some developing regions and countries are making progress toward these goals, but in many categories measured, including food security, the situation in Africa is stagnant or worsening. More than 200 million Africans now suffer from malnutrition. Policy choices and investments made now could substantially improve, or further worsen, the prospects for food security in Africa over the next two decades.

NOTES

1. To Prof. Sen a food centered view tells us rather little about starvation. Nor does it tell us even when starvation is accompanied by fall in food supply–why some groups had to starve while others could feed themselves (Sen, 1981).
2. A household has several entitlements at its disposal which can be used to produce or buy goods and services. The bundle of entitlements consists of various components: income from employment, the assets owned, the food produces for home consumption, etc.
3. Dreze and Sen (1989) emphatically distinguish between chronic hunger involving sustained nutritional deprivation on a persistent basis and famine involving acute starvation and a sharp increase of mortality.
4. For example, the UN launched the Central Emergency Response Fund (CERF) so that the response to future emergencies could be immediate—-under the previous setup, the funds had to be collected before any action could be taken. The UN suggested that $500 million was needed, but Oxfam agues this figure should be at least $1 billion. According to a recent UN news report, the fund has raised just over $260 million.
5. According to the Oxfam reports a temperature increase of 2.5 degrees centigrade by 2080 will put an estimated 60 million additional people in Africa at risk of hunger. A higher rise would put 80 million at risk. A separate report by Christian Aid estimates that climate change in Africa could lead to a further 185 million deaths from disease by the end of the century.
6. Corruption is perceived to be significant in many African countries. Transparency International's Corruption Perception Index, for example, rates 8 countries in Africa among the top 20 most corrupt countries world-wide.

REFERENCES

Beintema, N. and G.J., Stads (2004). *Investing in Sub-Saharan African Agricultural Research: Recent Trends,* 2020 Africa Conference Brief 8, Washington, DC: International Food Policy Research Institute.

Benson, T. (2004). *Africa's Food and Nutrition Security Situation: Where are We and How did We Get Here?* 2020 Discussion Paper No. 37, Washington, DC: International Food Policy Research Institute.

Breman, H. and S.K. Debrah (2003). *Improving African Food Security*, SAS Review 23 (1): 153-170.

Brown, L.R., H. Feldstein, L. Haddad, C. Peña, and A. Quisumbing (2001). *Generating Food Security in the Year 2020: Women as Producers, Gatekeepers, and Shock Absorbers*, in the Unfinished Agenda, ed. P. Pinstrup-Andersen and R. Pandya-Lorch, Washington, DC: International Food Policy Research Institute.

Dreze, J. and A., Sen (1989). *Hunger and Public Action*, Clarendon Press, Oxford.

Fishbein, R. (2003). *The State of Food Insecurity in the World 2003: Monitoring Progress Towards the World Food Summit and Millennium Development Goals*, Rome.

Food and Agriculture Organization, Sustainable Development Department (FAO-SDD), (1996), World Food Summit, *Technical Background Documents*.

International Food Policy Research Institute (IFPRI), (2000). *Women: The Key to Food Security*, Washington, DC.

Inter Academy Council, (2004). *Realizing the Promise and Potential of African Agriculture*, Amsterdam.

Kherallah, M., C. Delgado, E. Gabre-Madhin, N. Minot, and M. Johnson (2000). *The Road Half Travelled: Agricultural Market Reform in Sub-Saharan Africa,* Food Policy Report 10, Washington, DC: International Food Policy Research Institute.

Leipziger, D., M. Fay, Q. Wodon, and T. Yepes (2003). *Achieving the Millennium Development Goals: The Role of Infrastructure*, Policy Research Working Paper 3163, World Bank.

Maxwell, S. (1996). "Food Security: A Post-Modern Perspective,' *Food Policy*, Vol.21, No. 2, pp. 155-170.

Messer, E. and M.J., Cohen (2004). *Breaking the Links Between Conflict and Hunger in Africa,* 2020 Africa Conference Brief No. 10, Washington, DC: International Food Policy Research Institute.

New Partnership for Africa's Development (NEPAD), (2002). *Comprehensive Africa Agriculture Development Programme*, Rome: Food and Agriculture Organization of the United Nations.

Oxfam International and Save the Children, (2002). *HIV/AIDS and Food Insecurity in Southern Africa.*

Oxfam, (2002). *Rigged Rules and Double Standards: Trade, Globalization, and the Fight against Poverty*, Oxfam International.

Paarlberg, R.L. (2002). *Governance and Food Security in an Age of Globalization*, 2020 Discussion Paper 36, Washington, DC: International Food Policy Research Institute.

Reardon, T., E. Crawford, V. Kelly, and B. Diagana (1995). *Promoting Farm Investment for Sustainable Intensification of African Agriculture,* Policy Synthesis No. 3, East Lansing, MI, USA.

Rosegrant, *et al.*, (2005). *Looking Ahead: Long-Term Prospects for Africa's Agricultural Development and Food Security*, Washington D.C: IFPRI.

Sen, A. (1981). *Poverty and Famines—An Essay on Entitlements and Deprivation*, Clarendon Press, Oxford.

United Nations Development Programme (UNDP), (2003). Human Development Report, 2003, *Millennium Development Goals: A Compact Among Nations to End Human Poverty*, New York.

United Nations University, Institute for Natural Resources in Africa, and World Bank (UNU-INRA/World Bank), (1999). *Africa Can Feed Just 40 per cent of its Population in 2025,* Press Release for World Food Day, Legon, Ghana, and Washington, DC.

Weber, M.T. *et al.,* (1988). 'Informing Food Security Decisions in Africa: Empirical Analysis and Policy Dialogue,' *American Journal of Agricultural Economics*, Vol.70, No. 5, pp. 1044-1052.

World Bank, (2004). *Targets and Indicators for MDGs and PRSPs: What Countries have Chosen to Monitor,* Washington, DC: World Bank.

4

Origins of Agriculture and African Roots
An Enquiry in the Prehistoric World

4.1 INTRODUCTION

The vast majority of human history was as hunter-gathers; which extends back more than 4 million years. At the end of the Pleistocene[1] some human groups began to produce food rather than collect it and to domesticate wild plants and animals. The most remarkable transition of our entire prehistory is almost simultaneous appearance of domesticated plants and animals in several parts of the world between 10,000 and 5000 years ago (Price and Gebauer, 1995). The present chapter reviews the prehistoric origins of agriculture as part of human civilizations.

4.2 ARCHAEOLOGICAL PERCEPTIONS

Different concepts and methods are used by researchers to investigate agricultural societies. Paleolithic[2] archaeologists tend to excavate in natural stratigraphic levels, often in caves, paying careful attention to the distributions of bone and stone materials. Researchers focused on later agricultural peoples concentrate more on the stratigraphic levels revealed in the architectural remains of past structures, such as temples and houses. The latter must analyze pottery and metal works as well as stone and bone[3].

The differences in archaeological perceptions and practices reflect real changes in the nature of the archaeological record that began 10000-3000 years ago in many areas of the world. In most regions, Paleolithic sites tend to be small, this scatters of lithic materials, reflecting generally lower populations and the tendency for occupations to involve fewer people over shorter periods of time (Renfrew and Bahn, 1996). The low artifactual densities and the general absence of substantial structures at pre-farming sites also suggest greater residential mobility.

In many regions, the presence of residential and civic architecture and cemeteries at archaeological sites is unique to prehistoric farming societies. In addition, while the artifacts of Paleolithic-spearpoints, knives, and scrapers-tended to be largely for capturing energy (food), facilities or materials (stone bowls, ceramic containers) and features (pits) to store energy became much more important in later eras (Binford and Binford, 1966).

The archaeological record indicates that a more sedentary way of life, plant and animal domestication, and pottery were not adopted simultaneously in all regions (Childe, 1952). Sedentary villages preceded any evidence for plant domestication in South West Asia, while the domestication of maize, beans, and squash occurred prior to the earliest Mesoamerican villages. The Mesoamerican combination of beans and corn provides a complete protein source as well as adequate calories, some of the other staple grains such as barley and rice are high in carbohydrates but low in protein. The domestication of animals was a more significant part of the Neolithic transition in the Old World than in the Americas. Many of the regions of early, indigenous domestication were relatively arid as in the Near East and highland Mexico. But this was not the case in either South China or the riverine settings of eastern North America.

4.3 MASTERING THE ENVIRONMENT AND DOMESTICATION

Agriculture is a way of obtaining food that involves domesticated plants and animals. But the transition to farming entails major, long-term changes in the structure and organization of the societies that adopt this new way of life, as well as a totally new relationship with the environment. Hunter-gatherers largely live off the land in an extensive fashion, generally exploiting a diversity of resources over a broad area. However, farmers intensively utilize a smaller portion of the landscape and create a milieu that suits needs; humans began to truly master their environment.

Just because a species is exploited intensively by humans does not automatically mean it will become domesticated. Although oak trees have supplied acorns for humans for thousands of years, they have not been domesticated. Domestication changes the physical characteristics of the plant or animal involving both the inherent characteristics of the plant or animal species (generally length, life cycle, plasticity) and the intensity and nature of the human manipulation.

Agriculture requires several major practices for long-term success as given below (Sauer, 1952).

(i) *Propagation*: The selection and sowing of seeds or breeding of animals;
(ii) *Husbandry*: The tending of plants or animals during the growth period;
(iii) *Harvesting*: The harvesting of plants when ripe or the slaughter of animals at appropriate times; and
(iv) *Storage*: The storage of seeds and maintenance of animals through their non-productive periods to ensure annual reproduction.

Plant propagation and husbandry involve cultivation—clearing fields, preparing the soil, weeding, protecting the plants from animals, and providing water.

The evidence for early domesticated plants focuses on seed crops such as cereals—the grasses that produce large, hard-shelled seeds, nutritious kernels of carbohydrates that can be stored for long periods. The hard cereal grains and the stems of these plants were often burned during preparation or cooking in the past and thereby preserved to the present. Root crops are not well documented in the archaeological record as they lack hard parts that are more resistant to decay[4]. Root crops such as potatoes, yams, manioc, and taro may have been domesticated quite early and archaeologists have started to identify them from prehistoric sites recently.

Animals were apparently domesticated initially for meat, with the exception of the dog. Dogs were tamed from wolves very early, perhaps 14000 years ago in the Old World, and used for hunting and as pets, or even for food (Clutton-Brock, 1999). Subsequently several other animal species were added and herded for food and kept as beasts of burden. The earliest animals domesticated were pigs, goats, sheep, and cattle. The secondary products (such as milk, wool, horn, and leather) of these domesticated species also became important, as did their functions as beasts of burden.

The domestication of both plants and animals may be related to the storage of food. For instance cereals such as wheat, barley, corn, and rice have hard outer coverings that protect the nutritious kernel, permitting the seed to survive until the growing season and offering very good possibilities for storage (Harris and Hilman, 1989). Meat can be stored in the form of living, tame animals that are always available for slaughter. As such, storage provides a means to regulate the availability of food and to accumulate surplus.

4.4 PRIMARY CENTRES OF DOMESTICATION

Enquiries regarding the origins of agriculture must focus on primary centres where individual species of plants and animals were first domesticated. Primary centers for domestication were in the Near East, East Asia, Sub-Saharan Africa, Central America, South America, and North America (Redman, 1978). The earliest known domesticates-wheat, barley, peas, lentils, pigs, goats, sheep, and cattle appeared in the Old World, between the eastern Mediterranean sea and Afghanistan, shortly after 9000 B.C. Many other plants and animals such as bread wheat, rye, figs, olives, and flax were gradually added to this list. Secondary areas of agricultural development received plants and animals from elsewhere, although in many of these regions, some local plants and animals also were domesticated and used along with the introduced varieties.

Agriculture was also invented in the Far East, perhaps in two or three different areas, sometime before 6000 B.C (Legge and Rowley, 1967). Millet was first cultivated and pigs were domesticated in North China in early villages dating to roughly 6000 B.C (Cheny, 1966). Rice was initially cultivated in South China, possibly as early as the eighth or ninth millennium B.C and some what later in Southeast Asia, before 4000 B.C. In all probability, root crops were under cultivation in this area, along with rice, sometime between 7000 and 3000 B.C (Lechevallier and Ouivron, 1985). Since researches are continuing, we can expect the dates for all East Asia to be pushed back somewhat earlier. Plants such as African rice, sorghum, and pearl millet were domesticated in Sub-Saharan Africa after 2000 B.C (Binford, 1983). Cattle and goat herding were practiced in this area, where the new domesticates appeared.

In the New World, agriculture was first developed in Mexico, in northwestern South America, and in eastern North America. In Mexico, gourds and squash were cultivated during the eighth millennium B.C; avocados, chili peppers, beans, and possibly corn were cultivated later, before 5000 B.C (Flannery, 1986). These crops provide all the essential nutrients for a healthy diet, and as such meat protein was not necessary. Although turkeys, dogs, and the stingless honeybee were domesticated, these animals never provided an important part of the diet in this area.

Figure 4.1: Appearance of Domesticated Plants and Animals in the Prehistoric Era

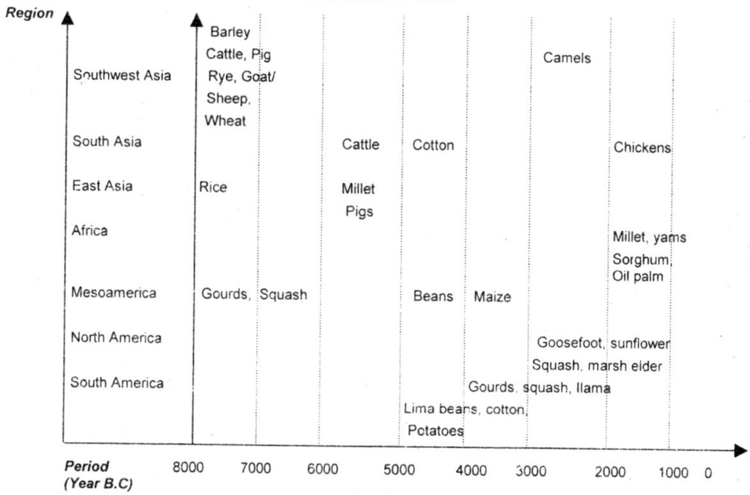

Source: Price, T.D. and G.M. Feinman, 1997.

Peru contains evidences for the early domestication of gourds, tomatoes, beans, and potatoes by 3000 B.C (Gabauer and Price). Some of these plants might have reached the mountains from an original habitat in the lowland jungles, but little is known about the prehistory of the Amazon Basin and other tropical areas of South America.

Potatoes might have been an indigenous crop; hundreds of varieties of wild and domesticated potatoes grow in this area today. In addition to plants, several animals were domesticated. The guinea pig was used for food, while the Ilama was probably domesticated and used to transport goods around the mountains of South America.

In addition to the above mentioned major centres of domestication, the origins of agriculture occurred in other areas shortly. Recent evidences from New Guinea suggests that agriculture was practiced very early in this area; a date of around 7000 B.C (White, 1982). These fields were probably used for fruit and tuber crops such as yams. In eastern North America, several local plants such as marsh elder, sunflower, and goosefoot were domesticated by 1000 B.C, long before the introduction of corn from Mexico. These evidences show that there was a trend toward domestication and agriculture on a global scale.

4.5 THEORIES REGARDING ORIGINS OF AGRICULTURE

It is remarkable that the process of domesticating plants and animals appears to have taken place separately and independently in a number of different areas at a few thousand years in a span of over 4 million years of human existence. Such dramatic shift in the trajectory of cultural evolution requires explanation. Explanations for the origins of agriculture continue to be revised and updated. We will try to review the ideas about the origins of agriculture from a historical perspective, considering the early theories first. Theories about the origins of agriculture have often focused on the earliest evidence from the Near East and, for that reason, may not be appropriate to all places where early domestication actually occurred.

During the first half of the twentieth century, the best information on early farming villages came from riverine areas or oasis with springs in North Africa and the Near East along the Nile River in Egypt or at Jordan valley (Redman, 1978). This was a period of increasing warmth and dryness in the earth's climate. Researchers reasoned that the ice ages were cold and wet, and they should have ended with higher temperatures and less precipitation. Given this view of past climate, logic suggested that areas such as the Near East (a dry region begin with) would have witnessed a period of aridity at the end of Pleistocene when vegetation grew only around limited water sources.

Following are the important theories related with the origins of agriculture:

(i) The Oasis Hypothesis

The Oasis hypothesis suggested a circumstance in which plants, animals and humans would have clustered in confined areas near water. Proponents of this idea (Childe, 1952) argued that the only successful solution to the competition for food in that period was for humans to domesticate and control the animals and the plants. As per this theory domestication emerged as a symbiotic relationship for the purpose of human survival.

(ii) The Natural Habitat Hypothesis

During the 1940s and 1950s new evidences came up indicating that there had been no major climatic changes in the Near East and the close of the Pleistocene; no crisis during which life would concentrate at oasis. Braidwood (1960) in his natural habitation hypothesis proposed that the earliest domesticates should have appeared where their wild ancestors lived. Braidwood and a large team of researchers excavated at the site of Jarmo in northern Iraq. The evidence from this early farming village supported his hypothesis that domestication did indeed begin in the natural habitat[5]. The theory concludes that once human societies recognized the possibilities of domestication, they would have immediately started farming.

(iii) The Population Pressure Hypothesis

Binford (1983) proposed the population pressure hypothesis. He argued that farming was back-breaking, time consuming, and labour-intensive. Citing studies of living hunter-gatherers, he pointed out that they spend only a few hours a day obtaining food; the rest of their time is for visiting, talking, gambling, and the general pleasures of life. Even in very marginal areas, such as the Kalahari Desert of South Africa, food collection is a successful adaptation, and people rarely starve. The theory pointed out that human group would not become farmers unless they had no other choice; that the origin of agriculture was not a fortuitous discovery, but a last resort.

Population pressure hypothesis is interpreted in terms of equilibrium between people and food, a balance that could be upset by either a decline in available food or an increase in the number of people. Since climatic and environmental changes appeared to be minimal in the near East, it must have been increased population size that upset the balance. Population pressure was thus introduced as casual agent for the origins of agriculture; more people required more food. The best solution to the problem was domestication, which provided a higher yield of food per acre of land (For details refer, Cohen, 1977a). At the same time, however, agricultural intensification required more labour to extract the food.

(iv) The Edge Hypothesis

It suggests that the effects of population pressure would be felt most strongly not in the core of the natural habitat zone, where dense stands of wild wheat and large herds of wild sheep and goats were available, but at the margins, where wild foods were less abundant (Binford, 1983). This theory, incorporating ideas about population pressure and the margins of the Fertile Crescent, has become known as the Edge hypothesis.

Binford's concern with population was elaborated by Cohen (1977b); who argued that an inherent tendency for growth in human population, a pattern responsible for the initial spread of the human species out of Africa, the colonization of Asia and Europe, and eventually of the New World. After about 10000 B.C all the inhabitable areas of the planet were occupied and population continued to grow. At that time there was an increase in the use of less desirable resources; land snails, shellfish, birds, and many new plants species were added to the human diet around the end of the Pleistocene. The only way for rapidly increasing species to cope with declining resources was to begin to cultivate the land and domesticate its inhabitants, rather than simply to collect the wild produce. As per this theory domestication was thus a solution to problems of overpopulation on a global scale.

(v) The Social Hypothesis

The critiques of farming and food storage versus environment and population have developed the social hypothesis for explaining the origins of agriculture. Bender (1978) has suggested that the success of food production may lie more in the ability of individuals to accumulate surplus of food and to transform that surplus into more valued items, such as rare stones and metals. From this perspective, agriculture was the means by which social inequality emerged and egalitarian societies became hierarchical.

(vi) Other Views

There are several other theories about why human societies adopted agriculture at the end of the Pleistocene. Carl Sauer (1952) suggested that agriculture began in the hilly tropics of Southeast Asia, where sedentary groups with knowledge of the rich plant life of the forest might have domesticated plants for poisons and fibers. David Rindos (1984) argued that domestication is a process of interaction between humans and plants, evolving together into a more beneficial symbiotic relationship.

4.6 EVIDENCES

Some of the issue with above theories can be seen in a brief consideration of the evidences from the Near East. The earliest agriculture villages were located at the margins of the natural habitat and attempts to artificially reproduce stands of wild wheat there may have resulted in domestication. Several sites show signs of abandonment in the levels beneath those layers that contain the first domesticated plants. The most recent climatic evidence indicates that there was, in fact, a period of slightly cooler and moister temperatures in the Near East at the end of the Pleistocene, which may have greatly expanded the geographic range of wild wheat and barley, making then available to more human groups, and fostering the process of domestication.

One theory may seem reasonable in one of the primary centres of domestication, but not in another. The sequence of events in the following two areas is of particular interest here.

(i) In the Near East, permanent settlements are known from 11000 B.C, prior to the presence of direct evidence for domesticated plants or animals. Cultivated plants appeared about 9000 B.C; animals were probably not herded until perhaps 8500 B.C. Pottery did not come into general use until around 7500 B.C (MacNeish, 1964).

(ii) However, in Mesoamerica the archaeological sequence reveals that domesticated plants first appeared around 3000 B.C, followed by pottery and permanent villages roughly 1000 years later. Domesticated animals were never important in this area (Beadle, 1980).

The differences in these two areas indicate that neither sedentism, the permanent settlement of communities, nor cultivation is totally dependent one upon the other. It is also clear that domesticated animals are not essential in all areas.

Due to the difficulties in excavating phenomena like social relations and population pressure, many of the current theories are hard to evaluate. Any adequate explanation of the agricultural transformation should deal not only with how it all began, but also why it happened rather suddenly around 10000 years ago (Price and Feinman, 1997). Population and climatic change certainly play a role in cultural evolution. But we cannot yet say precisely why plants and animals began to be domesticated shortly after the end of the Pleistocene.

The how and why of the Neolithic transition remain among the more intriguing questions in human prehistory. Simply put, there is, as yet, no single, accepted, general theory for the origins of agriculture. No common pattern of development is apparent in the various areas where domestication first took place.

4.7 ORIGIN OF AGRICULTURE: THE AFRICAN ROOTS

The first civilization in Africa is believed to have begun in the heart of the Sahara Desert, but which in 5200 BC was far more moist and densely populated. Several native species were domesticated, most importantly pearl millet, sorghum and cowpeas which spread through West Africa and the Sahel (Bailey, 2000). The Sahara at this time was like the Sahel today. Its wide open fields made cultivation easy, but the poor soil and limited rain made intensive farming impossible. The local crops were also not ideal and produced fewer calories than those of other regions. These factors limited surpluses and kept populations sparse and unurbanized.

North Africa took a very different route from the southern regions. Climatically it is closely linked to the Middle East and the Fertile Crescent and the agricultural techniques of that region were adopted wholesale. This included very different sets of crops, such as wheat, barley, and grapes. North Africa was also blessed by one of the richest agricultural regions in the world in the form of the Nile River Valley (Harlan, 1992). With the arrival of agriculture the Nile region quickly became one of the most densely populated in the world, and the Egyptians home to one of the first civilizations.

On the African continent, three areas have been identified as independently developing agriculture: the Ethiopian highlands, the Nile River Valley and West Africa. In East Africa we know that there was a lot of water to complete the neolithic life. Some studies have evidence of early agriculture in Upper Paleolithic times at Wadi Kubbaniya, on the Kom Ombos plateau, of Egypt, including a mortar and pestle, grinding stones, several harvesting implements and charred wheat and barley grains—which may have been introduced from outside the region. Carbon-14 dates range from 15,000 to 16,300 BC, showing that this early grain harvesting preceded that of the Middle East by about 5,000 years (Bellwood, 2004).

The archaeologists are of the opinion that these are not the only Late Paleolithic sites which have been discovered in Egypt along the Nile, nor are they alone in containing stone artifact assemblages which seem to indicate the harvesting of grain. Among others are several sites at Wadi Tushka, near Abu Simbel, at Kom Ombo, north of Aswan, and a third group (a whole series of sites) near Esna (Bailey, 2005). All these are in the Nile Valley[6]. While the flaked stone industries from them are different from those found at Kubbaniya, the Tushka site yielded several pieces of stone with lustrous edges, indicating that they were used as sickles in harvesting grain. Many such grinding stones are found with the early Egyptian Sebilian and Mechian cultures dating 10,000-13,000 BC (Cohen, 1977). With the benefit of hindsight we can see that many Late Paleolithic peoples in the Old

World were poised on the brink of plant cultivation and animal husbandry as an alternative to the hunter-gatherer's way of life. Unlike the Middle East, this evidence appears as a "false dawn" to agriculture, as the sites were later abandoned, and permanent farming then was delayed until 4,500 BC with the Tasian and Badarian cultures and the arrival of crops and animals from the Near East.

The drying of the Sahara created a formidable barrier between the northern and southern portions of the continent. Two important exceptions were Nubia that was linked to Egypt by the Nile and Ethiopia that could trade with the northern regions over the Red Sea (Fage, J.D., 2001). Powerful states grew up in these regions such as Kush in Nubia and Axum in Ethiopia. From these regions ideas and technologies from the Middle East and Europe could travel to Sub-Saharan Africa[7]. In Nubia and Ethiopia iron, trade, and agricultural surpluses lead to the establishment of cities and civilizations.

In the still more sparsely settled rest of the continent this same period sees the expansion of the Bantu speaking peoples. The Bantu expansion almost certainly began in Southern Cameroon around 4000 years ago. Bantu languages are spoken there today and there is archaeological evidence for incoming Neolithic farmers in Northern Gabon ca. 3800 BP. It is known that their expansion was extremely rapid and massive, but its exact engine remains controversial. This is too early for iron, which appears in the archaeological record by 2500 BP. One of the early expansions of Bantu was the migration of the Bubi to Fernando Po (Bioko) and they were still using stone technology at first European contact (Diamond, 2002). The difficulties of cutting down the equatorial forest for farming have led to the suggestion that the primary expansion was along river valleys, a hypothesis supported by studies of fish names. Another factor may have been the arrival of SE Asian food crops, notably the AAB plantain, the cocoyam and the water-yam (Wright, 1971). Linguistic reconstructions suggest that the only livestock possessed by the proto-Bantu was the goat. Over the centuries the entire southern half of Africa was covered, excluding only the Kalahari desert. This expansion only ended relatively recently. In the year 1000 Arab traders show that the Bantu had not reached as far as Mozambique, and European settlers observed the Bantu expansion into South Africa under the Zulu and others.

The importation Bantu pastoralism reshaped the continent's economy. Sometime in the first millennium and equally important change began as crops began to arrive from Southeast Asia. The Indian Ocean has always been far more open to trade than the turbulent Atlantic and Pacific. Traders could ride the monsoon winds west early in the year and return east on them later. It is guessed that these crops first arrived in Madagascar, which also adopted Southeast Asian languages, sometime between AD 300 and 800. From the island the crops crossed to East Africa. They included many crops, the most important being the banana. The banana and other crops allowed for more intensive cultivation in the tropical regions of Africa, this was most notable in the Great Lakes region, and area with excellent soil, that saw many cities and states form, their populations being fed largely by bananas.

Under colonial rule, Africa was mainly utilized by European powers for the purpose of growing cash crops such as cotton in West Africa and rubber in the Congo. The plantation system of farming was introduced in order to grow large quantities of these commodities employing cheap (often slave) native labour for export to the mother country without compensation (Pyne, 1997). Mining for gems and precious metals such as gold was developed in a similar way by wealthy European entrepreneurs such as Cecil Rhodes.

Today, many African economies suffer from the legacy of colonialism. The utilitarian attitude of European countries toward their colonial possesions stopped them from building adequate infrastructure in Africa. In agriculture, the plantation systems that they introduced are highly unsustainable and cause severe environmental degradation. For example, cotton severely lowers soil fertility wherever it is grown, and areas of West Africa that are dominated by cotton plantations are now unable to switch to more profitable crops or even to produce food because or the depleted soil (Rodney, 1982). Recently, more countries have initiated programmes to revert to traditional, sustainable forms of agriculture such as shifting cultivation and bush fallow in order to grow enough food to support the population while maintaining soil fertility to allow agriculture to continue in future generations.

4.8 SPREAD OF AGRICULTURE

Given the varied climatic, demographic, and cultural conditions of the early Holocene[8], the rapid spread of food production was a widespread phenomenon. In regions where indigenous resources were not domesticated, exotic cultigens and animals were introduced and adopted. Once domesticated, wheat and barley were transmitted rapidly to the Nile Valley, many parts of Europe, and North China as a supplement to millet (Smith, 1998). In the river valleys of eastern North America, maize from Mexico was incorporated into local agricultural complexes that included different combinations of oily seed plants, such as sunflower, marsh elder, and goosefoot.

The Neolithic transition apparently was an even more complex mosaic in Sub-Saharan Africa (Bender, 1978). Imported sheep and goats were introduced from Southwest Asia into diverse economies that locally domesticated more than a dozen different plant species, including finger millet (Ethiopia and northern Uganda), Sorghum (Lake Chad to the Nile), African rice (middle delta of the Niger), tiny-seeded teff (Ethiopia), and yams (West Africa). While domesticated sheep and goats were foreign, the origins of domesticated cattle in Sub-Saharan Africa are less certain; they ether were exotic or were domesticated independently in northern Africa, where they were present by the fifth millennium B.C. (Harris and Hilman, 1989). As in Japan, where ceramics preceded food production, pottery vessels were found at sites occupied by semi-sedentary fisher-forages from the fifth and sixth millennium B.C. in the Sudan, as well as along the margins of now-dry lakebeds south of the Sahara Desert.

4.9 SUCCESS AND CONSEQUENCE OF FOOD PRODUCTION

Food production emerged at a time of major cultural changes that have shaped the course of recent human history. Just as the Neolithic creates a divide in the archaeological record the beginnings of domestication are generally linked in time with more permanent or sedentary communities, changing social and political relationships, larger and denser populations, new technologies, and shifting networks of exchange and communication (Childe, 1952). The complexity of the relationships makes it difficult to decipher the exact causes for prehistoric changes. However, archaeologists have developed some models by studying contemporary people, particularly those who have recently shifted from a mobile hunting and gathering way of life to more sedentary and agricultural pursuits.

Figure 4.2: Population *Versus* Subsistence Strategies in the Prehistoric World

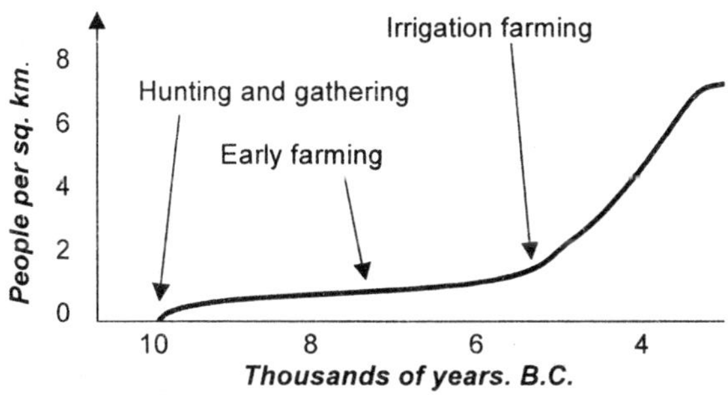

Source: Rindos, 1984.

During the Pleistocene, human populations grew at a slow pace. Based on the observations of modern hunter-gatherers populations it is reported that a few individuals may have separated from parent groups when resources were exhausted or when disputes became common. In larger campsites, the latter could have been a potential problem, because as the population grows, the number of interactions between individuals increases even more rapidly. By the end of the Pleistocene with the peopling of most of the continents (albeit at low densities), fissioning would have become less of an option for many groups. This pattern may partially account for observed late Pleistocene—early Holocene increases in local population densities, residential stability, greater reliance on lower-quality foods, and decreases in social group territory sizes (Jarriage and Meadow, 1989). Following the end of the Pleistocene, the more rapid rates of demographic growth may relate in part to changing patterns of child rearing and diet. Recently settled hunter-gatherers often witnessed a reduction in birth spacing[9].

More productive and storable food resources may have permitted larger communities and denser populations. For long-term maintenance and survival, larger communities would have required new mechanisms for integration, the resolution of disputes, and decision-making. Increase evidence for burials, ritual objects, non-residential structures, more formal patterns of exchange, and in some cases more unequal access to goods and labour would seem to signal these very significant changes in social and political relationships. Some of these new organizational forms were hierarchal, with more permanent, formal leadership roles instituted above the remainder of the population. Such leaders or decision-makers, in turn, may have fostered greater concentrations of resources and labour, leading to intensified production and even larger communities.

4.10 CONCLUSION

The origin of agriculture and sedentism occurred at the onset of a rapid succession of changes that have culminated in our modern world. The pace of these recent changes is truly remarkable when viewed from the perspective of all of human history. While neither domestication nor sedentism alone is necessary and sufficient to explain the formation of early cities and ancient states, both permanent communities and food production are critical elements of those very significant, later developments.

NOTES

1. The Pleistocene, beginning about 2 million years was marked by a series of major climatic fluctuations. Modern forms of the human species appeared toward the end of this epoch.
2. The first period of human prehistory, extending from the time of the first tools, more than 2.5 million years ago, until the end of the Pleistocene, 10,000 years ago; characterized by the use of flaked stone tools, it is also known as the Old Stone Age.
3. Because pre-Neolithic sits have fewer artifacts and are often deeply buried, systematic regional surveys, which find and map archaeological remains visible on the land surface, are rarely as practical or useful for the specialist in the Pleistocene as they are for many archaeologists who study later periods.
4. Because they produce asexually from shoots or cuttings, it is difficult to distinguish domesticated varieties from their wild ancestors. Asexually reproducing plants may maintain exactly the same genetic structure in many generations, because a piece of the parent plant is

used to start the daughter. Such plants may also exhibit great variation within a species, making domestication difficult to document.

5. Braidwood did not offer a specific reason as to why domestication occurred, other than to point out that technology and culture were ready by the end of the Pleistocene, that humans were familiar with the species that were to be domesticated. At that time, archaeologists and others considered farming to be a highly desirable and welcome invention, providing security and leisure time for prehistoric peoples.
6. The Egyptian Esna culture shows "extensive use of cereals," date from 13,000 to 14,500 years ago.
7. One of these was iron working that arrived, presumably from Sudan around 1200 BC and quickly spread to West Africa and reached South Africa by the fifth century AD. Some historians believe that iron working may have been developed independently in Africa. Unlike other continents Africa did not have a period of copper and bronze working before the Iron Age. Copper is quite rare in Africa while iron is quite common.
8. The most recent geological epoch, this began 10,000 years ago with the close of the Pleistocene and continues today. Some describe this epoch as a warmer episode between glacial periods. Also called Postglacial, Present Inter-glacial and Recent. The period witnessed the origins of agriculture, the first cities, and the industrial age.
9. A mobile way of life limits the number of infants a family group can transport and hence care for at any one time. Intensive exercise and prolonged breast-feeding have been suggested as factors that temporarily diminish a woman's fertility. With increased sedentism, storage, and domestication, both the frequency of intensive female activity and the length of the nursing cycle may have decreased. Twentieth-century hunter-gatherers tend to breast-feed for 2-6 years because of the frequent absence or unreliability of soft weaning foods. The storable, staple cereal grains provide such an alternative 'baby food' to mother's milk. In certain regions, animal milk also could be substituted.

REFERENCES

Bailey, Douglass (2000). *Balkan Prehistory: Exclusions, Incorporation and Identity.* Routledge.

Bailey, Douglass (2005). *Prehistoric Figurines: Representation and Corporeality in the Neolithic.* Routledge.

Beadle, G. (1980). 'The Ancestry of Corn,' *Scientific American*, 242:113.

Bellwood, Peter (2004). *First Farmers: The Origins of Agricultural Societies,* Blackwell Publishers.

Bender, B. (1978). 'Gatherer-hunter to Farmer: A Social Perspective,' *World Archaeology*, 10:204-222.

Binford, L.R. and S.R., Binford (1966). "A Preliminary Analysis of Functional Variability in the Monsterian of Levallois Facial,' *Recent Studies in Paleo-anthropology*, ed, J.D Clark and F.C Howell, American Anthropologist, Special Issue, 68 (2, 2), 238-295.

Binford, L.R. (1983). *In Pursuit of the Past*, Thames and Hudson, New York.

Braidwood, R.J. (1960). 'The Agricultural Revolution,' *Scientific American*, 203 (3), 130-148.

Cheng, T. (1966). *Archaeology in China: New Light on Prehistoric China*, W. Heffer and Sons, Cambridge.

Childe, V.G. (1952). *Man Makes Himself*, New American Library, New York.

Clutton-Brock, J. (1999). *A Natural History of Domesticated Animals*, Cambridge University Press, Cambridge.

Cohen, M. (1977). *The Food Crisis in Prehistory*, Yale University Press, New Haven, CT.

Cohen, M. (1977). 'Population Pressure and the Origins of Agriculture: An Archaeological Example from the Coast of Peru,' *Origins of Agriculture,* ed, C. Reed Mouton, The Hague.

Diamond, Jared (2002). *Evolution, Consequences and Future of Plant and Animal Domestication,* Nature Magazine, Vol. 418.

Fage, J.D. (2001). *A History of Africa*, Routledge, 4th edition.

Flannery, K.V. ed, (1986). *Guila Naquitz: Archaic Foraging and Early Agriculture in Oaxaca Mexico*, Academic Press, New York.

Gebauer, A.B. and T. Douglas Price, *Transition in Agriculture in Prehistory*, New York.

Harlan, Jack R. (1992). *Crops and Man: Views on Agricultural Origins* ASA, CSA, Madison.

Harris, D.R., and G.C. Hilman eds, (1989). *Foraging and Farming: The Evolution of Plant Exploitation*, Unwin Hyman, London.

Jarriage, J.F. and R.H., Meadow (1980). 'The Antecedents of Civilization in the Indus Valley,' *Scientific American*, 243: (2).

Lechevallier, M. and G., Ouivron (1985). 'Results of the Recent Excavations at the Neolithic Site (Mehrgarh, Pakistan),' *South Asian Archaeology*.

Legge, A.J. and Peter, A. Rowley (1967). 'Gazelle Drives in the Ancient Near East,' *Scientific American.*

MacNeish, R. (1964). 'The Origins of New World Civilization,' *Scientific American*.

Price, T.D. and A.B., Gebauer (1995). *Last Hunters-First Farmers: New Perspective on the Transition to Agriculture*, School of American Research, Santa Fe, NM.

Price and Feinman (1997). *Images of the Past*, Mayfield Publishing Company, California.

Pyne, Stephen J. (1997). *Vestal Fire: An Environmental History Told through Fire, of Europe and Europe's Encounter with the World*; University of Washington Press, Seattle.

Redman, C. (1978). The Rise of Civilization: From Early Farmers to Urban Society in the Ancient Near East, W.H Freeman and Company, New York.

Renfrew, C. and Paul, Bahn (1996). *From Archaeology: Theories, Methods and Practice*, Thames and Hudson, New York.

Rindos, (1984). *The Origins of Agriculture: An Evolutionary Perspective*, Academic Press, New York.

Rodney, Walter (1982). *How Europe Underdeveloped Africa*, Howard UP, Washington.

Sauer, C.O. (1952). *Agricultural Origins and Dispersals*, American Geographical Society, New York.

Smith, B.D. (1998). *The Emergence of Agriculture*, Scientific American Library, New York.

White, J. (1982). *Discovery of a Lost Bronze Age*, University Museum, University of Pennsylvania. Wright, Gary A, 1971, 'Origins of Food Production in Southwestern Asia: A Survey of Ideas' *Current Anthropology*, Vol. 12, No. 4/5 (October—December, 1971), pp. 447-477.

5

Relevance of Rainwater Harvesting in Eastern Africa

A Case Study

5.1 INTRODUCTION

In recent years rainwater harvesting, has been acquiring a higher social acceptance world-wide. Its main domestic form, roof water harvesting (DRWH), has been aided by the rapid growth in the use of hard roofing (usually corrugated iron sheeting) in areas formerly dependent on grass roofing. DRWH has thereby become feasible in most of Sub-Saharan Africa. It is a technique with the great attraction of delivering water to the very door of the user's house. Its main perceived disadvantages are its high cost and its individual nature. The former however only applies to some forms of DRWH, not all, and the latter's unattractiveness to promotional agencies like NGOs is diminishing as they lessen their former overwhelming emphasis on group enterprise.

Although numerous new water supplies have been constructed in rural Africa in recent years, population growth has resulted in only a small projected increase in the fraction (32% to ca 36%) of households having 'access to adequate quantities of safe water' (WHO/UNICEF, 2000). Official statistics are based on understandings of the words 'access', 'adequate' and 'safe' that seem inappropriate to rural Africa. 'Adequate' is taken to mean over 20 liters per person per day (lcd) and 'access' is taken to mean a water source within 1 km of the home (Ariyabandu R de D, 1999). Actually 20 lcd is well above current usage and immediate aspirations; it is quite incompatible with a carrying distance as long as 1 km. Collecting even only 10 lcd for a household with 6 members requires 3 round trips per day. If the source were 1 km away, this would take at least 2 woman-hours per day (collection is predominantly by women and children). "Water equals walking" has long been an accurate adage in rural Africa. It will be decades before point sources like wells or standpipes are sufficiently numerous, and hence close-spaced, that walking for water is no longer a major household burden. Yet most water programmes are still solely concerned with providing new point sources, often using techniques that have proven operationally unsustainable.

Several studies have found that DRWH development has reached a point where 'partial' DRWH systems could be affordable by the bulk of rural households in Africa[1]. Such systems would typically increase a household's annual water consumption by 50 per cent while reducing its water-fetching time by 70 per cent—at a cost as low as $ 40 US which equals about half the cost of roofing a small house (DTU). We may call this form of RWH 'very-low-cost' roofwater harvesting (VLC DRWH).

The objective of this chapter was to evaluate the potential of rainwater harvesting, which currently provides less than 2 per cent of household water needs in Eastern Africa because it is largely restricted to expensive forms. The purpose of the chapter was to assess the feasibility of VLC DRWH, examining its performance and its affordability by the bulk of rural households. The study was intended not only to assess the desirability of switching to much smaller DRWH designs than used hitherto, but also to prepare for a major programme with such agencies to kick-start the adoption of VLC DRWH in the region.

The area of study includes Western Uganda, Eastern Rwanda and North West Tanzania. The study areas have characteristics that make existing water sources rather unsatisfactory. Its poverty means that clean sources are few in number. Its topology results in a paucity of perennial streams and springs and arduous carrying conditions in most places. The water table is commonly deep except near swamps (where dwellings are understandably sparse) and in some areas the ground water is so mineralized that it is dangerous to ingest or objectionable in taste.

Box 5.1: Children and Water Collection

Children are collecting water in containers of varying sizes. The containers used from 3 litres to 10 litres for children below 8 years of age. Children above 8-10 years of age use larger containers and take on a more responsible role. Where water is close to the house, children may be the sole collectors of water. When water sources are more distant, women will help the children. During the dry spells, the men may also help as the nearest water source may be 4 kms or 5 kms distant. Men tend to use bicycles, carts or donkeys for water collection.Some children do not find water collection such a burden, as we see in the example below :

Moreen. Birere, a voung girl from Rukungiri was asked how she spends her time.

"Our parents are very strict, the only time to let us out from home is, when going to school, church or collecting water. It's harder in the holidays. The only chance to meet friends is at the spring (water collection)".

5.2 THE VLC DRWH TECHNOLOGY

A roof-water harvesting system comprises a roof, a storage tank and a means such as guttering of connecting the one to the other. Other possible components are filters or 'first-flush' diverters to reduce the quantity of dust or debris entering the tank, access points for cleaning, a means of extracting water from the tank and in-tank devices to aid water management or to maximize water quality.

The most costly system element is usually the store (tank), which in a 'stand-alone' system may be designed to hold all the water required throughout the longest expected dry season. Middle class households in the humid tropics might have upwards of 10000 litres of storage, while in a Monsoon storage may be two times larger. Such large structures are expensive unless use can be made of some natural rock foundation. Underground stores are less space-consuming and are generally cheaper, volume for volume, than surface mounted stores; however the former need a pump and are prone to failure modes that are difficult either to calculate or monitor (Rees D.G. & Thomas T.H., 1999).

A striking feature of DRWH systems is the strong law of diminishing returns that operates for tank sizing. As Figure 5.1 shows, a system containing a very small tank (holding only 7 day's household consumption) might yield 75 per cent of the water per year of a system with a very large tank (capable of holding 100 days' consumption). This suggests a route to cost minimization, provided that an alternative, albeit more costly per litre, alternative back-up water source is available. In rural areas such a back-up supply is likely to be the distant spring, well or pond formerly used.

Besides keeping tanks very small, economy measures in LDCs include constructing tanks more efficiently, using cheaper materials, devising slimmer gutters and down-pipes, substituting low-cost local labour for more capital-intensive production and devising management strategies that minimize the cost-benefit ratio.

Currently DRWH systems in developing countries commonly use, for their storage element, mortar jars, Ferro cement jars, cylinders and cuboid shapes of plastered brick, oil drums and corrugated iron cylinders, reinforced concrete tanks or (for richer households) plastic drums. Usually these are not tightly designed and have failure safety factors that are uneconomically high (very large tanks however need and get engineering design, as their failure can be dramatic and dangerous.) There is therefore considerable scope for material savings. Little used materials of promise are stabilised earth, plastic sheets and the ground itself, especially if designs separate the functions of strength and water-tightnes[2].

Figure 5.1: 'Diminishing Returns' Output *vs* Cost Curve

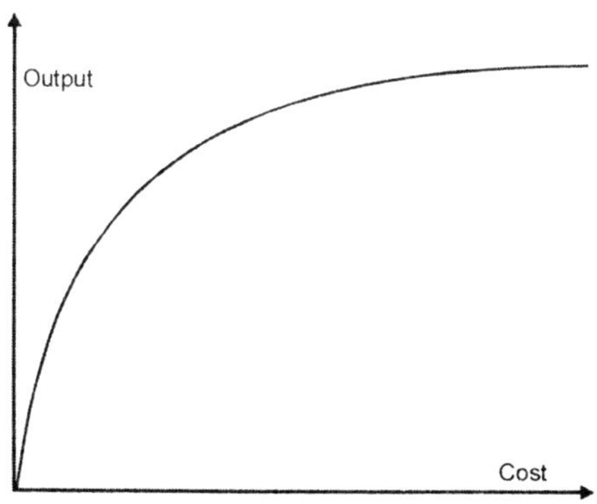

Development agencies are understandably nervous of involvement with technologies having a bias to the rich, and DRWH

has been accused of that tendency. Concentrating on small systems is one way of counteracting that danger. Developing the ability to service the grassroofs of the poorest would be another. Water can be collected from crude thatch, but it is coloured and turbid and its capture requires wide gutters. There are some directions for possible progress, including clarifying the stored water and employing sheet-plastic gutters. For the present study, ability to work with grassroofs was decided to be desirable but not essential if the fraction of homesteads with hard roofs were found to exceed 70 per cent and to be still rising. In fact the fraction of homesteads in the study area with at least one hardroof does generally satisfy this test: the prevalence of ironroofs in particular has risen dramatically in the last decade.

5.3 WATER NEEDS IN THE REGION AND THE POSSIBLE CONTRIBUTION OF VLC DRWH

(*i*) Rwanda

Data on water sources in the study area is not very readily available. In Rwanda there is a national register of springs; as per the 2001 census recorded data on Mbarara district, whose population was then 0.9 million people, is as shown in Tables 5.1 and 5.2. Piped water supplies in the few serviced urban areas in Uganda have improved. Nationally the fraction of the population having 'access' to clean water in 2004 was deemed to be 47 per cent for urban areas and 32 per cent for rural areas. For Africa as whole clean water coverage has changed little from 54 per cent over the last decade (WHO/UNICEF, 2000).

Locally in the Study Area there are areas like Rakai district where highly mineralized groundwater forces reliance on surface sources such as swamps. The building data indicates that only 38 per cent of roofs as being suitable for RWH whereas the proportion of dwellings for which at least one building has a hard roof is now probably over 65 per cent. None of the 12 NGOs, all working in DRWH, felt that absence of hard roofs was a serious restriction in the uptake of the technology. Corrugated ironroofs, that cost about £1 per square meter of building plan area, have become the norm for both housing and institutional buildings.

Table 5.1: Use of different water sources in Mbarara District (Rwanda Nat Census 2001)

Source Type	*Households Usage (%)*
1. Piped Water	3.3
2. Boreholes	5.5
3. Protected Well/Spring	8.6
4. Open Well/Spring	45.2
5. Stream/River	19.6
6. Lake/Pond/Dam	17.4
7. Total 'Clean'	17.5

Table 5.2: Distribution of Roofing Types in Mbarara District (Rwanda Nat Census 2001)

Roofing Type	*Percentage of Households Using*
1. Iron	37.2
2. Tile/Asbestos/Concrete	0.7
3. Total 'hard' Roofs	37.9
4. Grass/Papyrus	39.2
5. Banana	22.9
6. Total 'soft' Roofs	62.1

Rwanda is characterized by very steep but not mountainous terrain. In much of the country hillside springs have been the traditional water sources, augmented in the 1970s and 1980s by gravity-fed distribution piping. However since 1990 a growing fraction of the population may be found living considerably above the spring line and are carrying their water up through considerable heights. In the drier and flatter parts of the country to the East where springs are few, former National Park land has been recently settled by returned refugees. Rwanda was well-known for its attractive fired-tile roofing, however cheaper corrugated iron has gained in popularity recently.

(*ii*) Tanzania

In Tanzania the study area comprises Kagera Region, which is much wetter than the national average and thus more prone to have hard roofing (FAO, 1987). The terrain is less steep than in neighbouring Rwanda and good springs are far less common. Piped water is rarely encountered and shallow wells (some protected, some not) are widely used. The area is very 'peripheral', being 3 days journey from the capital, so material prices are relatively high.

In all three countries, water collection distances are significant and the terrain is rarely flat. A survey of 120 households in parts of the area is summarized in Table 5.3. From the table it can be seen that it took about 3.7 hours per household per day to collect water. These figures were based on a mean round trip speed on the flat of 65 metres/minute and lower speeds on slopes. This norm may be rather high although it is compatible with the few direct speed measurements made. Queuing time is not included and if it were collection times might be about 25 per cent higher.

In some well-populated plateau locations, water collection in the dry months is especially onerous because convenient sources dry up. The water has to be hauled up from valley sources as much as 5 km from (and 200 m lower than) the homestead.

Table 5.3: Analysis of Water Collection Distances/Times

Averages for all Households/People		
1. People per H/H	Number	6.3
2. Water per H/H	Litres/day	66.8
3. Time per H/H	Hour/day	3.7
4. Distance per H/H	Km/day	10.8
5. Water per Person	lcd	10.6
6. Time per Person	Hour/day	0.6
7. Distance per Person	Km/day	1.7

(*iii*) Uganda

Survey carried out in Kabarole district, Western Uganda, gives an idea of the benefits that can be obtained using small tanks. The survey analysis can be considered as a dry season analysis. The jars had been built as part of a study into water quality from cement jars and were 400-500 litres in size (the variation in size is due to manufacturing variability).

Table 5.4 shows the analysis of survey data collected from six villages, viz. Kandole, Katenta, Mugisa, Kaahwa, Karamagi, and Kayula. It is also worth pointing out that the survey form was designed to measure water carried from the traditional water source. The survey therefore measures the minimum benefit, as water consumption is likely to be higher when water is taken from the jar during the wet season.

Table 5.4: Analysis of Survey Data

		Sources					
		Kandole	*Katenta*	*Mugisa*	*Kaahwa*	*Karamagi*	*Kayula*
General Data	1. Distance to Source (m)	200.00	500.00	400.00	400.00	300.00	1500.00
	2. Number of Occupants	6.00	5.00	4.50	4.00	9.00	8.00
	3. Roof Area (m.sq.)	20.00	27.00	24.00	22.00	24.00	30.00
	4. Total Days Considered	106.00	106.00	92.00	85.00	92.00	106.00
	5. Rainy days during period	15.00	28.00	20.00	11.00	21.00	18.00
Calculated Data	1. Jerry cans carried from source (Daily average)	3.40	1.30	2.50	2.20	3.20	3.30
	2. Jerry cans consumed (Daily average)	5.40	3.00	5.30	3.00	4.90	5.00
	3. Average lpcd consumed	18.00	12.00	23.50	14.80	11.00	12.40
Estimated Savings	1. Litres (daily average)	40.70	34.50	57.50	18.10	35.50	34.80
	2. Kilometres walking (daily average)	0.81	1.73	2.30	0.73	1.07	5.21
	3. Minutes walking (daily average)*	19.50	41.40	55.20	17.40	25.60	125.10
	4. Percentage total water consumed	37.70	57.50	54.30	30.60	35.90	34.90

Note: *Assuming a walking speed of 2.5 kms per hour—in the majority of cases the terrain is steep.

It can be seen that the percentage coverage for the period looks quite low, only 35 per cent to 57.5 per cent. It should be noted, however, that the percentage of rainy days during the period (19% dry season) is low compared with the annual average (35%) and so the annual coverage figures will be higher (FAO, 1987). Also it can be noted that where the number of persons in the household is low, the savings are greater (with the exception of Kaahwa).

An indication of the walking time and walking distance shows that particularly high savings can be made when the distance to the traditional source is high (Katenta and Kayula), or where consumption is high (Mugisa). The actual daily time and walking saving are very significant—55 minutes and 125 minutes being the outstanding examples. It is interesting to note that there is no strong correlation between distances walked and consumed, which is generally believed to be the case.

5.4 ECONOMICS OF DRWH

In the study area all households already have some access to water from point sources. For some days per year, many also employ "informal" rainwater harvesting, placing bowls and jugs under eaves or even trees during rainfall.

The introduction of more formal (and productive) RWH will normally be accompanied by three benefits. The most obvious is a reduction in the time spent carrying water from point sources—a reduction more or less proportional to the volume of water no longer carried. The second is an increase in household water consumption wherever it was previously constrained by the effort of collection. The third is a common, although not invariable, increase in water quality. All these benefits rise with DRWH storage capacity, albeit in a way showing diminishing returns.

The increase in water consumption with VLC RWH has not been widely measured. Generally any increase is restricted to the wet seasons. DRWH (and VLC DRWH in particular) is not generally capable in the dry seasons of supplying quantities larger than already obtained from point sources: this means that it will be used to supplement, but not to substitute point-source water.

Figure 5.2: Value of Water

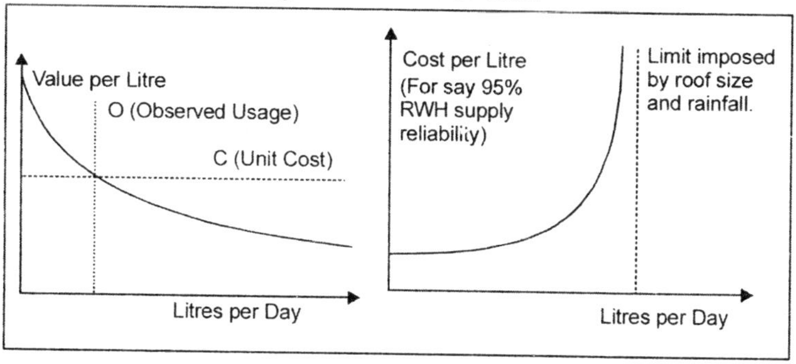

The costs of DRWH are overwhelmingly capital costs, as neither operation nor maintenance usually involves significant expenditure. Storage-tank cost is usually the dominant item, by contrast guttering accounts for only about 25 per cent of the total system cost. These capital costs are subject to economies of scale. The sensitivity (elasticity) of tank cost to storage capacity is about 0.8 (Rugasire, J.). The sensitivity of gutter cost to gutter capacity is even lower, so that it is usual to install gutters that are so large (e.g. designed for rainfall intensities up to 2 mm per minute) that they can catch all but 1 or 2 per cent of the annual run-off reaching them.

5.4.1 Value of Water

As with many other goods, water has a declining value with quantity. The first litre per day is worth more than the tenth. By examining the data that relates household consumption per day to the effective unit cost of water (*i.e.* cost per litre), we constructed a curve such as shown to the left in Figure 5.2. Each socio-economic group would have its own curve.

The cost line on the diagram is horizontal, which reasonably represents the situation where water is fetched, each successive litre requiring the same input of labour. Such a line does not fairly represent harvested roofwater, where the effective cost generally rises with daily consumption despite the economies of scale in tank construction. A typical cost v volume characteristic for RWH supply is shown left.

Sometimes we can find examples of water purchase and use them to infer the value of water. Richer households, or those experiencing illness, may pay for water to be brought to the house. More usually we have to infer costs indirectly through conversion of fetching distance/height into time and then time into money. Such costs, like the value of water, will be lower for poorer households than for richer ones.

5.4.2 Time Cost of Water Carriage

This is a function of a household's distance to, and height above, a water source, of the means of transport used, and of the persons involved in carriage and their respective unit time costs (actual or opportunity).

5.4.2.1 Haulage Distance

Table 5.4 shows the walking distances (users of 6 sources). Although there are some homesteads in the study area that haul water from distances greater than 5 km away in very dry months, the dry season average for 120 users of 6 point sources in the study area was 1.5 km to the source.

Box 5.2: Sickness and Water Collection

The elderly and the sick tend to suffer disproportionately. This is due to the fact that the sick find it difficult to collect water and usually carry smaller quantities of water.

Timanya: An elderly women of (65 yrs) in Kabale, Uganda.

"Water collection has become more of a problem than before in my life, I suffer from backache, all my grand children stay with their parents in turn, every day I collect 5 litres. At times children from the neighbours help me".

5.4.2.2 Height

Point water sources are generally lower than homes, so that the laden return journey is usually uphill. A round trip that comprises walking downhill with an empty water container and returning laden uphill is always slower than one of the same distance on the flat[3]. Experiments were undertaken to measure the effect of gradient on walking speed, but they gave rather inconclusive data because the samples were small and it proved impractical to control other variables such as youths' desire to impress, sense of urgency or tiredness etc.

5.4.2.3 Walking Speed

The speed of movement of a person collecting water depends upon many factors and varies between about 1.5 and 5 km/hour. For short haulage distances some people use a strategy of hurrying to minimise time or arm strain; this strategy cannot be maintained for more than about 200 m. Running down a gentle slope with an empty jerrycan, some young people exceed even 5 km/hour. Conversely, long uphill hauls require a slow steady pace with regular rests. Young children tire more quickly with distance than adults, even though they usually carry only 3 or 5 litre loads.

For distances over 1.5 km but only where slopes are gentle, pushed or pedalled bicycles are sometimes used to carry 1 or 2 × 20 litre jerrycans (especially by "commercial" water fetchers) at speeds of about 3.5 km/hour (Rugasira, L.). There is virtually no evidence of water carriage by pack animal in the target area—neither mules nor donkeys are commonly available. Such animals have to be driven slowly (3 km/hour) but carry up to 80 litres at a time (recent Mexican experience).

5.4.2.4 The Carrier's Age, Gender and Urgency

Water is most commonly carried by women and therefore by (in Africa) busy people. Babies may be left behind (a reason to increase speed) or may be carried (which reduces speed). Women often carry together, waiting at the source until a friend has filled her container (FAKT and KRA, 1997). School children regularly carry water (more often girls than boys) especially at weekends. In dry periods when distances are greater, men play a larger role in water fetching and probably travel a little faster than women. However, even strong men do not carry two jerrycans over any significant distance—the adult unit of water carriage is largely standardised at 20 litres (= 20 kg).

5.4.2.5 Total Time and Time Cost

The Appendix Table 5.1 indicates a mean time for water collection of 3.7 hours per household per day. In the drier months it is not uncommon to see a queue of 20 jerrycans at a source yielding under 5 litres per minute, implying a waiting time thereof 80 minutes. The queue rarely includes adults; women try to avoid such queues by fetching water before dawn, an expedient not without physical dangers (falls in the dark, snakebites etc.).

The opportunity cost of 3 hours per household is, in rural East Africa today, between $US0.2 and $US 0.6. The payment to a youth in a trading post to carry four jerrycans from a source 1.5 kms away is currently about $0.5.

5.5 THEORY OF COMBINING RWH WITH OTHER WATER SOURCES

For a given size and location of RWH system and for a given operating strategy, there will be a limit on the water it can supply per day, per week or per year. The maximum per year, corresponding to zero tank overflow, in litres will be the product of roof area (m^2), the annual rainfall (mm) and a run-off capture factor—typically 0.85 (For more details refer, Ariyabandu Ride D., 1999).

Consider first the situation where we can disregard seasonal factors, and assume that before RWH arrived, daily consumption from a point source was Q_P (litres/day). Q_P is determined by the interaction of the user's demand (cost v volume) curve and the unit cost C_P of supply from the point source. The daily cost to the user was therefore $Q_P \times C_P$.

If the water Q_R available per day from RWH is less than Q_P, then the users will draw Q_R from the RW system and the remainder Q_P-Q_R from the point source. The total consumption will not increase and the effective value of the harvested rainwater will be the saving $Q_R \times C_P$. If the water Q_R available per day from RWH is more than Q_P, then the users will increase their consumption from Q_P to Q_R and the rainwater will be worth more than the former total cost $Q_P \times C_P$. Exactly how much more will depend on the user's demand curve. The situation is represented in Figure 5.3, where Area (i) is the saving ($Q_P \times C_P$) while Area (ii) is the value of the extra water.

Note that Q_R is the daily amount available from RWH, whereas Q_P is determined by the price of supply (from non-RWH sources). The total value Area(i) + Area(ii) is less than ($Q_R \times C_P$) because the extra water is per litre less valuable to the user than the water "replaced".

Figure 5.3: Cost Per Litre

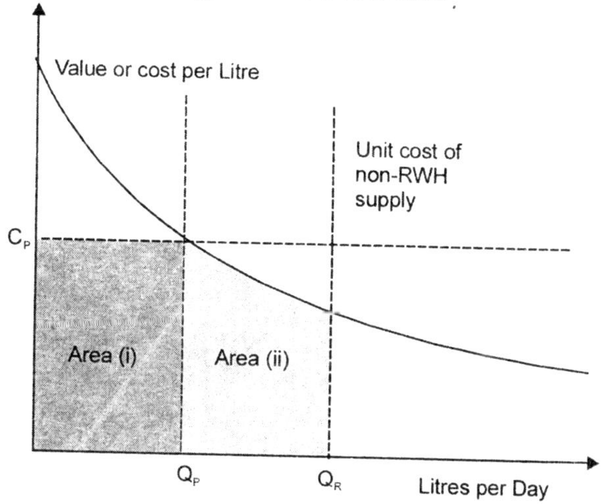

5.6 DOMESTIC WATER STORAGE FACILITY

In developing countries, technologies which are well-suited to improve the lives of rural poor are overlooked on occasions. There are a variety of reasons, the main reason usually being a poor access to knowledge and information, traditional cultural practices and lack of political will. Small-scale RWH is one such technology that has been largely overlooked by the majority of poor rural households in LDC's. In countries where the technology has been embraced (Thailand being the most prominent example), great benefits have been seen and large steps taken in alleviating the daily drudgery faced by householders in the task of meeting their water needs (Bradford, B., 1992).

5.6.1 Requirements of a Domestic Water Storage Tank

Any vessel used for storage of potable water in a domestic context should have certain attributes. These are investigated below in some detail:

5.6.1.1 Strength

Any tank that is to store water must have sufficient strength. Water pressure inside the tank creates stresses, which, if not dealt with properly, can cause the tank to fail, which could in turn lead to serious damage of the tank and injury to persons and/or damage to surrounding buildings. Ideally a full engineering analysis should be carried out for any new tank design and tests carried out to confirm the findings. In practice, tanks are usually designed and built, based on previous experience with the material being used and/or previous experience with similar vessels. A good safety factor is usually incorporated in such cases.

5.6.1.2 Impermeability

A water vessel should obviously be impermeable. This is achieved in one of a number of ways, depending on the material from which the tank is made. Some materials are inherently water proof e.g. corrugated steel sheets or fibre glass, and require no (or little) treatment to provide an impermeable barrier. Traditional materials, such as masonry and brick, are usually dealt with by applying an internal render of sand and cement, which can be treated with a water proofing agent or given a final coat of 'nil' (cement slurry). Ferrocement technology uses this concept by applying a cement slurry onto the wall of the tank when complete. Modern plastics may allow low-cost linings to be produced although little has been done in developing countries to develop a suitably sized off-the-shelf solution. Other modern materials, such as bituminous paints, suitable for use with potable water supplies, are slowly becoming available on the market in LDC's.

5.6.1.3 Durability

Engineering techniques for determining the durability (through accelerated ageing) are expensive and so the only way to properly 'test' a new technology is usually to apply the test of time. This is problematic when we are looking for a useful life of 20-30 years. Little information seems to be available on existing tanks and their useful life spans. The experience in Thailand shows how some unsuitable technologies can be widely disseminated before major flaws appear. In the Thai case more than 50,000 bamboo reinforced mortar jars were manufactured, many of which failed due to termite and fungal attack on the bamboo (Bradford, B., 1992).

> **Box 5.3:** Rainwater and Water Security
>
> Householders consider RWH to be a water source that is supplemented by other sources. This has been an advantage in the dissemination of small rainwater tanks, as the beneficiaries see the tanks as a partial supply and their expectations are not too high.
>
> Member of Rakai women's group (Uganda):
>
> "We know our jars are small, they cannot meet all our water demands, but we use the water sparingly, to prepare tea, drinking only after boiling".

5.6.2 Maintenance of Water Quality

A good storage vessel should maintain and improve the water quality. This is achieved in a number of ways (Cairncross, S. and Feacham, R., 1993):

- A good fitting, light-proof cover will prevent debris, animals or humans from entering the tank and prevent light from causing algae growth;
- Water quality can be enhanced by putting water into the tank and taking it out of the tank at the correct location—low-level tank entry and floating off-takes are devices designed to aid this approach;
- Good sanitary conditions around tanks will prevent disease being spread; and
- Water extraction should be such that the water is not contaminated while being drawn.

5.6.2.1 Health Risk Factor

Sometimes, with all good intentions, a water tank can become a serious health hazard. This is particularly the case when mosquitoes are allowed to breed in the tank. This can be avoided by sealing the tank well and preventing the mosquitoes entering and breeding by covering any openings with mosquito gauze.

5.6.3 Other DRWH System Components

5.6.3.1 Roofs

For domestic rainwater harvesting the most common surface for collection of water is the roof of the dwelling. Many other surfaces can be, and are, used: courtyards, threshing areas, paved walking areas, plastic sheeting, trees, etc. In some cases, as in Gibraltar and Zimbabwe for example, large rock surfaces are used to collect water which is then stored in large tanks at the base of the rock slopes (IRCA).

Most dwellings, however, have a roof. The style, construction and material of the roof affect its suitability as a collection surface for water. Typical materials for roofing include corrugated, galvanised, iron sheet (GI Sheet), asbestos sheet; tiles (a wide variety is found), slate, and thatch (from a variety of organic materials). Most are suitable for collection of roof-water, but only certain types of grasses e.g. coconut and anahaw palm thatched tightly, provide a surface adequate for high quality water collection (Gould and Nissen Peterson, 1999). The rapid move towards the use of GI sheets in many developing countries favours the promotion of RWH (despite the other negative attributes of this material).

Some work was carried out during the study to investigate the possibilities of using grass roofing for DRWH. Guttering was installed on one grass roof that had been constructed with a plastic membrane beneath it—this helps to prevent UV degradation of the plastic. The grass was loosely thatched and found locally. The plastic sheet guttering that was installed is shown in the Picture 4. It is designed to capture all the water falling on the thatch and passing through to the plastic sheet. It is fixed using two long poles, one suspended below the eaves and one on top of the thatch. It can also be designed to be demountable from the upper surface, such that it can be 'put away' under the eaves when there is no rain. Again this helps prevent degradation due to sunlight.

Guttering is used to transport rainwater from the roof to the storage vessel. Guttering comes in a wide variety of shapes and forms, ranging from the factory made PVC type to home made guttering using bamboo or folded metal sheet. In fact, the lack of standards in guttering shape and size makes it difficult for designers to develop standard solutions to, say, filtration and first flush devices. Guttering is usually fixed to the building just below the roof and catches the water as it falls from the roof.

5.6.3.2 Water Filtration

There are a wide variety of systems available for treating water before, during and after storage. The level of sophistication also varies, from extremely high-tech to very rudimentary. The simple trash rack has been used but this type of filter has a number of associated problems: firstly it only removes large debris; and secondly the rack can become clogged easily and requires regular cleaning.

The sand-charcoal-stone filter is often used for filtering rainwater entering a tank. This type of filter is only suitable, however, where the inflow is low to moderate, and will soon overflow if the inflow exceeds the rate at which the water can percolate through the sand (Rees D.G. and Thomas T.H., 1999). Settling tanks and partitions can be used to remove silt and other suspended solids from the water. These are usually effective where used, but add significant additional cost if elaborate techniques are used. Many systems found in the field rely simply on a piece of cloth or fine mosquito mesh to act as the filter (and to prevent mosquitoes entering the tank).

Post storage filtration includes such systems as the up-flow sand filter or the twin compartment candle filters commonly found in LDC's. Many other systems exist and can be found in the appropriate water literature.

5.6.3.3 First/foul Flush Systems

Debris, dirt, dust and droppings will collect on the roof of a building or other collection area. When the first rains arrive, this unwanted matter will be washed into the tank. This will cause contamination of the water and the quality will be reduced (For more details refer, IRCSA). Many RWH systems therefore incorporate a system for diverting this 'first flush' water so that it does not enter the tank.

There are a number of simple systems that are commonly used and also a number of other, slightly more complex, arrangements. The simpler ideas are based on a manually operated arrangement whereby the inlet pipe is moved away from the tank inlet and then replaced again once the initial first flush has been diverted. This method has obvious drawbacks in that there has to be a person present who will remember to move the pipe.

Other systems use tipping gutters to achieve the same purpose. The most common system uses a bucket that accepts the first flush and the weight of this water off-balances a tipping gutter which then diverts the water back into the tank. The bucket then empties slowly through a small-bore pipe and automatically resets. The quantity of water that is flushed is dependent on the force required to lift the guttering. This can be adjusted to suit the needs of the user.

Another system that is used relies on a floating ball that forms a seal once sufficient water has been diverted. The seal is usually made as the ball rises into the apex of an inverted cone. The ball seals the top of the 'waste' water chamber and the diverted water is slowly released, as with the bucket system above, through a small bore pipe.

Although the more sophisticated methods provide a much more elegant means of rejecting the first flush water, practitioners often recommend that very simple, easily maintained systems be used, as these are more likely to be repaired if failure occurs.

5.6.3.4 Treatment of Rainwater for Potable Supply

A number of post storage treatment techniques are recommended. Boiling water is the most commonly recommended, but it is seldom practiced. Ceramic candle filters are easily purchased in most major towns in Africa, but their cost is often prohibitive. A technique that is being widely recommended currently is solar disinfection or *SODIS*. This technique requires only clear glass or plastic bottles that are filled and then placed in the sun for one day. It is also worth remembering that in many cases contamination takes place during secondary storage or during water handling, due to unsanitary conditions.

5.7 REGIONAL EXPERIENCE OF PROMOTING DRWH

There is a surprisingly large number of organizations active in promoting domestic RWH in Eastern Africa, some of whom have been active for over decades. Moreover other sources indicate a steady growth in 'commercial' DRWH—e.g. the attaching of tanks to middle-class houses by their owners. The formation of the Uganda Rainwater Association in 1998 and the recognition of the technology by Government are further pointers to its growing popularity. It would seem that the proportion of households operating DRWH systems is rising steadily, perhaps by as much as 1 per cent per annum.

In the study area including Western Uganda, North West Tanzania and Eastern Rwanda has a total population of over 6 million and contains about 1 million residential homes. Against this figure, perhaps 2000 DRWH systems installed by the combined efforts of the NGOs represents a tiny impact—say 0.2 per cent penetration. Even if the seeds planted by training were to multiply vigorously, it seems unlikely that the number of DRWH systems disseminated by NGOs etc will catch up those in the private sector. In those same households the (purely commercial) penetration of ($100) iron roofing probably exceeds 60 per cent and of ($50) bicycles perhaps 25 per cent.

RWH generally treated as part of intensive rather than extensive interventions, but it also reported to be highly and permanently dependent upon availability of external subsidy. Repeatedly it was reported that it is too expensive for most of the population to purchase. The fraction of system hardware costs (*i.e.* excluding training and promotional costs) provided by beneficiaries in the interventions reported varied from about 10 per cent to 70 per cent (Rugasira, J). Thus there appears to be no sense that these interventions are for 'kick starting' a technology that is ready to run on its own.

DRWH, even in its very-low-cost (say $40) form is not affordably by the great bulk of its potential recipients in Eastern Africa. It is only a technique in a long-term programme of Government-funded or Agency-funded provision of better water supplies for those too poor to do other than collect from 'free' natural sources. It may often cost less per household than such alternatives as protecting more springs and wells, or extending gravity-flow schemes, but it is not sustainably affordable. Thus either: (a) DRWH should continue to be extended under substantial subsidy—perhaps over 50 per cent of the organizational and material costs of each installation—at the rate that the availability of such subsidy affords or (b) it should be deemed to have failed to affordably meet water needs and aid should be devoted to other more deserving ends.

An alternative view is that DRWH should be just left to commercially trickle down from higher-income to middle-income households in locations where other water sources are inadequate. A further option is to strive to reduce both the cost of individual systems and the cost of promoting/supporting them, so that far more poor households can be reached with a given financial resource. Moreover the threshold of affordability could also thereby be changed so that all but the poorest say 30 per cent of households could access water in this way without outside subsidy.

5.8 CONCLUSION

The present paper assess whether 'very-low-cost' domestic roof water harvesting has the potential for extensive acceptance in the Eastern Africa. It was found that 'informal' DRWH, using bowls or sometimes 200 litre drums, is already widely practised and that rainwater collection goods like gutters and GI tanks are on sale in many towns. Moreover a large (>65%) and growing fraction of households have at least one roof of GI sheets suitable for RWH.

A number of NGOs have been active in promoting DRWH amongst the rural poor in the Area. However it seems unlikely that their efforts have yet affected more than about 0.2 per cent of the households in East Africa, far fewer than the number practicing DRWH because they can afford its full cost. The NGOs generally hold that for poorer households DRWH can only be accessible if it is strongly subsidized. The activities of NGOs and local governments have made the DRWH option far better known and acceptable than a few years ago. Moreover DRWH has been used in a few cases to carry interventions aimed at enabling women to achieve greater status, skills and confidence.

The study indicated that a water store of capacity about 600 litres would enable most households to draw 65-75 per cent of their annual water from such stores, but would still need to collect the remainder from point sources like wells. This relief from water-carrying would be almost total in the wet seasons (about 2/3 of each year) but rather slight in the driest months when carrying distances and queuing times are at their longest. The average annual saving in distance walked corresponds (in the hilly terrain) to a mean time saving of about 700 hours per household per year, worth perhaps $70 at a realistic 'opportunity cost' for time. For households having to pay cash for their water carriage—at typically $0.1 per 20 liters—the benefits would be somewhat greater but at the expense of the income of professional carriers.

At present water consumption per capita is about 13 liters per day. With DRWH this is likely to rise significantly, but only in the wet seasons. From the data analysis, it appears that counting reduced walking time as the sole benefit, the 'payback time' for investment in VLC DRWH is about 1 year. This is an acceptable but not outstanding figure, indicating broad economic viability provided that promotion costs do not exceed say $10 per household. The availability of suitable credit would make take-up much easier for the poorest households. For households that are particularly poorly located with respect to point sources the payback period may be as low as 6 months. The benefits accrue more to women and school-age children than to men.

Overall it can be say that DRWH could bring considerable benefits to the majority of households in East Africa, is likely to continue to expand into higher-income households and has considerable potential for adoption by low-income households if artisan training and either credit or modest subsidy can be provided.

NOTES

1. In association with local organizations in Africa and tropical Asia, the Development Technology Unit at the University of Warwick has been researching DRWH systems for some years, looking for better understanding, lower costs and higher performance. It has been found that DRWH development has reached a point where 'partial' DRWH systems could be affordable by the bulk of rural households.
2. Prior to this Study the DTU had identified three promising designs for small stores (500-800 litres) as well as a large (8000 litre), but relatively low-cost, 'partly-underground' tank, with associated village-manufacturable pumps. It was estimated prior to the study that complete systems containing 750 litres (ca '7 days') of storage might be producible in the Study Area for $40US and 2000 litre

systems could cost under $80US. These estimates took into account the high prices of items like cement in the Area.

3. For calculation purposes it would be convenient either to replace any climb height by an extra horizontal distance of equivalent carriage time, e.g. "add 1 km for every 100 m climb". Alternatively we might assign a different round-trip mean speed for each gradient. It is likely that a very steep (return) uphill slope of say 1-in-5 will halve the round-trip mean speed, especially for climbs exceeding 100m. A gentle gradient of say 1-in-30 will have little effect on round trip time.

REFERENCES

Ariyabandu, R. de D. (1999). "Water Security through Rainwater Harvesting", *Integrated Development for Water Supply and Sanitation*, WEDC, Loughborough University, pp. 366 Ð 368.

Bradford B. July, (1992). "Focus on Thailand" *Raindrop, Rainwater Harvesting Bulletin*, Volume 7, pp. 1 Ð 11.

Cairncross S. and Feacham, R. (1993). *Environmental Health Engineering in the Tropics*, Wiley.

Development Technology Unit (DTU), University of Warwick, http://www.eng.warwick.ac.uk/DTU/Rainwater harvesting.

FAKT, and Kenya Rainwater Association (KRA), (1997), *Mvua ni maji Ð Rainwater harvesting by womenÕs groups in Kenya*, Video, FAKT, Stuttgart.

FAO, (1987). *Africa: Mean Annual Rainfall Map*, (Scale 1:1,000,000), Rome.

Pearce, E. A. and Smith C.G. (1998). The Hutchinson World Weather Guide, 4th Ed, Helicon.

Gould J. and Nissen-Petersen E. (1999). *Rainwater Catchment Systems for Domestic Supply*, IT Pubs.

International Rainwater Catchment Systems Association (IRCSA), http://www.ircsa.org.

Rees D.G. and Thomas T.H. (1999). "Low-cost Roofwater Harvesting in the Humid Tropics" *Integrated Development for Water Supply and Sanitation*, WEDC, Loughborough University, pp. 418-421.

Rugasira, J., *Rakai Women Groups involved in Rainwater Harvesting Activities (Women leading the development process in the new millennium)*, Uganda Rainwater Harvesting Association and SIDA.

WHO/UNICEF, (2000). *Water Supply and Sanitation Sector Monitoring Report, 2000*, Publication WHO/EOS/96.15; see also www.africanwater.org/csscoverage.htm#Africa

6

Sustainable Development of Rift Valley Bio-diversity

A Case of Nech Sar National Park in Ethiopia

6.1 INTRODUCTION

Nech Sar National Park (NSNP) is one of the eight national parks in Ethiopia covering an area of 514 sq. kms and is situated in one of the most scenic parts of the Ethiopian Rift Valley; locating around 500 km south of the Ethiopian capital Addis Ababa[1]. It is bordering with the 2000 feets high Amaro Mountains on the east, 1070 sq. kms wide Lake Abaya on the North, 350 sq. kms wide Lake Chamo on the West. The local people named the park "Nech Sar, which in the local language Amharic means 'white grass' because from a distance it is like an ocean of white grass as far as the eye can see (MFAE, 2002). The Park was established in 1974.

The dominant physiographic feature of the country around Nech Sar is the Great Rift Valley, one of the World's most fascinating geological events. The Rift Valley splits the great Ethiopian highland massif. The faulting and volcanic activities associated with it are the principal determinants of the Park's physical features. The steep escarpments that surround the park to the North, East and West mark fault lines and volcanic extrusions associated with the formations of the Rift. The Rift Valley was almost certainly the cradle of mankind and our first civilizations were the stone-age people who thrived long ago around the rich lakeshores of the many lakes strewn along the floor of the Rift Valley.

The NSNP planes are around 1108-1650 metres above the mean sea level and the major rivers originating from the park include Kulfo and Sermele. The western part of the planes along the hill is rich with undersurface water which feeds the large dense forest that has no match in the East African sub-continent. The natural block that separates Lake Abaya on the North and Lake Chamo on the South is known as 'Yegzier Dildiy', which in the local language means the 'bridge of the heaven' that offers a splendid view of the surroundings. The climate and temperature varies depending on the rainfall; the hottest season is between January and March when the temperature reach up to 35 °C and the coldest months are November and December (28 °C). The plane receives an average annual rainfall of 900 mm with highest intensity between March and May.

6.2 BIO-DIVERSITY

There is a great diversity of habitats in the NSNP planes including aquatic environment, marshy areas, ever green ground-water forest with a series of natural springs around and patches of tall gallery forest in the Seremelle valley. Ecologically the park lies in an arid eutrophic savannah characteristic of soils of medium fertility derived from ancient lake sediments.

It is the only national park in the world where the critically endangered Swayne's hartebeests still survives, the only known locality of the Nech Sar Nightjar, with large populations of hippo and crocodile (APF, 2005b). Although the larger mammals are locally extinct there are some 73 medium and small mammals and 343 bird species. The native Ibis, thick-billed raven are found in the Park and it is a sanctuary for lesser flamingoes, imperial eagle and the lesser kestrel. The Park supports Ethiopia's largest concentration of Burchell's zebra and is one of the best places to see greater Kudu. The Burchell's zebra is found on the central plain alongwith Grant's gazelle and kori bustard. It is one of the best places in Ethiopia to see klipspringer, dikdik, water buck, warthog, hippo, crocodile and many small mammals are common (Alison, M. Jones, 2005). There are bush pig and carnivores including lion, leopard, cheetah, wild dog, caracal, bat-eared fox, serval and many reptiles. The riverine forest has many colobus and vervet monkeys. Anubis baboons are very common.

'Azo Gebeya' is a place situated on the shore of Lake Chamo, where a great number of huge Nile crocodiles and Hippos crawl out of water and lie on the shore of the Lake. The crocodile farm near NSNP, established in 1984 breeds Nile crocodiles to export to foreign markets (Abate, Groum, 2004). Besides crocodiles and hippoes, tiger fish, cat fish, telepia and giant Nile Perch are found in Lake Abaya and Chamo (A Nile Perch fish that weighed as much as 110 kg was caught from the Lakes).

6.3 LOCAL COMMUNITY

Nech Sar lies between two culturally different groups of people. To the east in the beautiful Amaro mountains are the 'Korie' people, settled agriculturists with an economy based on a wide variety of grain and root crops, fruits and vegetables. The tuber of the false banana known as 'Enset' is the staple food of the "Korie'(For more details see, Plant, Martin, 2005). Coffee and chat are their principal cash crops. In the mountains to the west are the Gamo people with a similar economy to that of the 'Korie' but of very different origins (RI, 2005). To the North of the Korie is the "Guji-Oromo' part of the large Oromo nation.

6.4 SUSTAINABLE DEVELOPMENT OF THE NSNP

With the objective of insuring economic viability, African Parks (APs), a Company to protect the bio-diversity through community participation, took over the management of the Park for a specified period. APs envisioned NSNP to be one of the finest and most productive protected areas in Ethiopia that it delivers and demonstrates bio-diversity conservation and sustainable natural resources management for the benefit of the neighbouring communities[2]. One of the most important objectives is the betterment of the socio-economic conditions of communities in and adjacent to the Park.

The intention of APs is to make the NSNP a local engine of economic development and ensure that local communities benefit directly in the opportunities created by effective protected area management (APF, 2005a). This includes creation of job opportunities, development of reforestation that provide sustainable sources of fuel energy, browsing for livestock, soil conservation, small-scale business enterprises, creation of community conservation areas as buffer zones and social services development programmes. In addition, APs intends to establish a structure together with third parties that will focus on the establishment of small business groups, creation of employment opportunities and support of development programmes in the surrounding communities.

The major objectives of the sustainable bio-diversity conservation through community participation include the following (APF, 2006):

(i) The rights of the community to benefit from the Park are respected, which could be in the form of generation of employment opportunities at both first rate and self-employment and socio-economic development programmes such as health, education, agriculture, natural resources, etc.
(ii) The obligations of the community in the betterment of Park are met, which could be abstention from illegal utilization of resources bounded in the Park, promotion of environment conservation education and adoption of community wildlife conservation practice in areas adjacent to the Park.
(iii) Effective networking of all key stakeholders is created for the betterment of Park, and thereby ensuring proper monitoring and evaluation.

To achieve the above said objectives it is envisaged the following strategies with the participation of all stakeholders[3].

(i) Regular follow-up of Park management practices and the involvement of key stakeholders, especially the local community.
(ii) Alongwith local evaluation a joint evaluation of the performance of APs project with the participation of experts and resource agents at the national and international level will also be ensured.
(iii) Proper networking of the actions to abridge communication between different stakeholders.

6.5 CONCLUSION

The community oriented bio-diversity conservation for the sustenance of environment is a good lesson for other Rift Valley Sanctuaries and other bio-reserves. Alongwith environment protection, economic productivity and socio-cultural viability are all taken into account in this effort. When the world community celebrates World Environment Day every year we are forgetting per day deterioration of dense forest and the environment and the deprivation of the tribal communities. The NSNP model of APs' efforts is one of the innovative and good practices in this direction, which are reaping positive results throughout the world in our endeavour to protect and conserve the Mother Nature.

NOTES

1. The asphalt road from Addis Ababa to Arba Minch allows travellers to drive with maximum comfort. The newly built Arba Minch International Airport hosts inland flights from Addis Ababa.
2. The Article 7.3 of the Agreement Document signed by Federal Government, SNNPR state and APs PLC states, 'APF undertakes to take community interests into consideration, as far as, it is practically possible. To that effect, a Joint Liaison Committee (JLC) including representatives of SNNPR state has to be established with the local communities and existing CBOs, which meet on a quarterly basis. The establishment of the JLC will enable local communities to be the primary beneficiaries of the employment opportunities.'
3. Important actors include the Government (Zonal Justice and Administrative Affairs Office, Regional and Zonal Tourism, Parks and Hotels Commission, Regional/Zonal Rural Development Bureau, Woreda Administrative Office); local community (beneficiary groups such as co-operatives and small business enterprise, and traditional societal organizations from Kore, Guji, Arba Minch town and Chamo Leto communities); civil society organizations (South Portfolio-SNV, Forum for Environment, Arba Minch, etc.); and APs Nech Sar Project Office.

REFERENCES

Abate, Groum (2004). 'African Parks Strikes $1 Million Decide to Manage Nech Sar,' *Capital Ethiopia.com*, February 24.

African Parks Foundation (APF), (2005a). *Joint Liaison Committee for Nech Sar National Park Projects—APs (Ethiopia) PLC*, Proposal, Arba Minch.

African Parks Foundation (APF), (2005b). *Nech Sar National Park: Illegal Fishing*, October 23, Arba Minch.

African Parks Foundation (APF), (2006). *Nech Sar National Park: Annual Report 2006*, Arba Minch.

Alison, M. Jones (2005). 'A Proposed Management Plan for Ethiopia's Nech Sar National Park,' *Forest, Ecology and People: Principles and Practices*, Columbia University.

Ministry of Foreign Affairs of Ethiopia (MFAE), (2002). *Tourism, Investment and Banking System,* Addis Ababa.

Plant, Martin (2005). *People Problems for Ethiopian Game Park*, BBC News-Ethiopia, September, 26.

Refugees International (RI), (2005). Evictions from Nech Sar National Parks, Addis Ababa.

7

Environmental Refugees: Lessons from the Horn of Africa

A Case of Sudan

7.1 INTRODUCTION

Alongwith many of the problems that humans are facing in the new Millennium one of the latest additions is the phenomenon of environmental refugees. This is a situation where people who can no longer gain a secure livelihood in their homelands because of environmental disasters such as drought, soil erosion, desertification, deforestation and other environmental problems, together with population pressures and profound poverty. In their desperation, these people feel they have no alternative but to seek alternative shelter elsewhere, however hazardous the attempt. Not all of them have fled their regions or countries, many being internally displaced. But all have abandoned their homelands on a semi-permanent if not permanent basis, with little hope of a foreseeable return.

As far back as 1995 (latest date for a comprehensive assessment), these environmental refugees totalled at least 25 million people, compared with 27 million traditional refugees (people fleeing due to political oppression, religious persecution and ethnic troubles). The environmental refugees have doubled since 1995 and it will continue to increase because of global warming and other environmental hazards. Moreover, it could increase steadily for a good while thereafter as growing numbers of impoverished people press ever harder on over-loaded environments[1].

Of the 25 million environmental refugees in 1995, there were roughly five million in the African Sahel, where a full ten million people had fled from droughts, only half returning home. Another four million, out of eleven million refugees of all types, were in the Horn of Africa including Sudan. In other parts of Sub-Saharan Africa, where 80 million people were considered to be semi-starving due primarily to environmental factors, seven million people had been obliged to migrate in order to obtain relief food. In early 2000 Sudan featured eight million people who were officially considered at risk of starvation, with another six million in Somalia and three million in Kenya, plus several million others in other countries. A sizeable though undocumented proportion of these could be characterized as environmental refugees.

A number of commentators, journalists and analysts have recently focused on competition for natural resources, increasingly scarce due to global warming, as the trigger of the conflict in western Sudan. Among the earliest commentators to put a global warming spin on the Darfur crisis was economist Jeffrey Sachs. "Recent years have shown that shifts in rainfall can bring down Governments and even set off wars. The African Sahel, just south of the Sahara, provides a dramatic and poignant demonstration" (Jeffrey Sachs, 2006). The deadly carnage in Darfur, Sudan, which is almost always discussed in political and military terms, has roots in an ecological crisis directly arising from climate shocks. Darfur provides a case study of how existing marginal situations can be exacerbated beyond the tipping point by climate-related factors. It also shows how lack of essential resources threatens not only individuals and their communities but also the region and the international community at large. As the UN Secretary-General Ban Ki-moon wrote, "Amid the diverse social and political causes, the Darfur conflict began as an ecological crisis, arising at least in part from climate change" (Ban Ki-moon, 2007).

The UN Environment Programme (UNEP) report says competition over oil, gas, water, timber and land use are behind the "instigation and perpetuation" of decades of fighting throughout Sudan (UNEP, 2007). Environmental degradation is one of the root causes of the conflicts—alongside economic, political and social issues—as these natural resources are depleted. With more than five million internally displaced and international refugees, Sudan has the largest refugee population in the world today. There is the spread of deserts by an average of 100 km in the last 40 years, a loss of almost 12 per cent of forest cover in 15 years and overgrazing of fragile soil. Ignoring these environmental issues will ensure that some political and social problems remain unsolvable and even likely to worsen, as environmental degradation mounts at the same time as population increases.

The present chapter reviews the environmental factors underlying the crisis in Sudan and also assesses the economic forces and vicious circles including poverty.

7.2 GLOBAL SCENARIO

While Sub-Saharan Africa remains the prime locus of environmental refugees, there are sizeable numbers in other regions and countries. In China with its 120 million internal migrants, at least 6 million deserve to be regarded as environmental refugees, having been obliged to abandon their farmlands due to shortages of agricultural plots in the wake of decades of population growth. In Mexico there are 1 million new environmental refugees each year; some become assimilated in cities, and a few return home, leaving a cumulative total, as a bare minimum in 1995, of 2 million (UNDG, 1999). Finally there are those people displaced involuntarily by public works projects, notably large dams, and increasing by 10 million every year (with a cumulative total of 50 million in just China and India). Most of them resettle elsewhere, but the number remaining in a refugee-like situation totals at least 1 million.

The 1995 estimate of 25 million environmental refugees was cautious and conservative. Scattered throughout the developing world were 135 million people threatened by severe desertification, and 550 million people subject to chronic water shortages. While certain of these people would have been included in the 25 million figure, many could well have been driven to migrate without being counted as environmental refugees.

Of the nearly one billion people added to the global population during the 1990s, good proportions were among communities with a cash income of $1 per day or less. They include the people most likely to be subsisting, or rather struggling to survive, in environments too wet, too dry or too steep for sustainable agriculture. In Sub-Saharan Africa, these environments would have needed to support an extra 150 million people during the 1990s, and a similar total in India (WFP, 2002).

Poverty serves as an additional "push" factor associated with the environmental problems displacing people. Other factors include population pressures, malnutrition, landlessness, unemployment, over-rapid urbanisation, pandemic diseases and faulty Government policies, together with ethnic strife and conventional conflicts. In particular, it is sometime difficult to differentiate between refugees driven by environmental factors and those impelled by economic problems. In certain instances, people with moderate though tolerable economic circumstances at home feel drawn by opportunity for a better livelihood elsewhere. They are not so much pushed by environmental deprivation as pulled by economic promise. This ostensibly applies to many Hispanics heading for the United States. But those people who migrate because they suffer outright poverty are frequently driven also by root factors of environmental destitution. It is their environmental plight as much as any other factor that makes them economically impoverished. This generally applies to those refugees who migrate to areas where economic conditions are little if any better than back home, as is the case with many people who migrate within Sub-Saharan Africa and the Indian sub-continent. In this instance, with poverty and "life on the environmental limits" as the main motivating force, it matters little to the migrants whether they view themselves primarily as environmental or economic refugees.

On top of all these sub-problems is the lack of official recognition, whether on the part of Governments or international agencies, that there is an environmental refugee problem at all. Of course the above is not to overlook parallel problems in OSCE countries; very much on the contrary. Well known is the displacement of tens of thousands of people in the environs of the Aral Sea and as a result of desertification and general land degradation in other parts of Central Asia. Of course "tens of thousands" of these environmental refugees does not compare with the tens of millions of such refugees in Africa and elsewhere in the developing world, but it is specially significant, obviously enough, for the people concerned.

7.3 SUDAN: A VICTIM OF ENVIRONMENTAL DESTRUCTION

Sudan is situated in northern Africa, bordering the Red Sea and it has a coastline of 853 km along the Red Sea. With an area of

2,505,810 sq. kms., it is the largest country in the continent and tenth largest in the world. It borders the countries of Central African Republic, Chad, Democratic Republic of the Congo, Egypt, Eritrea, Ethiopia, Kenya, Libya and Uganda. It is dominated by the River Nile and its tributaries. The terrain is generally flat plains, broken by several mountain ranges; in the west the Jebel Marra is the highest range; in the south is the highest mountain Mount Kinyeti Imatong, near the border with Uganda; in the east are the Red Sea Hills.

In its 50 years of independence, Africa's largest country has been plagued by conflicts rooted in the economic, political, social and military domination of the country by a narrow elite within northern Sudan. Civil war has touched the ten southern states, also the west (all three Darfur states), the centre (Blue Nile and Southern Kordofan States), the east (Kassala State) and the northeast (Red Sea State). Fighting in Darfur has occurred intermittently for atleast thirty years. Until 2003, it was mostly confined to a series of partly connected tribal and local conflicts, and then these hostilities escalated into a full-scale military confrontation in all three Darfur States, which also frequently spills into neighbouring Chad and the Central African Republic (Aisha Abdella, 2006).

The Blue and White Niles meet in Khartoum to form the River Nile, which flows northwards through Egypt to the Mediterranean Sea. Blue Nile's course through Sudan is nearly 800 km long and is joined by the rivers Dinder and Rahad between Sennar and Khartoum. The White Nile within Sudan has no significant tributaries. The amount of rainfall increases towards the south. In the north there is the very dry Nubian Desert; in the south there are swamps and rain forest. Sudan's rainy season lasts for about three months (July to September) in the north, and up to six months (June to November) in the south. The dry regions are plagued by sand storms, known as haboob, which can completely block out the sun. In the northern and western semi-desert areas, people rely on the scant rainfall for basic agriculture and many are nomadic, travelling with their herds of sheep and camels (UNEP, 2007). Nearer the River Nile, there are well-irrigated farms growing cash crops. There are several dams on the Blue and White Niles. Among them are the Sennar and Roseires on the Blue Nile, and Jebel Aulia dam on the White Nile. There is also Lake Nubia on the Sudan-Egyptian border. Rich mineral resources are available in Sudan including: petroleum, natural gas, gold, silver, chromite, asbestos, manganese, gypsum, mica, zinc, iron, lead, uranium, copper, kaolin, cobalt, granite, nickel and tin.

Box 7.1: Sudan Floods: A Show Case for Environmental Destruction

Floods that have left thousands of families homeless in July 2007 in Sudan reached critical stage in several states. The river levels have exceeded those of previous years, especially in the Nile River State of Northern Sudan. The level of the Blue Nile at Khartoum, the capital, was "far above" the record levels seen at this time of year in 1988. Readings from several monitoring stations show the Nile to be more than a metre higher than in 1988. At least 59 people have been killed and more than 35,000 families left homeless by rains and floods affecting 12 of the 26 States. About 134 public buildings, including schools, health centres, police stations and other Government facilities had collapsed.

The International Federation of Red Cross and Red Crescent Societies reported that it affected 2.4 million people across 16 States. The causalities were more where the White Nile and Blue Nile rivers meet, with more than 13,000 families affected, followed by North Kordofan State in Central Sudan. Weather reports indicate that rainfall will be very high in the coming years due to global warming and the White Nile and Blue Nile will reach unprecedented levels.

In Southern Sudan, nearly 10,000 people have been affected by floods in Unity and Upper Nile States. The floods have hit hardest in Renk county in Upper Nile, where the effect of heavy rains has been compounded by natural drainage systems being disrupted by road construction. A recent study by the UN Environment Programme stated that road construction (often connected to the oil industry) in Southern Sudan could have wide-ranging environmental effects, including flooding, erosion and watercourse siltation.

Desertification is a serious problem in Sudan. There is also concern over soil erosion. Agricultural expansion, both public and private, has proceeded without conservation measures. The consequences have manifested themselves in the form of deforestation, soil desiccation, and the lowering of soil fertility and the water table.

The nation's wildlife is threatened by hunting. As of 2001, twenty-one mammal species and nine bird species are endangered, as well as two types of plants. Endangered species include: the waldrapp, northern white rhinoceros, tora hartebeest, slender-horned gazelle, and hawksbill turtle. The Sahara oryx has become extinct in the wild (UNSS, 2005). In May, 2007, it was announced that hundreds of wild elephants have been located on a previously unknown, treeless island in the Sudd swampland region of Southern Sudan. The exact location was kept secret to protect the animals from poachers.

7.4 CAUSES OF THE PRESENT CRISIS

The violence has claimed at least 400,000 lives, displaced 2.5 million people and left more than 3.5 million men, women and children struggling to survive amid violence and starvation (Brian D. Pellot, 2007). Flooding, deforestation, overgrazing due to explosive livestock growth and a marked decline in rainfall as a result of regional climate change are identified as significant stress factors in Sudan's largely pastoral society.

Competition between pastoralists and agriculturalists is key to so many conflicts in East Africa, including the crisis in Darfur. Violence between tribes and ethnic groups are the most visible dividing lines, but the stories of these conflicts cannot be told without including underlying environmental and demographic stresses. Sudan, along with other countries in the Sahel belt, has suffered several long and devastating droughts in the past few decades. The most severe drought occurred in 1980-84 was accompanied by widespread displacement and localised famine. There is the erosion of natural resources caused by climate change as among the root causes of social strife and conflict. The scale of historical climate change, as recorded in Northern Darfur, is almost unprecedented: the reduction in rainfall has turned millions of hectares of already marginal semi-desert grazing land into desert. The impact of climate change is considered to be directly related to the conflict in the region, as desertification has added significantly to the stress on the livelihoods of pastoralist societies, forcing them to move south to find pasture.

The great drought and famine of 1984-85 led to localised conflicts that generally pitted pastoralists against farmers in a struggle for diminishing resources, culminating in the Fur-Arab War of 1987-89. Important causes include historical grievances, local perceptions of race, demands for a fair sharing of power between different groups, the inequitable distribution of economic resources and benefits, disputes over access to and control over increasingly scarce natural resources (land, livestock and water), the proliferation of arms and the militarisation of young people, the absence of a democratic process and other governance issues (UNDP, 2002). Local issues have been politicised and militarised, and drawn into the wider political dynamics of Sudan.

Data collected since 1917 in El Fasher, capital of North Darfur, showed that the average annual rainfall had halved. UNEP has identified categories of natural resources that have been linked to the various conflicts in Sudan[2]: oil and gas reserves; Nile water; hardwood timber; range-land and rain-fed agricultural land, and the associated water points (UNEP, 2007). The rural ethnic and livelihood structures of Sudan are so complex and area-specific that any summary of the issue of resource competition on a national scale is, by definition, a gross simplification. For instance, traditional pastoralist and agricultural societies in Sudan are not always clearly separated: in many areas, societies (families, clans and even whole tribes) practice a mixture of crop-growing and animal-rearing.

Major social groups include predominantly sedentary crop-rearing societies/tribes; nomadic livestock-rearing societies/tribes; and owners of, and workers in, mechanised agricultural schemes. These three groups depend all on rainfall for their livelihood. Most of the recorded local conflicts take place within and between the first two groups. The third group—the mechanised farming group—is generally not directly involved in conflict, but has played a very strong role in precipitating it in some States, by uncontrolled land grabs from the other two groups[3]. Throughout Sudan's recorded history, pastoralists resisting the shrinkage and degradation of range-lands have been at the centre of local conflicts: competing with other groups for choice grazing land; moving and grazing livestock on cropland without consent; reducing competition by forcing other pastoralists and agriculturalists off previously shared land.

Studies conducted in the Um Chelluta region of Southern Darfur showed that rain-fed agricultural land increased by 138 per cent between 1973 and 2000, while range-land decreased by 56 per cent and closed woodland shrank by 32 per cent. UNEP warned that the historical, ongoing, and forecast shrinkage and degradation of remaining range-lands in the northern part of the Sahel belt was set to exacerbate the situation (Brian D. Pellot, 2007). The fighting in Darfur was often characterised by a 'scorched earth' campaign, carried out by militias over large areas, which not only resulted in a significant number of civilian deaths, but the widespread destruction of villages and forests, and the displacement of victims fleeing to camps for protection, food and water. So environmental degradation is one of the driving forces of displacement and the environment is being further undermined by the sheer number of displaced people and refugees.

Refugee camps set up to provide shelter and care for the 2.4 million people who fled their homes amid the ongoing violence are causing further damage (UNHCR, 2006). Boreholes dug to provide much-needed water supplies are depleting underground water reserves, and forests are disappearing as trees are chopped for firewood used by the refugees. And as families attempt to rebuild their lives when the conflicts end, there will be a further drain on scarce resources such as land and wood. The tragedy in Darfur could be repeated throughout North Africa and the Middle East as growing populations fight for limited water supplies. The environmental impact of a refugee camp is often high: For instance extensive deforestation could be found as far as 10km from a camp; in some the situation was being aggravated by brick-making[4].

It is the need of the hour to control and address the situation, including investment in environmental management, climate adaptation measures; capacity-building of national and local Government in environmental affairs, and the integration of environmental factors in all UN relief and development projects. The total cost of these measures is estimated at approximately US$120 million over three to five years (UNEP, 2007). These are not large figures when compared to the Sudanese GDP in 2005 of $85.5 billion. Conflicts ultimately become inevitable if systems become so pressurized and social, economic, and institutional systems are not able to adapt.

The UN recommends Sudan to reduce the environmental impact of its oil industry and agricultural practices, and prevent local conflicts over natural resources. It says rising oil revenues mean the country should be able to invest in these practices. It also says all UN aid projects in the country should improve environmental practices in their operations.

7.5 POVERTY DIMENSIONS

Poverty in Sudan is deeply entrenched and is largely rural. In 2002 some 20 million people were living below the poverty line of less than US$1 a day (Ali Abdel, 2006). About 19 million people—85 per cent of the rural population—are estimated to be living in extreme poverty. Most of them struggle to feed themselves and their families and have little or no access to safe drinking water and health services. The United Nations Development Programme's Human Development Index ranks Sudan 61st among the 77 least developed nations in the world.

Viewing the extent and severity of poverty in Sudan in the last 15 years, it is quite notable that poverty—by any indicators used—has recently increased both in its extent and severity. Studies conducted in Sudan suggest that inspite of its huge agricultural resources, it stand among the poorest nations of earth. The percentage of people who live in poverty has recently increased; some studies estimated the percentage of people under poverty line to be 90 per cent out of total population of Sudan (Aisha Abdalla Hommaida, 2006). In some region of Sudan the severity of poverty increased to reach the stage of famine. Some regions have experienced the situation of famine twice in the last 15 years (Southern Sudan, North Darfur and the Red Sea Hills Area). While NGOs efforts in the area of food subsidies and food aid is increasing to the limit that the country has become one of the major food aid receivers, still the situation of food insecurity and food related poverty is existing (WFP, 2002). Many areas still unrecalled by either Government or NGOs food aid.

The policies of 1990s in Sudan have contributed to the issues of poverty, civil war and so on[5]. With regard to the Red Sea Hills much of Government attention and concern have been paid to ensure food subsidies to the urban areas as against rural areas and remote regions. This combined with the neglect of small and traditional producers in the agricultural sector aggravated the situation. In the absence of clear policy to deal with food shortages, these factors have led to the failure and the lack of commitment of the State towards the poorest population, which worsened the situation of poor and increased the severity of poverty to the extent of famine.

The incidence of poverty varies considerably according to region. Economic growth has been unevenly distributed along with economic and social devastation caused by the conflict in certain parts of the country. Severe inequalities in terms of access to education, sanitation and clean water, to infrastructure and natural resources, income opportunities, justice and political protection exist between regions (Aisha Abdalla Hommaida, 2006). For example, health services in Southern Sudan only reach about 25 per cent of the population. People living in areas that have been or continue to be affected by drought and conflict—particularly the South and Darfur—are the most vulnerable to poverty.

A rapidly growing population is putting significant pressure on already fragile ecosystems, a situation which has been exacerbated by the displacement of peoples, either by drought or conflict (UNFPA, 2002). In addition, erosion, loss of soil fertility and damage to watersheds are affecting resources. Agricultural productivity is decreasing as a result of lack of technological break-throughs in rain fed agriculture, and as a result food security and livelihoods are threatened. Malnutrition, tuberculosis and malaria have become rampant. Around 22 per cent of children in the South and Darfur are suffering from acute malnutrition, and the incidence of diarrhea in children may be as high as 45 per cent in Southern Sudan (WHO, 2003).

In general, small-scale farmers and herders in the traditional rain- fed farming and livestock sectors are more prone to poverty than those in irrigated areas. Those without land are dependent on cash earnings from casual labour, such as collecting firewood and making charcoal. Many depend on humanitarian aid. In 2006 about 2.5 million people in Darfur, and nearly 3 million in the South, east and transitional areas received food assistance (USAID,

2004). Isolation is one of the key factors affecting poverty. Settlements located away from main thoroughfares have little or no access to social services and markets. Within rural communities, households without assets and labour power are the poorest—consisting of elderly or disabled people, or households headed by women with young dependants. Women and girls are the most disadvantaged members—less than one third of them have access to education.

7.6 AGRARIAN STRUCTURE AND POVERTY

More than two decades of civil unrest in the Sudan have cost the lives of about 1.5 million people and had a devastating effect on the well-being of the population. Protracted civil conflict in Sudan generally has its origin in socio-economic inequities caused by neglect of the agricultural sector, misguided land reforms, unfair distribution of resources for development between urban and rural areas and for irrigated and traditional farming, and exclusion of local communities from decision-making (IFAD, 2002). These policies have led to the development of an economy-based mainly on export and lease of natural resources, to competition over access to scarce land and water, and to inadequate nation-building[6].

Inadequate development strategies, slow adaptation to climatic volatility, and erosion of natural resources are the root causes of poverty. These causes have also fuelled the prolonged civil conflicts that have had a devastating effect on the rural population. Poverty levels in the country are closely linked to the strengths and weaknesses of agricultural productivity. In 1970s Sudan along with many countries of Sub-Saharan Africa, began to introduce large-scale mechanized farms and to expand the irrigation sector in a bid to increase crop production, especially cash crops. The new farming systems and land allocation policies displaced subsistence farmers and nomads from their land, and dismantled traditional systems of communal ownership and management that had previously discouraged local conflict. They proved inappropriate for ecologically fragile areas that are much better suited to traditional agricultural methods characterized by livestock herding and the mobility of farmers.

Small-holder farmers are hindered by the limited size of their land holdings, low rates of productivity and an inability to improve their incomes. Because of the lack of rainfall and domestic water supplies, for most farmers the growing season is brief and crop failures are frequent. Pests and disease are problems they are ill-equipped to combat. Existing systems for research and agricultural support are unable to produce and disseminate new technical packages capable of overcoming these problems (ADB, 2003). Since they have limited access to credit, distribution and marketing channels, and because of their inadequate technical knowledge and poor skills in production and marketing, farmers find it difficult to break out of the cycle of low productivity and income. Seasonal migration in pursuit of wage labour opportunities on mechanized and irrigated farms and in urban areas has become widespread.

7.7 CONCERNS FOR ENVIRONMENTAL SECURITY

The issue of environmental refugees promises to rank as one of the foremost human crises in the new Millennium. To date, however, it has been viewed as a peripheral concern, a kind of aberration from the normal order of things—even though it is an outward manifestation of profound deprivation and despair. While it derives primarily from environmental problems, it generates myriad problems of political, social and economic sorts (Brain D. Pellot, 2007). As such, it could readily become a cause of turmoil and confrontation, leading to conflict and violence. Yet as the problem becomes more pressing, our policy responses fall ever-further short of measuring up to the challenges. Unfortunately in most of the developing countries environmental refugees have still not been officially recognized as a problem at all.

At the same time, there are limits to host countries' capacity, let alone willingness, to take in outsiders. Immigrants aliens present abundant scope for popular resentment, however unjust this reaction. In the wake of perceived threats to social cohesion and national identity, refugees can become an excuse for outbreaks of ethnic tension and civil disorder, even political upheaval. This is already the case in those developed countries where immigrant aliens increasingly prove unwelcome, as witness the experience of Haitians in the United States and North Africans in Europe. Almost one third of developed countries are taking steps to further restrict immigrant flows from developing countries. Yet measures to relieve the plight of refugees of whatever kind have drastically diminished in relation to the growing scale of the problem.

Although the annual budget of the United Nations High Commissioner for Refugees was recently boosted somewhat, the agency is increasingly unable to supply food and shelter for refugees of traditional kind alone, much less to invest in rehabilitation or repatriation of these refugees (UNHCR, 2006). Meantime the world's refugee burden is borne primarily by the poorest sectors of the global community. In the year 2000 the twenty countries with the highest ratios of official (traditional) refugees had an annual per-capita income of only $850.

7.8 ENVIRONMENTAL REFUGEES AND INTERNATIONAL MIGRATION

The most prominent concentrations of environmental refugees are located in developing regions, the western developed countries might respond that the "over there" problem has little to do with them in practical terms. True, they may sense a humanitarian reaction and supply aid for that reason, but it is likely to remain limited, at best, in relation to "bigger picture" factors, which should be viewed as exceptionally significant. Developed countries cannot isolate themselves from distress and disaster in developing countries: already there are sizeable numbers of environmental refugees who have made their way, usually illegally, into developed countries—and today's stream will surely come to be regarded as a trickle when compared with the floods that will ensue in decades ahead.

For instance, the case of Italy, a country well placed for North Africans who can clandestinely cross from Tunisia to Sicily in a three-hour voyage. They number at least 120,000 per year, and their cumulative total has exceeded 1 million. Spain is an even easier target for North Africans, who readily cross the 15 kilometres of the Straits of Gibraltar; the numbers involved match those of Italy (EC, 2005). A still more facile opportunity awaits Hispanics from Mexico and Central America who cross the Rio Grande into the United States with numbers of atleast 0.5 million per year, and with a cumulative total of 6 million.

Thus the environmental refugees' problem is not a problem confined to developing countries alone. This problem will surely grow bigger fast. Morocco, Tunisia and Libya are each losing over 1000 square kilometers of productive land a year to desertification. In Egypt, which is uniquely dependent upon irrigation, half of irrigated croplands suffer from salinization—and Egypt already imports a huge share of its food. Turkey has lost 160,000 square kilometres of farmlands to soil erosion. These environmental pressures are aggravated by population pressures[7].

7.9 POLICY ACTIONS

There is much scope for preventive policies, with the aim of reducing the need to migrate by ensuring acceptable livelihood in established homelands. First of all, we need to expand our approach to refugees in general in order to include environmental refugees in particular. We cannot continue to ignore environmental refugees simply because there is no institutionalised mode of dealing with them. If official standing were to be accorded to these refugees, this might help to engender a recognised constituency for instance those 900 million people who endure desertification, 4 million of whom have become environmental refugees in the Sahel alone. While desertification entrains costs of $42 billion a year just through the loss of agricultural produce, the United Nations' Anti-Desertification Action Plan would cost no more than $22 billion a year (UNDP, 2002). Yet the amount subscribed so far falls far short of the target, ostensibly on the grounds that arid-land dwellers have no constituency and hence lack political leverage.

Secondly, we need to widen and deepen our understanding of environmental refugees by establishing the root causes of the problem—not only environmental causes but associated problems such as security concerns, plus the interplay of the two sets of forces. There are many conceptual grey areas as concerns proximate and ultimate causes, the contributory roles of population pressures and poverty, the linkages to ethnic tensions and conventional conflict, and so lengthily forth. Consider too the root causes of famine. If a famine has been human-made, it can be human-unmade, whereas natural factors can only be managed and accommodated (DFID, 2006). Just as the recurrent droughts in Sub-Saharan Africa cannot all be blamed on climate, so the recurrent famines cannot all be blamed on drought—and the same must apply, to some degree atleast, to droughts (plus desertification) in Central Asia. Drought has often served to trigger famines by disrupting the social, economic and political processes that would normally ensure sufficient access or entitlement to food (WFP, 2002).

Probably most important of all is that there can be little progress except within an overall context of what has come to be known as Sustainable Development. This applies notably to reliable access to food, water, energy, health and other basic human needs—lack of which is behind many environmental refugees' need to migrate (UNEP, 2007). In big picture terms, Sustainable Development represents a sound way to preempt the environmental refugee issue in its full scope over the long-run. As a prime mode to tackle the issue, then, there would be a handsome payoff on investment to foster Sustainable Development in developing countries through greater policy emphasis on environmental safeguards, together with efforts to stem associated problems such as poverty, population and landlessness.

7.9.1 Initiatives in Sudan

The present crisis in Sudan is to be resolved through both internal and external adjustments in social, economic, political and environmental institutions, by giving emphasis to poverty reduction. The Government of Sudan has taken initiatives in making structural reforms and addressing the root causes of poverty in the country. The North-South Peace Agreement has allowed the Government to take a new direction in addressing pressing socio-economic concerns. The tenets of the peace agreement have been designed to redistribute wealth and authority more evenly, and surplus revenue from oil exports will be allocated for poverty reduction.

In 2004 the Government of Sudan and the Sudan People's Liberation Movement reached an agreement regarding the main objectives of the policy framework for a National Poverty Eradication Strategy (PES). The PES has two overall objectives:

- Achieving lasting peace and reducing the risk of future conflicts; and
- Making substantial progress towards reducing poverty and other developmental goals.

The strategy is based upon the need to share the benefits of economic growth widely and equitably throughout the country so as to break the vicious circles of poverty, environmental destruction, famines and refugees. Rural development priorities focus on poverty reduction, restoration of livelihoods, provision of essential infrastructure and services and investments in agriculture, especially the rain-fed sector. The PES addresses rural development from a number of aspects that are relevant to the structural causes of rural poverty, by:

- Building a decentralized and multi-layered governance structure that is characterized by transparency, accountability and adequate resource allocation;
- Implementing comprehensive capacity-building and institutional strengthening programmes;
- Creating an enabling environment for private sector development with special emphasis on rural development;
- Empowering local communities and vulnerable and marginalized social groups including women and young people; and
- Implementing environmentally sound management of natural resources.

In 2006 the Government of National Unity launched an investment campaign known as the Agricultural Revival, in which substantial fund was directed towards the water sector and mechanization as a matter of priority. Studies have shown that Sudan needs to attain, and sustain, a GDP growth rate of about 7 per cent per annum to achieve the MDG on poverty. It will take Sudan, growing at a per capita GDP rate of 2.2 per cent per annum (equivalent to a GDP growth rate of about 5 per cent per annum) about 28 years to achieve the MDG on poverty (Ali Abdel Gader Ali, 2006). If the country is able to maintain its growth rate of the second half of the

1990s it will be able to achieve the MDG of reducing poverty by half by the year 2015.

Alongwith these an effective UN High Commissioner for Refugees (UNHCR) is so critical to the success of the entire operation in South Sudan because within the UN system the agency has the most in-house expertise on protecting refugees and internally displaced persons and managing large-scale returns. UNHCR must fulfil their protection mandate, as the displaced people of Sudan are depending upon UNCHR to help them to return home safely[8]. Regarding UNCHR the following areas need immediate attention.

- The High Commissioner of UNHCR should strengthen the management of UNHCR's Sudan program;
- UNHCR officials in Geneva, Khartoum, and South Sudan work together to share information so decisions about new responsibilities are based upon realistic assessments of capacity to fulfil them;
- UNHCR focus on its core competencies, and ensure that its resources are directed to fulfilling its protection mandate; and
- Donor countries to review their funding priorities to ensure that UNHCR receives adequate support.

7.10 CONCLUSION

In conclusion, we can recommend the pragmatic mode of promoting Sustainable Development, whether in the Horn of Africa or Central Asia, whether in the Himalayan foothills or the borderlands of the Caucasus mountains. A prime way to tackle desertification, salinization, in fact several sorts of land degradation, is through planting trees for shelter belts, to retain soil moisture, and to resist soil erosion. Certain types of trees offer additional benefits, e.g. leguminous species add nitrogen to infertile soils, or they supply built-in insecticides, or they offer industrial timber. Probably the biggest benefit lies with reforestation in montane areas, in order to rehabilitate hydrological systems and watershed functions, and thus avoiding floods and drying-outs for river systems downstream. At the same time the traditional and indigenous socio-political and economic institutions are to be equipped to face the challenges in the environment front through transparent and holistic measures.

NOTES

1. When global warming takes hold, there could be as many as 200 million people overtaken by disruptions of monsoon systems and other rainfall regimes, by droughts of unprecedented severity and duration, and by sea-level rise and coastal flooding.
2. But when we say that the conflicts started because of resources we are not denying the Government did not make massive errors, and ethnicity had no role to play: all these things found a fertile soil in a situation which was already tense because of the demand for resources.
3. In the Nuba Mountains and in Blue Nile State, combatants reported that the expansion of mechanised agricultural schemes onto their land had precipitated the fighting, which had then escalated, and coalesced with the major north-south political conflict.
4. One large tree is needed to provide the fire to make around 3,000 bricks. In addition, the clay needed for brick-making can damage trees by exposing roots, and also create pits in which water collects and mosquitoes can thrive.
5. In contrast to other cases, where famine is considered in many areas as an issue related to failure of subsistence, failure of coping strategies, failure of entitlements, to the limit that people reaches the state of destitution. In Sudan 1990s poverty and famine has been highly politicized and then they have turned to become more than a complex issue. Policies such as State food policy, food pricing, food provision, and agricultural and producing policies—food export and food thrifts have also accentuated the problem.
6. After decades of internal conflict Sudan signed a peace agreement in January 2005 and the new Government of National Unity and Government of Southern Sudan have launched a six-year recovery, peace-building and development plan. International donors have pledged to contribute to the massive costs entailed in reconstructing the country.
7. North Africa today features 152 million people, and the eastern Mediterranean 100 million, with a joint total of 252 million. Contrast to the European Union 459 million, a good deal larger. But the Mediterranean countries are growing much faster. By 2025 the North Africa/Eastern Mediterranean will grow to 333 million people, an increase of 32 per cent, whereas the European Union is projected to grow to 470 million, an increase of 2 per cent. Across the Atlantic, Mexico/Central America/Caribbean today totals 185 million, way

behind the United States with 294 million. But a 2025 projection that Mexico/Central America/Caribbean will grow to 235 million, for an increase of 27 per cent, whereas the United States will grow to 349 million for an increase of 19 per cent.

8. The signing of the Comprehensive Peace Agreement (CPA) in January 2005 between the Government of Sudan and the Sudan People's Liberation Movement brought the 21-year civil war to an end, creating the conditions for the return of approximately four million refugees and internally displaced people to South Sudan. Although basic services are missing throughout the region and international agencies face serious logistical obstacles to establishing their presence, Sudanese are courageously "voting with their feet" and opting to return. The process will rival that of Afghanistan as the largest return process in recent decades.

REFERENCES

African Development Bank (ADB), (2003). *Sudan Country Dialogue Paper 2003-2004.*

Aisha, Abdalla Hommaida (2006). *Poverty in Sudan*, Institute of African and Asian Studies, University of Khartoum, Sudan.

Ali, Abdel Gader Ali (2006). *Can the Sudan Reduce Poverty by Half by the Year 2015*, Working Paper Series, Arab Planning Institute, Kuwait.

Ban, Ki-moon (2007). *Washington Post.*

Brian, D. Pellot (2007). *Report on Sudan's Environment Degradation*, UN Environment Programme, United Nations.

Department for International Development of the United Kingdom (DFID), (2006). *Country Engagement Plan.*

European Commission (EC), (2005). *Country Strategy Paper and National Indicative Programme 2005-2007.*

International Fund for Agricultural Development (IFAD), (2002). *Country Strategic Opportunities Paper-2002.*

Jeffrey Sachs, (2006,). *Scientific American Website.*

UNEP, (2007). Sudan: *Post-Conflict Environmental Assessment- 2007.*

United Nations Development Group (UNDG), (1999). *Common Country Assessment* 1999.

United Nations Development Programme (UNDP), (2002). *Common Country Assessment and United Nations Development Assistance Framework 2002-2006.*

United Nations Population Fund (UNFPA), (2002). *Proposed Projects and Programmes 2002-2006.*

United Nations Refugee Agency (UNHCR), (2006). *Country Operations Plan -2006.*

United Nations System in Sudan (UNSS), (2005). *Work Plan for Sudan-* 2005.

United State Agency for International Development (USAID), (2004). *Interim Strategic Plan for Sudan, 2004-06.*

World Food Programme (WFP), (2002). *Country Programme 2002-06.*

World Health Organization (WHO), (2003). *Country Cooperation Strategy for WHO and Sudan 2003-07.*

8

Employment Potential of Sub-Saharan Africa in the New Millennium

Problems and Prospects

8.1 INTRODUCTION

African economies are potentially rich in human resources; however, the human potential is relatively neglected due to poor education and health facilities with their capacities frequently underused. The consequence is low labour productivity and lack of competitiveness compared with countries where human resources are more fully developed and better used. The poor development of human resources in Sub-Saharan Africa has its origin in colonial history (Lall, S., 1989). The extent of utilization of human resources is reflected in the labour market through high levels of unemployment and poverty rates; which is found to be highly complicated in the Sub-Saharan Africa even in the early years of New Millennium.

The global employment situation has not improved much in the beginning of the New Millennium despite a pick-up in economic growth world-wide. Unemployment grew slightly despite a world-wide growth in GDP of 3.2 per cent and a slight increase in trade from 2.5 per cent in 2002 to 3.0 per cent in 2003 (WTO, 2003). Sub-Saharan Africa has slightly reduced its unemployment rate but not enough to improve its high incidence of working poverty. In addition, the region has to face the enormous pressure that the HIV/AIDS pandemic is placing on labour markets. This, together with the continuing 'brain drain' is depriving the region of much needed human capital, making it unlikely to reach the Millennium Development Goals. The present chapter analyzes the trends, problems and prospects of employment situation in the Sub-Saharan region; which is trying for a take off in the New Millennium.

8.2 GLOBAL EMPLOYMENT SCENARIO

The ILO estimates show that in 2003 around 186 million individuals were searching for employment, which is the highest-level ever-recorded (GET, 2003). The increase was reported to be more pronounced among young people, escalating the world youth unemployment rate to 14.4 per cent, over twice as high as the world unemployment rate of 6.2 per cent. Although the world headcount of female unemployment decreased minimally between 2002 and 2003, women generally remain those groups most strongly affected by unemployment and annual unemployment growth rate was highest among the females. On the other hand youth unemployment among females was marginally lower than the male counterparts. Table 8.1 and Figure 8.1 brief the world unemployment scenario.

In parallel to the deteriorating employment situation, the size of the informal economies expanded in developing regions with low GDP growth rates. Workers in the informal economy carry a high risk of becoming working poor with earnings insufficient to raise themselves and their families above the poverty line (say US$ 1). This is the general situation in economies with lack of extensive unemployment insurance systems or other forms of suitable social welfare measures. Continued stagnancy in the employment situation would make it impossible to achieve the United Nations Millennium Development Goals of halving world poverty by 2015.

Table 8.1: Unemployment in the World, 1993 and 2003 (Millions)

Category	*1993*	*2003*	*Annual Growth Rate (%)*
1. Total Unemployment	140.5	185.9	3.23
2. Unemployed Males	82.3	108.1	3.13
3. Unemployed Females	58.2	77.8	3.37
4. Youth Unemployment	69.5	88.2	2.69
5. Youth Unemployment Among Males	41.2	52.4	2.72
6. Youth Unemployment Among Females	28.3	35.8	2.65

Source: ILO, Global Employment Trends, 2003.

Figure 8.1: Annual Growth Rate of Unemployment in the World, 1993-2003 (%)

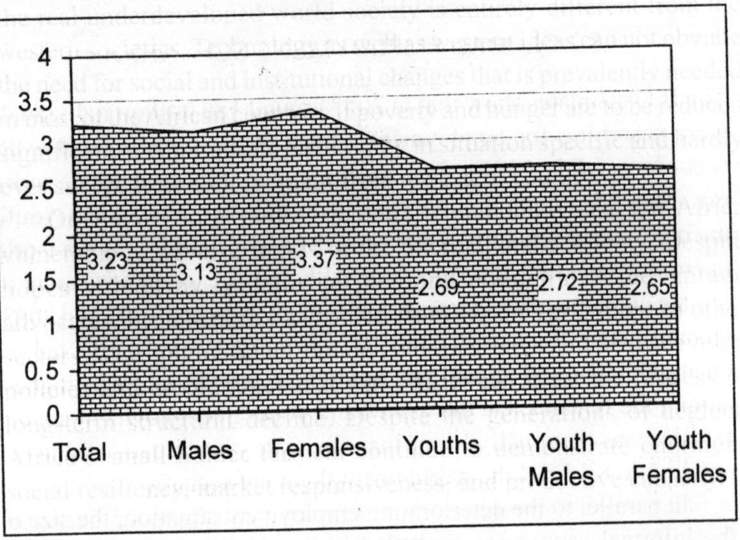

In terms of global growth, the picture brightens in 2004; with the growing demand in the industrialized world, trade increases and its positive effect on the GDP growth in the industrialized economies as well as in the developing regions. The growth rates achieved during 2003 was 3.6 per cent in Sub-Saharan Africa, 4.4 per cent in Middle East and North Africa, 1.6 per cent in Latin America and Caribbean, 5.1 per cent in South Asia, 4.1 per cent in South-East Asia, 7.1 per cent in East Asia, 4.1 per cent in Transition economies, 1.8 per cent in industrialized economies and with a world average of 3.2 per cent (Table 8.2).

The likelihood of reaching the Millennium Development Goal of halving poverty by 2015 and of creating the number of new jobs needed to halve unemployment and poverty depends on achieving faster growth in the world economy, specifically in the industrialized economies. Increasingly it also depends on the development of rapidly growing economies such as China and India, not only because it accounts for 40 per cent of the world's workforce but also because the region as a whole benefits from the growing demands, with concomitant positive impacts on their labour markets.

Table 8.2: Regional Economic Growth in the New Millennium, 2000-2003

Regions	*Year*			
	2000	*2001*	*2002*	*2003*
1. Sub-Saharan Africa	2.7	3.4	3.2	3.6
2. Middle East and North Africa	4.5	3.2	3.2	4.4
3. Latin America and the Caribbean	4.0	0.6	-0.1	1.6
4. South Asia	5.3	4.1	4.8	5.1
5. South-East Asia	5.7	2.8	4.4	4.1
6. East Asia	8.2	6.6	7.6	7.1
7. Transition Economies	6.6	5.1	4.1	4.1
8. Industrialized Economies	3.6	0.8	1.7	1.8
9. World	4.7	2.3	3.0	3.2

Source: ILO, Global Employment Trends Model, 2003

The world economy has been able to achieve somewhat attractive growth in the beginning of the New Millennium; however, it is insufficient to absorb the increasing labour force and thereby reducing the stipulated poverty reduction rates. The overall challenge is to absorb the 514 million new entrants to world labour markets and to reduce working poverty by 2015. How well GDP growth will translate into employment growth depends on the efforts of policy-makers to prioritize the importance of employment policies and to put them on equal footing with macro-economic policies.

8.3 EMPLOYMENT SCENARIO IN SUB-SAHARAN AFRICA

Many scholars have forecasted that Sub-Saharan Africa will emerge as a major potential supplier of cheap labour to the world economy in the New Millennium; however, the recent analyses show that African development will continue to lag that in Asia for the next few decades in the New Millennium (See for example, Ghai, D., 1987). However, expansion of unskilled labour-intensive manufacturing for export has become a realistic prospect for much of Sub-Saharan Africa.

With a labour force growth rate of 2.8 per cent, an ever-increasing number of people are competing for a very limited number of jobs in the formal economy, which remains of concern for labour markets in Sub-Saharan Africa (KILM, 2003). The other pressing concern is the impact of HIV/AIDS on labour markets; by forcing people out of work, the epidemic is having long-lasting negative effects on labour markets and economic growth. The problems of unemployment as well as underemployment are largely structural in nature. Majority of them are employed in low-productivity, low-income and survivalist-oriented activities in the small-holder or subsistence agricultural sector; which characterizes seasonal underemployment. Most small-holders do not earn enough to sustain a decent living. Working poor account for almost 45 per cent of the total number of employed.

In Sub-Saharan Africa unemployment rates have not improved much in the first years of New Millennium. The average rate of unemployment stayed at 10.8 per cent, leaving 29.7 million people without work. In famines and political instability-stricken countries, the long-term effect on unemployment is devastating as in Angola[1]. Unemployment and underemployment of young people is a compelling problem in most parts of the region. Estimates show that unemployment rates for the 15 to 24 age group are twice as high as for the overall labour force (ERA, 2003). In times of economic slowdown, young people's likelihood of becoming or staying unemployed is higher than that for adults. In 2003, 18.6 million young people had no job, 7.2 million of whom were women, with an unemployment rate of 21 per cent (GET, 2003). Table 8.3 captures the labour market and economic indicators of Sub-Saharan Africa.

Table 8.3: Labour Market and Economic Indicators in Sub-Saharan Africa, 1993 and 2003

Sub-Regions	*Unemployment Rate (%)*		*Employment-Population Ratio (%)*		*Annual Labour Force Growth (%)*	*Annual GDP Growth Rate (%)*
	1993	*2003*	*1993*	*2003*	*1993-2003*	*1993-2003*
1. Eastern Africa	10.3	11.0	71.5	73.3	3.0	3.5
2. Central Africa	12.8	9.4	62.1	61.0	2.0	1.6
3. Southern Africa	27.1	31.6	45.7	42.8	2.1	2.8
4. Western Africa	7.1	6.7	66.2	66.0	2.9	3.3
Sub-Saharan Africa	11.0	10.8	65.6	66.0	2.8	2.9

Source: ILO, KILM 2003.

Sub-Saharan Africa's progress in education is very slow, especially for women, but literacy rates have been showing signs of improvement since the 1980s. An additional problem is that the few young people with higher education tend to leave the region because of lack of suitable work opportunities. Table 8.4 examines the youth unemployment rate in the region as a comparison to the world average.

The heavy reliance on rain-fed agriculture in Sub-Saharan Africa has a significant effect on labour use in agriculture, which tends to be concentrated in peak periods of relatively short-duration, with typically 30-50 per cent of total annual labour concentrated in a two to three months period (Woodhouse, 1988). This pattern of labour absorption permits about a third of the rural workforce to engage in seasonal or part-time non-agricultural activities. Non-farm activities are important as they provide employment for disadvantaged groups in the rural community, especially women and the landless[7]. Labour use/absorption in agriculture varies with the type of cropping practice; for instance, in rice cultivation, the shift from forest fallow to annual cultivation is associated with an increase in total labour input per hectare from 770 hours in Liberia to 3300 hours in Cameroon (Ruthenberg, 1980).

Table 8.4: Youth Unemployment Rates in Sub-Saharan Africa, 1997-2003

(Selected Years) *Percentage*

Year		*Sub-Saharan Africa*	*World*
1997	Total	20.7	12.9
	Female	17.9	12.6
	Male	22.9	13.1
2001	Total	20.6	13.9
	Female	17.8	13.7
	Male	22.7	14.0
2002	Total	21.1	14.3
	Female	18.4	14.1
	Male	23.2	14.5
2003	Total	21.0	14.4
	Female	18.4	14.2
	Male	23.1	14.5

Source: GET, 2003

8.4 ECONOMIC PERFORMANCE

Sub-Saharan Africa's performance in the economic front in the first years of New Millennium is continued to be below the other developing regions. Real GDP grew by an average of 2.9 per cent in the first years (See Table 8.3 and Figure 8.2). Those economies that are more integrated to world trade are affected by a slow recovery from the global downturn as well as by low commodity prices in the early years of the Millennium. Southern Africa had a slight decline in GDP in the early years, in particular in 2002-03. In the sub-region, Botswana had the highest increase in GDP followed by Namibia, South Africa experiencing a decline.

The Western Africa grew by more than 4 per cent in 2003 and was mainly due to the increase in growth in Nigeria, the largest economy in the sub-region, along with the higher growths in Guinea-Bissau, Senegal and Liberia. The growth rate during the same period in Eastern Africa was 2.6 per cent, which is due to Madagascar's rebound in growth after substantial fall in output in the previous year and the performance of the Eritrean economy. However, the Zimbabwe's economy did not grow as anticipated. The Central Africa grown at 5.3 per cent in 2003, which was lesser than that in the previous year; mainly because of the declines in Equatorial Guinea, Congo and Angola.

Figure 8.2: SSA's Economic and Employment Scenario, 2003

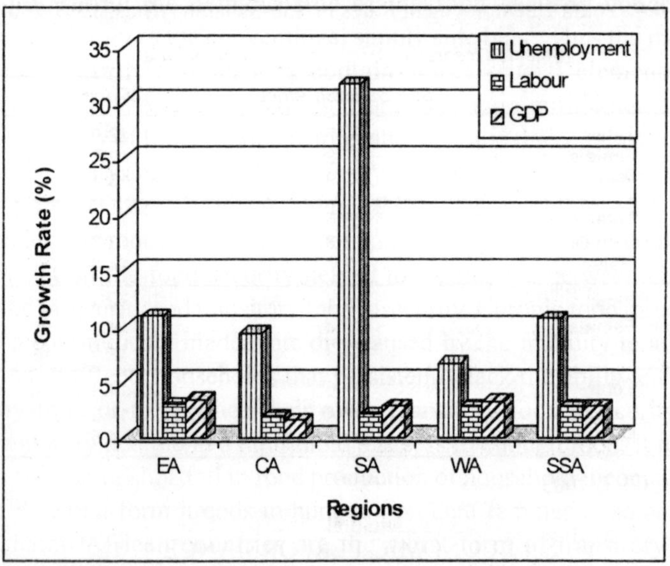

Legend: EA—Eastern Africa, CA—Central Africa, SA—Southern Africa, WA—Western Africa, SSA—Sub-Saharan Africa.

In the sub-region, among the five regions, Sub-Saharan Africa holds number three in most of the indicators including unemployment rate, GDP growth, and annual labour force growth. The Sub-Saharan region's economic performance mainly depends on progress in peace agreements, the number of African economy's eligible for debt relief under the Heavily Indebted Poor Countries (HIPC). Initiative, growth in the developed world, anticipated aid from several advanced economies to help fight against militant groups and to discourage militant groups and unstable African countries from providing safe havens to terrorist.

Sub-Saharan Africa is on the receiving end of a donor-driven model of long-term technical assistance and overseas training that is not coming to grips with the political, financial and structural reforms necessary to stem the brain drain and develop Africa's institutional capacity to train the growing human capital, carry out basic and applied researches and retain gifted scientists in the region. In theory, technical assistance is designed to develop national and regional capacity through the permanent transfer of skills and expertise to local scientists, teachers, managers and institutions; however, it has become technical assistance par excellence!

8.5 REFLECTION OF ECONOMIC PERFORMANCE ON THE LABOUR MARKET

The interaction between labour market and the economic development as reflected through entrepreneurial, technical and managerial skills required for agricultural progress, industrialization and service sector growth arises from previous experience of commerce and industry; however, Africa has in comparison with other developing regions, been particularly unfortunate in this respect. Experience is only one source of capability acquisition; education and training are the most important, but the precise link between particular types of education and specific levels or forms of economic activity in particular industrialization are not easy to trace (King, 1984). The educational structure of Sub-Saharan Africa is reported to be unsuitable for industrialization and sustainable economic progress, to find connection between the higher levels of unemployment and economic performance. If the region were to emulate some of the dynamic growth and diversification there would have to be a phenomenal rise in the quantity, quality and completion rates in education relevant for employment generation.

Figure 8.3: Unemployment Trend: SSA *vs* World 1997-2003

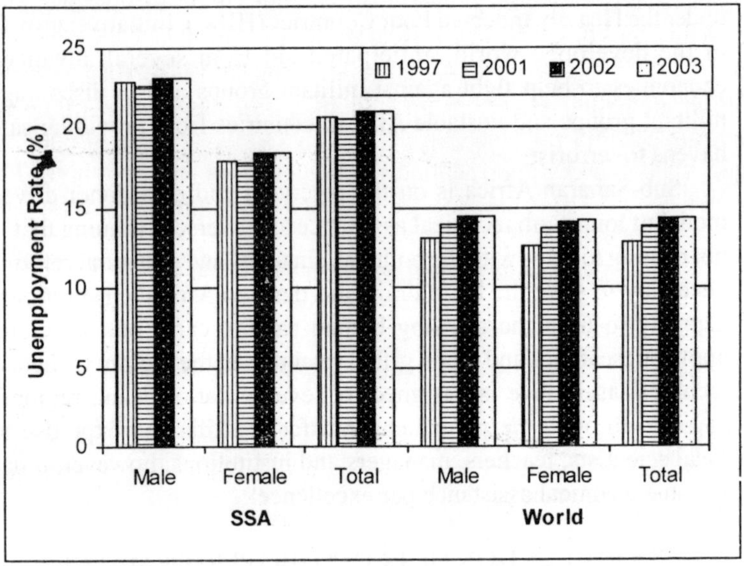

The average unemployment rate (10. 3 per cent as mentioned in Table 8.3) is expected to decline atleast marginally due to anticipated increase in GDP growth in the region and the increased political stability in some of the former conflict economies. The youths will gain less from this improvement than adults and the likelihood of being without a job will remain at a level over twice as high for youth than for the overall labour force. Over 29 million people are expected to be unemployed in the coming years; of those who are employed, 110 million will be working poor and unable to provide their families with decent living conditions (GET, 2003).

The employment generation in rural areas should focus on development of agriculture and the non-farm sector; agriculture remains important in terms of employment accounting for over two-thirds of the total labour force in Sub-Saharan Africa. Non-agricultural sector provides additional regular employment and income opportunities in the face of rising population and provide seasonal and part-time employment for farm workers during off-peak farming seasons. As mentioned earlier, while agricultural activities indisputability dominates employing between 70-80 per cent, the non-farm sector provides primary employment between 6 and 26 per cent of Africa's rural labour force, with significant inter-country differences (Milimo, J. and Fisseha, Y., 1986). The total numbers employed in rural manufacturing activity exceed those employed in urban manufacturing in most of Sub-Saharan region.

In the non-farm sector, the labour intensity is found to be more in small firms than in the larger ones in the Sub-Saharan Africa. Studies in Ghana, Sierra Leone, Kenya and Ethiopia find a positive correlation between farm size and capital intensity; initial capital cost per worker Ghana averaged US$ 435 in firms with family labour and no wage workers while it was about US$ 9000 per worker in firms employing over 100 workers (Byerlee *et al.,* 1977). The family provides the major source of labour for African rural industries; owners plus family workers operate over one-half of rural industrial establishments in Africa. It point towards potential of non-farm sector in generating employment in the capital scarce Sub-Saharan Africa.

The long-run growth of labour force is forecasted to be 366 million in 2015, from 271 million in 2003, which is mostly contributed by the urban labour force (around 50% of the total) by exerting strong pressure on the urban labour markets (KILM, 2003). It point towards the necessity to create nearly 8 million additional jobs per year to absorb the rapidly growing job seekers (labour force is projected to grow 2.5 per cent/annum until 2015). The reduction of unemployment atleast to half by 2015 requires that the GDP growth should triple, which will be an unrealistic goal for most of the economies.

Although the region has made some progress in economic development as well as in human capital improvements, it is still the poorest region in the world. The higher incidence of HIV/AIDS in the Sub-Saharan Africa further magnifies the complexity of the employment situation. GDP per capita has seen almost no improvement during the 1990s and the first years of this millennium; unless progress is made in terms of creating productive employment opportunities for the increasing job seekers the gravity of the socio-economic balance will further worsen and will affect the overall progress of the community at large.

8.6 CONCLUSION

Widespread unemployment and underemployment remain a regional challenge for the Sub-Saharan Africa; poverty along with growing unemployment inhibits further growth in the labour market. Backwardness in education, health and empowerment has weakened the people's potential to lift themselves from vicious circles of poverty and unemployment. All these invite the attention of the Governments, policy-makers and all those stakeholders to the need for creating employment opportunities to help women in particular and the society in general to secure productive and remunerative work in conditions of freedom, security and human dignity.

The youth unemployment in the region need special attention, since underutilization of the high potential of young people is not only a waste but also a threat to future prosperity. Young people without jobs either become frustrated, stay in the educational system much longer than they wish or lose their capabilities by not using them. Unless solutions are found for this challenge, the long-term socio-economic implications will not be favourable for the economies.

To enable the Sub-Saharan African countries to face the challenges, major packages through international assistance are needed to increase access to western markets and to reduce foreign debts, by freeing resources for reform programmes targeted on improved governance, employment generation and poverty reduction. All the challenges we discussed in this chapter can be addressed only if policy-makers give proper importance to 'decent work', the ILO's global employment agenda, in the concerned country's economic and social policies. The creation of decent work implies not only decline in poverty but at the same time provides the essential platform for future growth.

NOTES

1. The 27 years of conflict (Ceasefire reached in 2002) resulted in the deaths of 1.5 million people, displaced 2-4 million and has blighted employment prospects for the immediate and long-term future. Hundred of thousands of Angolans remain displaced within their economy, crowded into camps outside large townships. In addition, around 0.47 million Angolans are returning from neighbouring

economies at an increasing rate. They have no hope of finding jobs that can keep them and their families out of poverty.

2. In Kenya, the proportion of female owners in the market centres of Central Province ranged from 3.6 per cent in wood and metal activities to 40.9 per cent in vending, with an overall average of 25.1 per cent. In Malawi, the proportion of women in non-agricultural activities is about 12 per cent. Elsewhere, female participation is much higher: in Ghana and Zambia for example, about two-thirds of the female labour force are engaged in non-farm, activities. Female participation tends to dominate activities that can be conveniently operated in the household. For example, beer brewing is an exclusively female concern in Botswana, Burkina Faso, Malawi and Zambia. Female workers also form the majority in fish processing in Ghana and Senegal; pottery making in Malawi, rice husking in Tanzania and retailing and vending in general. For more details, refer Haggblade, *et al.* (1987), Milimo and Fisseha (1986) and ECA (1984).

REFERENCES

Byerlee, D. Eicher, C., Liedholm, C. and Spencer, D.S.C. (1977). 'Rural Employment in Tropical Africa: Summary of Findings,' *Africa Rural Economy Working Paper No. 20*, Michigan State University, East Lansing.

Economic Commission for Africa (ECA), (1984). *Women in the Artisanal Fishing Industry in Senegal and Ghana*, Research Centre for Women, Addis Ababa.

Ghai, D. (1987). 'Economic Growth, Structural Change and Labour Absorption in Africa: 1960-85', *UNRISD Discussion Paper No. 1*, Geneva.

Haggblade, S. Hazell, P. and Brown, J. (1987). 'Farm-Non-farm Linkages in Rural Sub-Saharan Africa: Empirical Evidence and Policy Implications,' *Discussion Paper*, Agriculture and Rural Development Department, The World Bank, Washington, DC.

ILO (GET), (2003). *Global Employment Trends 2003*, Geneva.

ILO (KILM), (2003). *Key Indicators of the Labour Market*, 3rd Edition, CD-ROM, Geneva.

King, (1984). 'Science, Technology and Education in the Development of Indigenous Technological Capability,' in M. Fransman and K. King (eds), *Technological Capability in the Third World*, Macmillan, London.

Lall, S. (1989). 'Human Resource Development and Industrialization with Special Reference to Sub-Saharan Africa,' *Journal of Development Planning*, No. 19.

Milimo, J. and Fisseha, Y. (1986). 'Rural Small-Scale Enterprises in Zambia: Results of a Country-wide Study,' *MSU International Development Working Paper 28*, Michigan State University, East Lansing.

Ruthenberg, H. (1980). *Farming Systems in the Tropics*, Clarendon Press, Oxford.

UN Economic Commission for Africa (ERA), (2003). *Economic Report on Africa 2003*, Addis Ababa.

Woodhouse, P. (1988). 'The Green Revolution and Food Security in Africa: Issue in Research and Technology Development,' *Development Policy and Practice Research Group Working Paper No. 10*, Open University, Milton Keynes.

WTO (ITS), (2003). *International Trade Statistics*, New York.

9

Decentralized Governance in an African Federal System

Regionalization in Ethiopia

9.1 INTRODUCTION

Decentralization is an instrument to give opportunities for people at the local level to be involved in determining their economic and political choices. Decentralization is directly and indirectly associated with many aspects of good governance, including consensual decision making, equity, representation, accountability and responsiveness of public institutions to community concerns (Olowu, 1993). The positive aspects of democratic governance have added to the theoretical and practical aspect of decentralization as an attractive political instrument to bring Government closer to the people. Countries world-wide have embraced the policy of decentralization as a means of advancing participatory development and governance. Democratic African countries are also not an exception in this political process at least at the national level. The present chapter reviews the decentralization process in the East African country of Ethiopia, and analyses the nature of self-rule and decision-making power of local government institutions.

9.2 NATURE OF DECENTRALIZATION

Since 1991, Ethiopia has been experimenting with a policy of regionalization, which aimed at devolving governmental power from the Centre to the regions. The policy has created nine ethnic-based regional state governments and two autonomous administrative areas that comprise the Ethiopian federal structure. All regions are given considerable degree of internal self-rule, including the authority to raise local revenue and administer their own budgets and development plans. Each region has a number of zonal, *woreda* and *kebele* tiers of administration to which it must transfer responsibilities and resources to promote decentralized governance at all levels of Government[1].

Ethiopia's regionalization policy is intended to enable the different ethnic groups to develop their culture and language, manage socio-economic development in their respective areas, exercise self-rule and bring about an equitable share of national resources among the regions (MEDAC, 1998). A democratic local government that is accountable to the people and that enhances public participation in governance is a sine-qua-non for effective decentralization. The extent of decision-making authority and fiscal and budgetary autonomy at the local level are major criteria that are increasingly being used to measure the success of decentralization process in bringing about democratic self-governance.

9.3 ORGANIZATIONAL STRUCTURE

Following the fall of the *Derg* Government, the Transitional Government of Ethiopia (TGE) was established in 1991 under the leadership of the Ethiopian People's Revolutionary Democratic Front (EPRDF)[2]. Ethiopia was declared a federal republic following the adoption of yet another new constitution in 1995. The current Ethiopian state structure has five tiers of Government viz. the federal, regional, *woreda* and *kebela* levels (See Appendix)[3]. The 1995 Federal constitution, which is Ethiopia's fourth, recognizes only the federal and regional State Governments.

Apart from ethnic and linguistic diversity, Ethiopia's regional states are vastly different in terms of population and territory. The regional State of Oromia, with an estimated population (1998-99) of nearly 22 million and an area of 3.53 lakhs sq. km, contrast with that of Harari Regional State with a population of 1.5 lakh and area of about 311 sq. km (Table 9.1).

Table 9.1: Details of Regional State Governments and Autonomous Administrative Areas, 1998-99

State/Administrative Area	*Population (Lakhs)*	*Area ('000 sq. km)*	*Number of Zones*	*Number of woredawotch*
1. Tigray	33.58	60.20	4	35
2. Afar	11.31	77.00	5	28
3. Amhara	147.69	188.80	10	130
4. Oromiya	200.13	360.00	12	176
5. Somale	19.79	215.90	9	47
6. Benishangul/Gumuz	4.93	46.80	3	13
7. SNNPRS	110.65	112.00	9	76
8. Gambella	1.95	26.10	4	8
9. Harrari	1.44	0.31	3	19
10. Addis Ababa	23.42	0.54	6	28
11. Dire Dawa	2.77	1.60	4	23
Total	557.66	1089.25	66	556

Source: MEDAC, Dept. of Regional Planning and Development, 1998.

The regional State Governments have considerable degree of self-rule, including elected regional council and executive administration[4]. It is also empowered to prepare and approve its own budget and economic plans and programmes (For details see, FDRE, 1995). Both the federal and regional State Governments have legislative, executive and judiciary functions. As in any federal system, state sovereignty has been constitutionally apportioned between the Central Government and the nine regional States that constitute the Ethiopian Federation[5].

9.4 FEATURES OF DECENTRALIZATION

The current structure of Ethiopia's state governance can be called as ethnic federalism and is not that much effective in the devolution of powers and responsibilities to the lower tiers of administration. Regional State Governments are still dominant and exercise significant control over the sub-national governments' affairs. However, the present system has laid a strong foundation for federal system of participatory governance (Barkan, *et al.*, 1998). From an institutional angle the current federal structure in Ethiopia can be characterized as authoritarian ethnic federalism. An important feature of this evolving system has been the Central Government control of regional State Governments through the instrument of single ethnic based parties affiliated to the ruling EPRDF[6].

The top down character of decentralized governance in Ethiopia is also manifested by the heavy dependence of regions on the federal government for budgeting allocations. Underdevelopment of the country, paucity of national revenue sources and the limited capacity to mobilize adequate resources for development, all accentuated the fiscal dependence of the regions on the Central Government. During the last few years the regional governments are able to finance only an average 17 per cent of their expenditures from their own revenues (Table 9.2). The allocation of budgetary and national revenues on the basis of geographical and demographic factors obviously favours bigger regions. In addition to their dependence on the federal government for budgetary transfers, regional governments are also subject to substantial control by the Centre.

Table 9.2: Revenue Sharing between Federal and Regional State Governments in Ethiopia

Year	*Federal Government Revenue (Birr*)*	*Share of Regional State Government*	
		Amount (Birr)*	*%*
1994-95	5912.6	886.6	14.9
1995-96	6965.9	1129.4	16.2
1996-97	7877.4	1352.4	17.2
1997-98	8412.8	1595.2	18.9
1998-99	9362.1	1516.1	16.2
1999-2000	10430.6	1813.9	17.4
Average	8160.2	1382.2	16.9

Note: * One dollar = 8.616 birr.

Source: Bahru Zewde, *et al.* (Ed), Ethiopia: The Challenge of Democracy from Below, Elanders Gotab, Stockholm, 2002.

The extent of supervision and monitoring of regions by the Central Government varies from region to region. State Governments that have sufficient administrative and institutional capacity, including manpower, better infrastructure and resources base enjoy a relatively higher degree of autonomy and independence than others[7]. The challenge for the present Ethiopian federal system is to correct regional disparities and bring about even and balanced development among the different regions (Teshome, 1994). Unless the government is able to provide equal development opportunities, the persistence of regional economic differences can generate resentment that can threaten the viability of the federal arrangement.

9.5 WOREDA LEVEL GOVERNANCE

The Woreda is a multipurpose local government unit in the current state structure in Ethiopia. Although not mentioned in the federal constitution, it is recognized by all regional constitutions and has been given elaborate powers and responsibilities (Pausewang, *et al.*, 2002). As an autonomous self-governing unit, it has an elected council, executive committee and administrative structure. Formally, Woreda government can prepare and approve its own budget, prepare and implement economic and social development projects, set up and manage public services and exercise democratic decision-making at the local level. In addition, it has an independent court structure and has been given the authority to mobilize the people for participatory governance and development.

Woreda governments have extensive formal powers and responsibilities. Its responsibilities include the running socio-economic development programmes such as agriculture, health, education and infrastructure development. However, in practice it is subject to the control and supervision of the zonal administration and the regional governments in matters ranging from budget preparation and approval to undertaking socio-economic development projects (Mandefro, 1998). In addition, all economic and social plans have to be submitted to the zonal administration and also conduct periodical evaluations of Woreda.

An important issue that needs to be addressed is the legal status and function of municipalities in the evolving local government structure. Most municipalities and urban bodies in Ethiopia are not recognized as distinct authorities of local administration (ESSWA, 1998). As much they are subject to dual authority on the one hand, lacking separate legal status, they are supervised by predominantly rural Woreda councils; and on the other hand, they are subject to the technical and administrative supervision of Zonal Bureaus of Works and Urban Development.

9.6 KEBELEWOTCH[8] AT THE GRASSROOTS LEVEL GOVERNANCE

The Kebele is the lowest tier of administration in Ethiopia's decentralized governance structure. Even though it is an important unit of local governance, its role and function in the current system of governance are not clear. In many instances, Kebelewotch have served as basic units of grassroot democracy and enhanced the community participation in governance. Presently there is no clear authority and functional relationship between the Kebelewotch on the one hand and the Woreda administration and the Municipality on the other (Vestal, 1999). In addition, there is a problem of jurisdiction as to whether Kebelewotch are under the Woreda or the Municipal administration. In relative terms, the status of rural Kebelewotch is clear because they are under the supervision of the Woreda administration. However, urban ones are subject to dual supervision by the Woreda council and the Municipality.

The goal of decentralization or so called regionalization in Ethiopia is to progressively transfer the delivery and management of public services from the Central Government to democratic sub-national governments. The constitution and various policies provide for the formal transfer of powers and responsibilities from the Central Government to the regional, zonal and Woreda levels of administration. However, in reality there has been very little devolution of authority and functions from regional governments to Woreda levels of administration, although not constitutionally recognized, have been superimposed and acts as a brake on the autonomy and independence on Woreda Governments[9]. As such, Woredawotch do not have sufficient decision-making authority to serve as autonomous institutions of decentralized governance, nor do they manage public and community services on their own without strict guidance and supervision by zonal administrations.

9.7 CONCLUSION

From the above discussion in this chapter it can be seen that the emerging pattern of decentralized governance has affected the independent decision-making power of the Woreda level of government; which are supposed to be more close to the common man. Even though, in theory, the Woreda Government has been given full powers to exercise complete decision-making authority, in practice, command and instructions flow from top to bottom in an unbroken bureaucratic line from the regional government to the zones, Woredawotch and Kebelewotch. The bureaucratic chain of command has limited the local discretionary powers and decision-making authority of the Woreda tiers of government. Decentralized governance can promote a system where people are empowered to decide on economic and political issues affecting their well-being.

NOTES

1. At present Tigray, Afar, Amhara, Oromia, Somale, Southern Nations Nationalities and Peoples (SNNP), Benishagul-Gumuz, Gambella and Harrari are the regional States and Addis Ababa and Dire Dawa are the two autonomous administrative areas.
2. The country was divided into twelve self-governing ethno-linguistic regional states and two special autonomous administrative areas. The number was later reduced to nine regional states following the controversial merger of the numerous ethnic and nationality groups encompassing many regions in the South into one regional government.
3. An earlier legislation, Proclamation No. 7/92, makes reference to all and assigns powers and duties to each of them. All echelons of government below the regional level are the responsibilities of regional state governments, and their organization, powers and functions are defined in regional constitutions.
4. In addition, each region can also be considered as having semi-sovereign status because it has a constitution, a flag and regional language to be used in schools, courts and public administration.
5. Central and regional government powers and responsibilities have also been defined in the constitution. Accordingly, national defense, foreign policy, currency, inter-regional trade and citizenship are major functions left for the Central Government. Regional governments are made responsible for executing economic and social development policies, strategies and plans of the region, and establishing and administering a regional police force and maintaining public order.
6. Each region is ruled by an ethnic-based party that has established structures at the level of zones, Woredawotch and Kebelewotch. The overwhelming majority of elected and appointed local government officers and administrators are members of the ruling party. Since

the regional ethnic-based party is a member of the ruling EPRDF coalition, the system maintains a monolithic structure that ensures the heavy influence of the center on the periphery.

7. For instance, Amhara, Oromia and Tigray are not subject to the same degree of interference and supervision by the center as the man-power deficient regions such as Gambella, Afar, Benishagul-Gumuz and Somale.
8. Kebelewotch is the plural of Kebele and Woredawotch that of Woreda.

REFERENCES

Barkan, *et al.*, (1998). 'Decentralization and Democratization in Sub-Saharan Africa,' *Occasional Papers: 45-49*, International Programmes, University of IOWA.

ESSWA (Ethiopian Society of Sociologist, Social Workers and Anthropologists), (1998). *The Role of Indigenous Associations and Institutions in Development*—Abstracts, Workshop Organized by ESSWA, Addis Ababa, June 25-26.

FDRE (Federal Democratic Republic of Ethiopia), (1995). 'Proclamation of the Constitution of the Federal Democratic Republic of Ethiopia,' *Negarit Gazetta*, No. 1, Addis Ababa.

Mandefro. (1998). *Ethiopia: Anatomy of a Traditional Polity*, Clarendon Press, Oxford.

MEDAC (Ministry of Development and Co-operation), (1998). *Regional Development in Ethiopia: An Overview*, Department of Regional Planning and Development, Addis Ababa.

Olowu, Delele. (1993). *African Local Governments as Instruments of Economic and Social Development*, International Union of Local Authorities, Hague.

Pausewang, *et al.* (2002). *Ethiopia Since the Derg: A Decade of Democratic Pretension and Performance*, ZED Books, London.

Teshome, Teshale. (1994). *The Making of Modern Ethiopia: 1896-1974*, Red Sea Press, Lawrenceville, N.J.

Vestal, Theodore M. (1999). *Ethiopia: A Post Cold War African State*, Pracger, London.

APPENDIX FIGURES

Figure 9.A.1: Organizational Structure of Decentralized Governance in Ethiopia: Federal Level

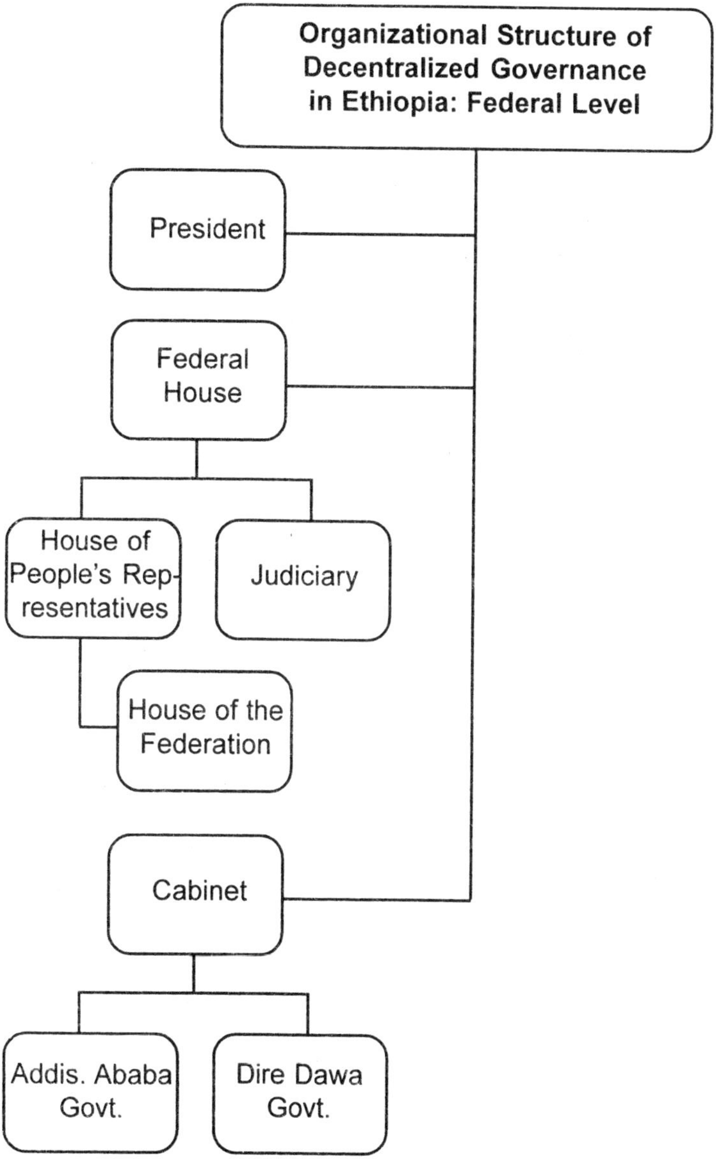

Figure 9.A.2: Grassroots Level Governance

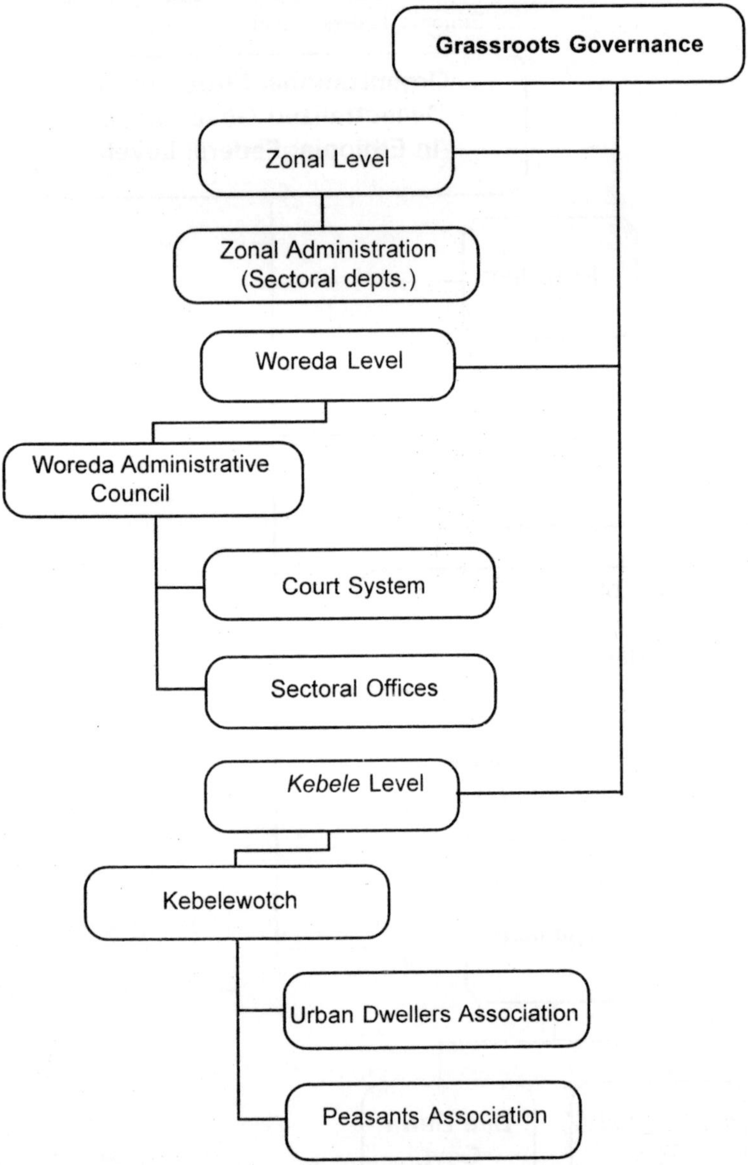

Figure 9.A.3: Structure of Regional Level Government

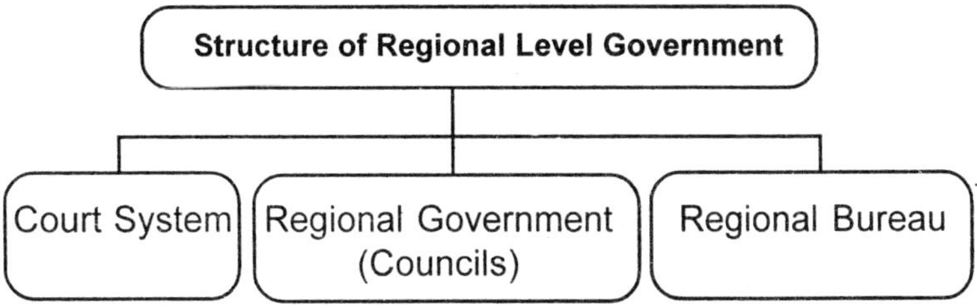

10

Socio-Economic Impacts of HIV/AIDS Menace in Africa

10.1 INTRODUCTION

Sub-Saharan Africa has been worst affected by the global AIDS epidemic and has caused vast amounts of human suffering. Nearly two-thirds of all HIV positive people live in this area, although it contains little more than 10 per cent of the world's population (UNAIDS, 2006). The most obvious effect of this crisis has been illness and death, but the impact of the epidemic has certainly not been confined to the health sector; households, education, workplaces and economies have been significantly affected, along with other sections of society. During 2005 alone, an estimated 2 million adults and children died as a result of AIDS in Sub-Saharan Africa. Since the beginning of the epidemic more than 15 million Africans have died from AIDS.

The present chapter discusses the social and economic impacts of the HIV/AIDS in Africa. It also gives special attention to the impacts on the health sector, education, labourforce and also review the required interventions.

10.2 IMPACT ON THE HEALTH SECTOR

In many countries of Sub-Saharan Africa, AIDS is erasing decades of progress in extending life expectancy. Some studies show that the average life expectancy of individuals living in Sub-Saharan Africa has fallen by five years since the early 1990's, mainly because of AIDS (Business Day, 2006). The impact the AIDS has had on average life expectancy is partly attributed to child mortality, as increasing numbers of children are born with HIV due to the fact that their mother was infected. The biggest increase in deaths, however, has been among adults aged between 20 and 49. This group now accounts for 60 per cent of all deaths in Sub-Saharan Africa, compared to 20 per cent between 1985 and 1990, when the epidemic was in its early stages[1]. By affecting this age group so heavily, AIDS is hitting adults in their most economically productive years and removing the very people who could be responding to the crisis.

In all affected countries the AIDS epidemic is bringing additional pressure to bear on the health sector. As the epidemic matures, the demand for care for those living with HIV rises, as does the toll among health workers. In Sub-Saharan Africa, the direct medical costs of AIDS (excluding antiretroviral therapy) have been estimated at about US$30 per year for every person infected, at a time when overall public health spending is less than US$10 per year for most African countries (UNAIDS, 2006).

As the HIV prevalence of a country rises, the strain placed on its hospitals is likely to increase. In Sub-Saharan Africa, people with HIV-related diseases occupy more than half of all hospital beds. Government-funded research in South Africa has suggested that, on average, HIV-positive patients stay in hospital four times longer than other patients[2]. Hospitals are struggling to cope, especially in poorer African countries where there are often not enough beds available. This shortage results in people being admitted only in the later stages of illness, reducing their chances of recovery. As the epidemic worsens, more complex cases of HIV and AIDS are likely to arise, taking up more hospital time and further reducing the standard of care provided.

While AIDS is causing an increased demand for health services, large numbers of healthcare professionals are being affected by the epidemic[3]. Healthcare workers are already scarce in most African countries. Excessive workloads, poor pay and the temptation of migrating to richer countries once trained are factors that have played a role in this shortage.

Although the recent increase in the provision of antiretroviral drugs (ARVS, which significantly delay the progression from HIV to AIDS) has brought hope to many in Africa, it has also put increased strain on healthcare workers. Providing ARVs requires more time and training than is currently available in most countries—for instance, in Tanzania it has been estimated that providing treatment to all those who need it would require the full-time services of almost half the existing health workforce.

10.3 SOCIAL IMPACTS

The toll of HIV and AIDS on society can be very severe. Although no part of the population is unaffected by HIV, it is often the poorest sectors of society that are most vulnerable to the epidemic and for whom the consequences are most severe. In many cases, the presence of AIDS means that the family will dissolve, as parents die and children are sent to relatives for care and upbringing. A study of rural South Africa suggested that households where an adult had died from AIDS were four times more likely to dissolve than those where no deaths had occurred (Hosegood and Mc Grath, 2004). Much happens before this dissolution takes place; AIDS strips families of their assets and income-earners, further impoverishing the poor.

(i) Family Incomes

In Botswana it is estimated that, on average, every income earner is likely to acquire one additional dependent over the next ten years due to the AIDS epidemic. A dramatic increase in destitute households—those with no income earners—is also expected. Other countries in the region are experiencing the same problem, as individuals who would otherwise provide a household with income are prevented from working by HIV and AIDS—either because they are ill themselves or because they are caring for another family member who is. Such a situation is likely to have repercussions for every member of the family. Children may be forced to abandon their education and in some cases women may be forced to turn to sex work. This can lead to a higher risk of HIV transmission, which further exacerbates the situation. AIDS will not only reverse progress in poverty reduction, but will increase the percentage of people living in extreme poverty.

(ii) Basic Necessities

A study in South Africa found that already poor households coping with members who are sick from HIV or AIDS were reducing spending on necessities even further. The most likely expenses to be cut were clothing (21%), electricity (16%) and other services (9%). Falling incomes forced about 6 per cent of households to reduce the amount they spent on food and almost half of households reported having insufficient food at times (HJKFF, 2002).

(iii) Food Production

The AIDS epidemic adds to food insecurity in many areas, as agricultural work is neglected or abandoned due to household illness. In Malawi, where food shortages have had a devastating effect, it has been recognised that HIV and AIDS are fuelling the country's poor agricultural output (bbc.co.uk, 2005). It is thought that by 2020, Malawi's agricultural workforce will be 14 per cent smaller than it would have been without HIV and AIDS. In other countries, such as Mozambique, Botswana, Namibia and Zimbabwe, the reduction is likely to be over 20 per cent.

Food production in households where the head of the family died of AIDS was affected in different ways depending on the sex of the deceased. As in other Sub-Saharan African countries, it was generally found that the death of a male reduced the production of 'cash crops' (such as coffee, tea and sugar), while the death of a female reduced the production of grain and other crops necessary for household survival.

(iv) Health Care Expenses

Taking care of a person sick with AIDS is not only an emotional strain for household members, but also a major strain on household resources. Loss of income, additional care-related expenses, the reduced ability of caregivers to work, and mounting medical fees push affected households deeper into poverty. It is estimated that, on average, HIV-related care can absorb one-third of a household's monthly income (Steinberg, *et al.*, 2002). The financial burden of death can also be considerable, with some families in South Africa spending three times their total household monthly income on a funeral.

(v) Impact on Children

It is hard to overemphasise the trauma and hardship that children affected by HIV and AIDS are forced to bear world-wide. The epidemic not only causes children to lose their parents or guardians, but sometimes their childhood as well. As parents and family members become ill, children take on more responsibility to earn an income, produce food and care for family members. It is harder for these children to access adequate nutrition, basic health care, housing and clothing. Fewer families have the money to send their children to school. Often both of the parents are HIV-positive in Africa. Consequently, more children have been orphaned by AIDS in Africa than anywhere else. Many children are now raised by their grandparents or left on their own in child-headed households.

As projections of the number of AIDS orphans rise, some have called for an increase in institutional care for children. However this solution is not only expensive but also detrimental to the children. Institutionalisation stores up problems for society, which is ill equipped to cope with an influx of young adults who have not been socialised in the community in which they have to live[4]. The way forward is prevention. Firstly, it is crucial to prevent children from becoming infected with HIV at birth as well as later in life. Secondly, if efforts are made to prevent adults becoming infected with HIV, and to care for those already infected, then fewer children will be orphaned by AIDS in the future.

10.4 IMPACT ON THE EDUCATION SECTOR

The relationship between AIDS and the education sector is circular—as the epidemic worsens, the education sector is damaged, which in turn is likely to increase the incidence of HIV transmission. There are numerous ways in which AIDS can affect education, but equally there are many ways in which education can help the fight against AIDS. The extent to which schools and other education institutions are able to continue functioning will influence how well societies eventually recover from the epidemic.

(i) On Children

A decline in school enrolment is one of the most visible effects of the epidemic. This will in itself have an effect on HIV prevention, as a good basic education ranks among the most effective and cost-effective means of preventing HIV. There are numerous barriers to school attendance in Africa. As discussed earlier children may be removed from school to care for parents or family members, or they may be living with HIV themselves. Many are unable to afford school fees and other such expenses—this is particularly a problem among children who have lost their parents to AIDS, who often struggle to generate income.

Studies have suggested that young people with little or no education may be 2.2 times more likely to contract HIV as those who have completed primary education (GCE, 2004). In this context, the devastating effect that AIDS is having on school enrolment is a big concern. In Swaziland and the Central African Republic, it has been reported that school enrolment has fallen by 25-30 per cent due to AIDS.

(ii) On Teachers

HIV/AIDS does not only affect pupils but teachers as well. In the early stages of the African epidemic it was reported that teachers were at a higher risk of becoming infected with HIV than the general population, because of their relatively high socio-economic status and a lack of understanding about how the virus is transmitted. This trend appears to have changed, as evidence increasingly shows that the more educated an individual is, the more likely they are to change their behaviour (Boler and Jellema, 2005). But HIV and AIDS are still having a devastating affect on the already inadequate supply of teachers in African countries; for example, a study in South Africa found that 21 per cent of teachers aged 25-34 are living with HIV (UNAIDS, 2006).

Teachers who are affected by HIV and AIDS are likely to take increasing periods of time off work. Those with sick families may also take time off to attend funerals or to care for sick or dying relatives, and further absenteeism may result from the psychological effects of the epidemic (World Bank, 2002). When a teacher falls ill, the class may be taken on by another teacher, may be combined with another class, or may be left untaught. Even when there is a sufficient supply of teachers to replace losses, there can be a significant impact on the students. This is particularly concerning given the important role that teachers can play in the fight against AIDS.

The illness or death of teachers is especially devastating in rural areas where schools depend heavily on one or two teachers. Moreover, skilled teachers are not easily replaced. Tanzania has estimated that it needs around 45,000 additional teachers to make up for those who have died or left work because of HIV and AIDS[5].

10.5 IMPACT ON THE LABOUR FORCE

HIV and AIDS dramatically affect labour, setting back economic and social progress. The vast majority of people living with HIV in Africa are between the ages of 15 and 49—in the prime of their working lives. AIDS weakens economic activity by squeezing productivity, adding costs, diverting productive resources, and depleting skills. Company costs for health-care, funeral benefits and pension fund commitments are likely to rise as the number of people taking early retirement or dying increases. Also, as the impact of the epidemic on households grows more severe, market demand for products and services can fall. The epidemic hits productivity through increased absenteeism. Comparative studies of East African businesses have shown that absenteeism can account for as much as 25-54 per cent of company costs.

A study in several Southern African countries has estimated that the combined impact of AIDS-related absenteeism, productivity declines, health-care expenditures, and recruitment and training expenses could cut profits by at least 6-8 per cent (UNAIDS, 2006). Another study of 1006 companies in Southern Africa found that 9 per cent had suffered a significant negative impact due to AIDS. In areas that have been hit hardest by the epidemic, it found that up to 40 per cent of companies reported that HIV and AIDS were having a negative effect on profits. Despite this, only 13 per cent of the companies surveyed that had less than 100 workers had a company policy in place to deal with HIV and AIDS.

Some companies have implemented successful programmes to deal with the epidemic. An example is the gold-mining districts in South Africa. The gold mines attract thousands of workers, often from poor and remote regions. Most live in hostels, separated from their families, and as a result a thriving sex industry operates around many mines and HIV is common. In recent years, mining companies have been working with a number of organisations to implement prevention programmes for the miners. These have included mass distribution of condoms, medical care and treatment for sexually transmitted diseases, and awareness campaigns (WHO, 2007). Some mining companies have started to replace all-male hostels with accommodation for families, in order to reduce the transmission of HIV and other sexually transmitted diseases.

In Swaziland, an employers' anti-AIDS coalition has been set up to promote voluntary counselling and testing. The coalition not only includes larger companies but also small and medium sized enterprises. In Botswana, the Debswana diamond company offers all employees HIV testing, and if they are HIV positive then they and their spouses are offered HIV antiretroviral drugs. This policy was introduced in 1999 when the company found that many of their workforce were HIV positive. With a skilled workforce, it is financially worth their while to protect the health and therefore the productivity of their workers.

10.6 ECONOMIC IMPACTS

Through its impacts on the labour force, households and enterprises, AIDS has played a more significant role in the reversal of human development than any other single factor (UNDP, 2005). One aspect of this development-reversal has been the damage that the epidemic has done to the economy, which, in turn, has made it more difficult for countries to respond to the crisis. One way in which HIV and AIDS affect the economy is by reducing the labour supply through increased mortality and illness. Amongst those who are able to work, productivity is likely to decline as a result of HIV-related illness. Government income also declines, as tax revenues fall and Governments are pressured to increase their spending to deal with the rising HIV prevalence.

The abilities of African countries to diversify their industrial base, expand exports and attract foreign investment are integral to economic progress in the region. By making labour more expensive and reducing profits, AIDS limits the ability of African countries to attract industries that depend on low-cost labour and makes investments in African businesses less desirable (Rosen, *et al.*, 2004). HIV and AIDS therefore threaten the foundations of economic development in Africa.

The impact that AIDS has had on the economies of African countries is difficult to measure. The economies of the worst affected countries were already struggling with development challenges, debt and declining trade before the epidemic started to affect the continent. AIDS has combined with these factors to further aggravate the situation. It is estimated that the yearly impact of AIDS on Sub-Saharan Africa's Gross Domestic Product (GDP) is 1 per cent. While this is a relatively modest effect, it will build in significance over time, especially in countries where HIV prevalence is rising. One way in which this impact can be reduced is through the provision of antiretroviral drugs to people living with HIV. If the proportion of those in need of ARVs who are receiving them increased to 50 per cent, the effect of the epidemic on economic growth would be reduced by 17 per cent (BER, 2006).

Studies have shown that there is a strong correlation between a population's health and the capacity of its Government to function effectively[6]. It had previously been thought that health was a more or less passive factor, that it would improve as development progressed. But, as a population's health declines it will have a significant negative effect on the functioning of the State. This is already happening in several of the States of Southern Africa.

There are 700,000 orphans in Zimbabwe and 600,000 in South Africa. These numbers are expected to grow geometrically in the next 8-10 years (Shelton and Johnston, 2001). It is likely that many will turn to crime to survive, destabilizing the society. They are also likely to turn to political radicalism. Orphan populations provide fertile ground for the recruitment of disaffected youth to radical causes and political organizations. Long-term effects of the plague spell the destruction of a large portion of the region's human capital. This will diminish production and GDP.

Economic consequences that are frequently ignored are depletion of national savings, increased deficit spending, and increased aggregate debt. Foreign investors are pulling back from the region, and where they will invest they are demanding that local governments or entrepreneurs put up a significantly larger share of the operation than in the past.

Security and social services will also decline as a consequence of AIDS. Military and police forces are weakened. Declining revenues from a shrinking tax base lowers the ability to provide education and health-care. People will increasingly see the Government as illegitimate. Further, because the burden of disease falls primarily on the poor and lower middle classes, the epidemic will increase class inequalities and deepen the deprivation of the lower middle class and the very poor.

10.7 INTERVENTIONS

(i) International Support

One of the most important ways in which the situation in Africa can be improved is through increased funding. More money would help to improve both prevention campaigns and the provision of treatment and care for those living with HIV. Developed countries have increased funding for the fight against AIDS in Africa in recent years, perhaps most significantly through the Global Fund to fight AIDS, Tuberculosis and Malaria. The Global Fund was started in 2001 to co-ordinate international funding and has since approved grants totalling US $3.3 billion to fight HIV and AIDS in Africa (GFFA, 2005). Around 60 per cent of the fund's grants have been directed towards Africa and 60 per cent has been put towards fighting AIDS. This funding is making a significant difference, but given the massive scale of the AIDS epidemic more money is still needed.

Among other things, organisations like PEPFAR[7] and the Global Fund provide vital support to local and community groups that are working 'on the ground' to provide relief in Africa. These groups are directly helping people in need, and many rely on international funding in order to operate. However, getting money from large, international donors to small, 'grassroots organisations' can present a number of difficulties though, as money is lost or delayed as it is passed down large funding chains.

(ii) Domestic Commitment

More than money is needed if HIV prevention and treatment programmes are to be scaled up in Africa. In order to implement such programmes, a country's health, education, communications and other infrastructures must be sufficiently developed. In some African countries these systems are already under strain and are at risk of collapsing as a result of AIDS. Money can also only be used efficiently if there are sufficient human resources available, but there is an acute shortage of trained personnel in many parts of Africa.

In many cases, African countries also need more commitment from their Governments. There are promising signs that some Governments are starting to respond and becoming more involved in the fight against AIDS, and this commitment needs to be sustained if the severe impact of Africa's AIDS pandemic is to be reduced.

(a) Reducing Stigma and Discrimination

HIV-related stigma and discrimination remains an enormous barrier to the fight against AIDS. Fear of discrimination often prevents people from getting tested, seeking treatment and admitting their HIV status publicly. Since laws and policies alone cannot reverse the stigma that surrounds HIV infection, more and better AIDS education is needed in Africa to combat the ignorance that causes people to discriminate (WHO, 2007). The fear and prejudice that lies at the core of HIV/AIDS discrimination needs to be tackled at both community and national levels.

(b) Helping Women and Girls

In many parts of Africa, as elsewhere in the world, the AIDS epidemic is aggravated by social and economic inequalities between men and women. Women and girls commonly face discrimination in terms of access to education, employment, credit, health-care, land and inheritance. These factors can all put women in a position where they are particularly vulnerable to HIV infection. In Sub-Saharan Africa, around 59 per cent of those living with HIV are female (Kaisernetwork.org, 2005). In many African countries, sexual relationships are dominated by men, meaning that women cannot always practice safe sex even when they know the risks involved.

Attempts are currently being made to develop a microbicide—a cream or gel that can be applied to the vagina, preventing HIV infection—which could be a significant breakthrough in protecting women against HIV (WHO, 2007). Women could apply such a microbicide without their partner even knowing. It is likely to be some time before a microbicide is ready for use, though, and even when it is, women will only use it if they have an awareness and understanding of HIV and AIDS. To promote this, a greater emphasis needs to be placed on educating women and girls about AIDS, and adapting education systems (which are currently male-dominated) to their needs.

10.8 CONCLUSION

Although both international and domestic efforts to overcome the crisis have been strengthened in recent years, the epidemic is showing no signs of diminishing, and the people of Sub-Saharan Africa will continue to feel the effects of HIV and AIDS for years to come. It is clear that as much as possible needs to be done to minimise this impact. As access to treatment is slowly expanded throughout the continent, millions of lives are being extended and hope is being given to people who previously had none. Unfortunately majority of people in need of treatment are still not receiving it, and campaigns to prevent new are lacking in many areas. HIV and AIDS in Africa are linked with many other problems, such as poverty and poor public infrastructures. Efforts to fight the epidemic must take these realities into account, and look at ways in which the general development of Africa can progress.

Tackling the AIDS crisis in Africa is a long-term task that requires sustained effort and planning—both within African countries themselves and amongst the international community. One of the most important elements of the fight against AIDS is the prevention of new HIV infections. HIV prevention campaigns that have been successful within African countries need to be highlighted and repeated. The other main challenge is providing treatment and care to those living with HIV in Africa, in particular ARVs, which can allow people living with HIV to live long and healthy lives. Many African countries have made significant progress in their treatment programmes in recent years and it is likely that the next few years will see many more people receiving the drugs. HIV/AIDS is acting as the single biggest barrier to Africa's development. Unless the crisis is addressed, untold suffering will continue to take its toll on this region.

NOTES

1. In Swaziland it has previously been estimated that life expectancy at birth, which is currently just 33, would be 66 without AIDS.
2. It is predicted that patients affected by HIV and AIDS will soon account for 60-70 per cent of hospital expenditure in South Africa.
3. Botswana, for example, lost 17 per cent of its healthcare workforce due to AIDS between 1999 and 2005. A study in one region of Zambia found that 40 per cent of midwives were HIV-positive.
4. There are other alternatives available. One example is the approach developed by church groups in Zimbabwe, where they recruit community members to visit orphans in their homes, where they live either with foster parents, grandparents or other relatives, or in child-headed households.
5. The greatest proportion of staff that have been lost, according to the Tanzania Teacher's Union, were experienced staff between the ages of 41 and 50.
6. Price-Smith painted a grim picture of the many repercussions of the AIDS pandemic, spreading out to undermine all aspects of society. "Southern Africa is the global center of the pandemic," Price-Smith said, "with Botswana leading with 36 per cent of the adults HIV positive; South Africa is at 26 per cent."
7. The US Government has shown a commitment to fighting AIDS in Africa through the President's Emergency Plan for AIDS Relief. Started in 2003, PEPFAR provides money to fight AIDS in numerous countries, including 15 focus countries, most of which are African. In 2005, PEPFAR allocated US $1.1 billion to these African focus countries (PEPFAR, 2006). The US Government is also the largest contributor to the Global Fund.

REFERENCES

Bbc.co.uk, (2005). *Malawi issues food crisis appeal*, October.

Boler, T. and Jellema, A. (2005). *Deadly Inertia: A Cross Country Study of Educational Responses to HIV/AIDS.*

Bureau for Economic Research (BER), (2006). *The Macro-economic Impact of HIV/Aids under Alternative Intervention Scenarios (with Specific Reference to ART) on the South African Economy*, Stellenbosch University.

Business Day, (2006). *Sub-Saharan Lifespan Down by Five Years*, June.

Food and Agriculture Organization of the United Nations (FAO), (2001). *Rural Women Carry Family Burdens: Focus, AIDS—A Threat to Rural Africa.*

GCE, (2004). *Learning to Survive.*

Global Fund to Fight AIDS, Tuberculosis and Malaria (GFFA), (2005). *Grants to Countries in Africa, Rounds 1-5 Funding*, September.

Henry, J. Kaiser Family Foundation (HJKFF), (2002). *Hitting Home: How Households Cope with the Impact of the HIV/AIDS Epidemic*, October.

Hosegood, V. and McGrath, N. *et al.* (2004). 'The impact of adult mortality on household dissolution and migration in Rural South Africa', *AIDS*, July 23rd, Vol. 18, issue 11.

Kaisernetwork.org, (2005). *US has Increased Global Condom Distribution in Recent Years, Targeting Mostly High-Risk Groups*, September.

PEPFAR, (2006). *Action Today, A Foundation for Tomorrow: Second Annual Report to Congress on the President's Emergency Plan for AIDS Relief*, February.

Rosen, S. *et al.* (2004). 'The cost of HIV/AIDS to Businesses in Southern Africa', *AIDS*, 18 : 317-324.

Shelton, J.D. and Johnston, B. (2001). *Condom Gap in Africa: Evidence From Donor Agencies and Key Informants.*

Steinberg, M. *et al.* (2002). *Hitting Home: How Households Cope with the Impact of the HIV/AIDS Epidemic*, The Henry J Kaiser Foundation, October.

UNAIDS, (2006). *Report on the Global AIDS Epidemic.*

United Nations Development Programme (UNDP), (2005). *Human Development Report 2005*, Overview.

WHO, (2007). *Towards Universal Access: Scaling Up Priority HIV/AIDS Interventions in the Health Sector*, April.

World Bank, (2002). *Education and HIV/AIDS: A Window of Hope.*

11

Zimbabwe's Mounting Inflation
A New History in the Economic Theory of Inflation

11.1 INTRODUCTION

For untold numbers of Zimbabweans, toilet paper and bread, margarine, meat, even the once ubiquitous morning cup of tea had become unimaginable luxuries. Zimbabwe has been tormented this entire decade by both deep recession and high inflation, and in recent months the economy seems to have abandoned whatever moorings it had left. The national budgets are insufficient and Government services have crumbled. The purity of Harare's drinking water, siphoned from a lake downstream of its sewer outfall, has been unreliable for months, and dysentery and cholera swept the city. The city suffers rolling electrical blackouts. Mounds of uncollected garbage pile up on the streets of the slums.

Public-school fees and other ever-rising Government surcharges have begun to exceed the monthly incomes of many urban families. The jobless—officially 70 per cent of Zimbabwe's 4.2 million workers, but widely placed at 80 per cent when idle farmers are included—furtively hawk tomatoes and baggies of ground corn from roadside tables, an occupation banned by the police (Michael Wines, 2006). Those with spare cash put it not in banks, which pay a paltry 4 to 10 per cent annual interest on savings, but in gilt-edged investments like bags of corn meal and sugar, guaranteed not to lose their value.

All are casualties of the hyperinflation that is roaring toward 1,000 per cent a year, a rate usually seen only in war zones. Zimbabwe's inflation is currently the world's highest, and has been for some time[1]. The present chapter analyses the status, causes and consequences of mounting inflation in Zimbabwe. It also reviews the long-term impact of globalization and the structural adjustment programmes, including the land reforms on the socio-economic institutions.

11.2 POLITICAL ECONOMY OF THE ZIMBABWEAN CRISIS

Although there is no credible threat to Robert G. Mugabe's 26-year rule, Zimbabwe's political opposition is calling for mass protests against the economic situation. So Mugabe has tightened his grip on power even further, turning the economy over to a national security council of his closest allies. In addition, he has seeded the Government's civilian ministries with loyal army and intelligence officers who now control key functions, from food security to tax collection. At the same time, Mugabe's Government has printed trillions of new Zimbabwean dollars to keep ministries functioning and to shield the salaries of key supporters—and potential enemies—against further erosion. The Government tripled the salaries of 190,000 soldiers and teachers. But even those Government workers still badly trail inflation; the best of the raises, to as much as $33 million a month, already are slightly below the latest poverty line for the average family of five. This only worsened the inflation, for printing too many worthless dollars is in part what got Zimbabwe into this mess to begin with. Zimbabwe fell into hyperinflation after the Government began seizing commercial farms in 2000. Foreign investors fled, manufacturing ground to a halt, goods and foreign currency needed to buy imports fell into short supply and prices shot up.

Inflation, about 400 per cent per year from November 2005, edged over 600 per cent in January 2006, but began to soar after the Government revealed that it had paid the International Monetary Fund $221 million to cover arrears that threatened Zimbabwe's membership in the organization. In February 2006, the Government admitted that it had printed at least $21 trillion in currency—and probably much more, critics say—to buy the American dollars with which the debt was paid. By March 2006, inflation had touched 914 per cent a year, at which rate prices would rise more than tenfold in 12 months. The annual rate of price growth was 1,042.9 per cent in April 2006, the Central Statistics Office (CSO) said, having risen 129 percentage points from March. It means average goods are about 11 times as expensive in April 2006 as they were 12 months earlier. In April 2007 inflation rate jumped up from the 2,200 per cent recorded March 2007. The inflation for the month of June 2007 was more than 13,000 per cent (Paul Nyaka Zeyar, 2007).

In the midst of this craziness, some Harare enclaves seem paradoxically normal. North of downtown, where diplomats and aid workers are financed with American dollars, and generators and bottled water are the norm, the cafes still serve cappuccino and the markets sell plump roasting chickens, albeit $1 million chickens. Everywhereelse, the hardship is inescapable. Millions of Zimbabweans survive these days on the kindness of outsiders—foreigners who donate food or medicine and, more important, family members who have fled the nation for better lives abroad (The Economist, 2007). As many as three million Zimbabweans now live in foreign countries such as Britain, South Africa and the United States. They remit as much as $50 million a month to their families—equivalent of one sixth of the gross domestic product.

Indeed, life for many may be better in the nation's impoverished rural areas, where subsistence farming is the only industry and millions of people are guaranteed free monthly rations from the United Nations and other donors. In the cities, little is free. Hyperinflation is a cradle-to-grave experience in Zimbabwe. The Government increased the price of childbirth, from $7 million in 2006, by 463 per cent. Funeral costs also doubled over the same period. In rural areas, even the barest funeral costs atleast $6 million, or about US $28.50—well beyond most families' means. The dead are buried in open fields at night.

Following the Lancaster House Agreement in December 1979, the transition to majority rule in early 1980, and the lifting of sanctions, Zimbabwe enjoyed a brisk economic recovery. Real growth for 1980-81 exceeded 20 per cent. However, depressed foreign demand for the country's mineral exports and the onset of droughts cut sharply into the growth rate in 1982, 1983, and 1984. In 1985, the economy rebounded strongly due to a 30 per cent jump in agricultural production (UNCTAD, 2000). However it slumped in 1986 to a zero growth rate and registered negative of about minus 3 per cent in 1987 due primarily to drought and foreign exchange crisis faced by the country. Growth in 1988-1990 averaged about 4.5 per cent.

Box 11.1: Witnesses of Mounting Inflation in Zimbabwe

In Glen Norah, a dense suburb of thousands of tiny homes southwest of Harare, 58-year-old Ayina Musoni and her divorced daughter Regai, 26, share their five-room house with Regai's two children and three lodgers. The lodgers, two security guards and a teacher, pay monthly rent totaling Z$3 million, or about $14.25 in American money. Mother and daughter make as much as $10 in American money each week by selling vegetables, from 7 a.m. to 6 p.m. daily. But the profits are being consumed by rising costs at the farmers' market where they buy stock. "Like potatoes," Regai said; "I went last week, and it was Z$500,000 for a packet. And when I went this weekend, it was Z$700,000".

Ms. Musoni's latest monthly bill for services from the Harare City Government was Z$2.4 million. The refrigerator in her closet-size kitchen is empty except for a few bottles of boiled water. Christmas dinner was sadza, or corn porridge, with hard-boiled eggs. For Easter, there was nothing.

Unity Motize, 64, lives with her 65-year-old husband, Simeon, in Highfield, a middle-class suburb turned slum not far south of town. The couple occupies one room of their three-room house. The second sleeps two sons, their wives and their two infants, all left homeless in May 2005 after riot police bulldozed the homes of hundreds of thousands of slum-dwellers. A 23-year-old son and an unemployed daughter sleep in the living room.

Zimbabwe has adequate internal transportation and electrical power networks. Paved roads link the major urban and industrial centres, and rail lines managed by the National Railways of Zimbabwe tie it into an extensive Central African railroad network with all its neighbours. In non-drought years, it has adequate electrical power, mainly generated by the Kariba Dam on the Zambezi River but augmented since 1983 by large thermal plants adjacent to the Wankie coal field. However, things have changed over the years. As of 2006, crumbling infrastructure and lack of spare parts for generators and coal mining means that Zimbabwe imports 40 per cent of its power[2].

With considerable hydroelectric power and plentiful coal deposits for thermal power stations, Zimbabwe is less dependent on oil as an energy source than most other comparably industrialized countries. Only about 15 per cent of Zimbabwe's total energy consumption is accounted for by oil, all of which is imported. Zimbabwe imports about 1.2 billion litres per year. Dependence on petroleum is managed through the price controls for vehicle fuels, the use of gasohol, and the substitution of diesel-electric locomotives on the railway system. Zimbabwe also has substantial coal reserves that are utilized for power generation, and recently discovered in Matabeleland province are coalbed methane deposits greater than any known natural gas field in Southern or Eastern Africa. In recent years poor economic management and low foreign currency reserves have led to serious fuel shortages.

Agriculture was once the backbone of the Zimbabwean economy. Due to large scale eviction of white farmers and the Government's land reform efforts, this is no longer the case. Reliable crop estimates are not available due to Zimbabwe Government's attempts to hide the realities following the evictions (Van Zyl, *et al.,* 2001). The ruling party banned maize imports, stating record crops for the year of 2004. Maize was the country's largest crop prior to the farm evictions and tobacco was the largest export crop followed by cotton. Poor Government management has exacerbated meager harvests caused by drought and floods, resulting in significant food shortfalls beginning in 2001. The land redistribution has been generally condemned in the developed world[3]. However, it has found considerable support in Africa and a few supporters among African-American activists.

11.3 SOCIO-ECONOMIC CRISIS

As a whole, the nation has now sunk to standards common elsewhere in Africa. The Government has reached the limit of its ability to do anything about it. Cutting spending seems impossible, and raising taxes further is unthinkable. That leaves one option much more inflation. The inflation was caused by flight of foreign capital, shortages and steep increase in the money supply, seizure of commercial farms alongwith rise in interest rates, economic slowdown, and price controls.

Zimbabwe is suffering from shortages of food, fuel and foreign currency. The Government blames domestic and foreign enemies for the problems. According to the International Monetary Fund, Zimbabwe suffers the highest rate of inflation in the world. Many analysts put the responsibility firmly at the ruling party's door, claiming the Government made the situation worse when it seized control of land owned by white farmers, which triggered a sharp drop in production and exports of agricultural goods (Potts, 2000).

Zimbabwe is a country that is blighted by crumbling urban infrastructure. Housing, education and transport costs also have jumped, while the unemployment rate means that almost two out of every three Zimbabweans are out of work. The country is struggling to pay civil servants and is planning to owe money to neighbours such as South Africa and Mozambique from whom it is been importing electricity and fuel.

The International Monetary Fund (IMF) and other international bodies are calling for reforms, but Mugabe is unwilling to accept outside help or interference (Blessing Zulu, 2007). The surging cost of domestic electricity, food, fuel and commuter transport fares were at the heart of price surges. Economists believe that these price increases will continue because Zimbabwe will be forced to import maize, a basic food staple, to make up for lack of home-grown produce. The Government has also warned of shortages of bread and flour, which may cause even more hardship. Some studies reveal that only 10 per cent of the country's winter wheat crop had been planted due to shortages of fuel and fertilizer. Households in Zimbabwe were given four hours electricity supply a day in a move designed to support the country's wheat farmers, who need power to irrigate their crops.

Rampant inflation is a clear sign of a deep economic crisis. Critics have blamed President Robert Mugabe's policies, particularly the seizure of white-owned farms, for damaging the once self-sufficient country—in the past described as the bread basket of Africa. The Government has a plan to revive the economy. That plan, the latest of perhaps seven in 10 years, would quickly raise billions of American dollars to end a chronic foreign currency shortage, cut the inflation rate to double digits and an end to the recession that has gripped Zimbabwe, halving its economic output, since 1999. The Zimbabwean Reserve Bank warned in 2005 that the inflation target would only be achieved if the Government avoided supplementary budgets and gratuity pay-outs. It also warned Government for unplanned benevolent or gratuity payments that are unrelated to current production activities for real economic growth.

Table 11.1: Important Economic Indicators of Zimbabwe

Indicator	*Values*
1. GDP (PPP)	USD $25.690 billion (2005) (107th)
2. GDP Growth	5.7% (2007) -3.6% (2008) (IMF est.)
3. GDP Per Capita	USD $2,607 (2005 est.)
4. GDP by Sector	Agriculture: 17.3%, Industry: 24.5%, Services: 58.3% (2003)
5. Inflation (CPI)	7,634.8% (official—July 2007); 13,000% (CCZ—June 2007); 6,430% (2008—IMF est.)
6. Population below Poverty Line	80% (June 2007) earn below ZWD 8.2 million per month (USD $27.33)
7. Labour Force	4.23 million (2004 est.)
8. Labour Force by Occupation	Agriculture: 60%, Services: 9%, Wholesale, Retail, Hotels, Restaurants: 4%, Manufacturing: 4%, Mining: 3% (2003)
9. Unemployment	80% (2005 to 2007 est.)
10. Main Industries	Mining (coal, gold, platinum, copper, nickel, tin, clay, numerous metallic and non-metallic ores), steel; wood products, cement, chemicals, fertilizer, clothing and footwear, foodstuffs, beverages, etc.
11. Exports	USD $1.644 billion (2005 est.)
12. Export Goods	Cotton, tobacco, gold, ferroalloys, textiles/clothing
13. Main Export Partners	South Africa 33.3%, China 7.5%, Japan 6.4%, Netherlands 4.9%, US 4.7%, Italy 4.3%, Zambia 4.2%, Germany 4.1% (2005)
14. Imports	USD $2.059 billion (2005 est.) f.o.b.
15. Import Goods	Machinery and transport equipment, other manufactures, chemicals, fuels, etc.
16. Main Import Partners	South Africa 43%, China 4.6%, Botswana 3.3% (2005)
17. Public Debt	Domestic: ZWD $1 trillion (rev) (April 2007) International: USD $5.2 billion (September 2006).

Source: The Economist (2007).

11.4 ROAD TO THE CRISIS

In recent years, poor management of the economy and political turmoil has led to considerable economic hardships. The Government of Zimbabwe's chaotic land reform programme, recurrent interference with, and intimidation of, the judiciary, as well as maintenance of unrealistic price controls and exchange rates have all led to a sharp drop in investor confidence[4]. Between 2000 and 2007, the national economy contracted by as much as 40 per cent; inflation vaulted to over 4530 per cent, and there were persistent shortages of foreign exchange, local currency, fuel, and food.

Direct foreign investment has all but evaporated. Billions were spent in the country's involvement in the war in the Democratic Republic of the Congo. Price controls have been imposed on a wide range of products including food (maize, bread, steak), fuel, medicines, soap, electrical appliances, yarn, window frames, building sand, agricultural machinery, fertilisers and school textbooks. Mugabe's supporters maintain that economic hardship has been brought about by Western backed-economic sanctions instituted through the United Nations[5].

As of February, 2004 Zimbabwe's foreign debt repayments ceased, resulting in compulsory suspension from the International Monetary Fund (Blessing Zulu, 2007). This, and the United Nations World Food Programme stopping its food aid due to insufficient donations from the world community, has forced the Government into borrowing from local sources. Zimbabwe began experiencing severe foreign exchange shortages, exacerbated by the difference between the official rate and the black market rate in 2000 (See Table 11.2). In 2004 a system of auctioning scarce foreign currency for importers was introduced, which temporarily led to a slight reduction in the foreign currency crisis, but by mid 2005 foreign currency shortages were once again chronic. The currency was devalued by the Central Bank twice, first to 9,000 to the US$, and then to 17,500 to the US$ on 20 July, 2005, but at that date it was reported that that was only half the rate available on the black market.

In July 2005 Zimbabwe was reported to be appealing to the South African Government for US$ 1 billion of emergency loans, but despite regular rumours that the idea was being discussed no financial support has been obtained from South Africa. The official Zimbabwean dollar exchange rate had been frozen at Z$101,196 per U.S. dollar since early 2006, but as of 27 July 2006 the parallel (black market) rate has reached Z$550,000 per U.S. dollar (Paul Nyakazeya, 2007). By comparison, 10 years earlier, the rate of exchange was only Z$ 9.13 per USD.

In August 2006 the RBZ revalued the Zimbabwean Dollar by 1000 ZWD to 1 (revalued) dollar. At the same time Zimbabwe devalued the Zim Dollar by 60 per cent against the USD. New official exchange rate revalued ZWD 250 per USD. The parallel market rate was about revalued ZWD 1,200 to 1,500 per USD. In November 2006 it was announced that sometime around December 1 there would be a further devaluation and that the official exchange rate would change to revalued ZWD 750 per USD. This never materialized. However, the parallel market immediately reacted to this news with the parallel rate falling to ZWD 2,000 per USD and by year end it had fallen to ZWD 3,000 per USD. On April 1, 2007 the parallel market was asking ZWD 30,000 for $1 USD. By June 25 it was down to ZWD 400,000. See Table-11.2 for more details.

Table 11.2: Devaluation of Currency in Zimbabwe

Year	*Parallel exchange rate*	*Official exchange rate*
2000	56—70	38
2001	70—340	55
2002	380—1740	55
2003	1400—6000	55; 824
2004	5500—6000	824—5730
2005	6,400—100,000	5,730—26,003
2006	100,000—550,000 (550—3,000 revalued dollars)	85,158—101,196 (250 revalued dollars)
2007	3,000—400,000 revalued dollars	250 revalued dollars 15,000 revalued dollars (special rate)

Note: Official rates quoted are Government set exchange rates. Parallel (Black market) rates differ significantly.

Poverty and unemployment are both endemic in Zimbabwe, driven by the shrinking economy and hyper-inflation. Both unemployment and poverty rates run near 80 per cent. As of January 2006, the poverty line was ZWD 17,200 per month (The

Economist, 2007). As of June 2007 this had risen to ZWD 5.5 million per month (US $14.00). The average farm worker's monthly wage was under ZWD 100,000 per month (US $0.25) and the average worker's monthly wage was ZWD 500,000 (US $1.25). The lowest 10 per cent of Zimbabwe's population consume only 1.97 per cent of the economy, while the highest 10 per cent consume 40.42 per cent (1995). The current account balance of the country is negative, standing at around US –$517 million.

11.5 GLOBALIZATION AND THE ZIMBABWEAN CRISIS

For political and economic crises as severe as Zimbabwe's, domestic causes are central, at the same time it is regional and international too. In that sense, it is a post (political) apartheid struggle. Analyzing the international context of the crises is not to deny the importance of national policies necessary for the long-term stability of Zimbabwe and of Southern Africa. As the Africa Union proposes, change must emerge from internal strengths and resources (Adams, *et al.*, 2001). Taking an international perspective, however, delineates the context and the constraints on *any* Government, labour, or farm leaders in Zimbabwe, as they face enormous problems for land and economic reforms.

Harsh as it was to eradicate political apartheid in Southern Africa, involving many deaths and torture, those involved thought it would be relatively easy in comparison with eradicating economic apartheid. They knew that this struggle would be very long and very brutal. By focusing on the international, this analysis raises the question whether any elected Government in Zimbabwe can implement reforms, without equally fundamental change in policies of dominant powers, such as the United States and Europe. For Zimbabwe, land hunger, along with the Economic Structural Adjustment Programme (ESAP), intensified real hunger. Without addressing the persistence of economic apartheid in the region and inequalities of ESAP, however, the current debates remain a historical. International analysts frequently reiterated that the Government of Zimbabwe had 20 years to promote land reform, but only engaged seriously in 1998 (Moyo, 2000b). They then write it off as an election ploy, during the first parliamentary elections in 2000 and then presidential elections in 2002.

Part of the legacies is the unfulfilled commitments of the United States and United Kingdom[6]. The Lancaster House constitution did not permit the Zimbabwean Government to pursue any land reform that was not willing seller-willing buyer. The government could not even visit the vast estates, such as that of the Anglo-American Corporation, without permission of the owner of the land, to assess what was utilized or unutilized land.

Because much of the land was in the hands of those with close links to apartheid South Africa (in 2000, the Oppenheimers still owned 960,000 hectares in Zimbabwe), it would have been extremely dangerous to take land except on a willing seller basis. During the 1980s, apartheid commando raids came regularly, all the way to Harare (Moyo, 2000a). During the 1980s, however, land reform was quite successful, a fact also not well acknowledged during this current crisis. Although falling short of unrealistic targets, by 1990 the Government had purchased and redistributed an impressive 3.3 million hectares to 52,000 families. During this time, large estates went to political cronies (estimates vary widely), but what was redistributed to needy farmers did increase quality of life. This relative success, however, probably increased expectations for land among Zimbabwean destitute. In addition, because of the willing seller-willing buyer requirement, seventy per cent of the prime land was untouched.

In 1990 when Zimbabwe signed on to the ESAP, the number one Government expenditure was education, defense number two, and health-care three. The IMF required user fees for rural clinics and primary education in 1992, during the worst regional drought of the century. The impoverishment of Zimbabweans under ESAP is now well documented. Before ESAP Zimbabwe recorded impressive achievements in decreasing crude death rates (from 10.1 to 6.1/1000) and infant mortality (from 86 to 61/1000 births) while improving life expectancy (55 to 59 years) and adult literacy (PRFIDS, 1999). Expenditures in health rose throughout the 1980s, reaching 3.1 per cent of GDP in 1990 (The WHO recommends at least 2.5 per cent of GDP be allocated to the health sector of developing countries.) The health delivery system was "turned on its head" with the majority of funds going to rural clinics and district, not urban, hospitals. Primary education was free and compulsory, with special emphasis for sending girls to school. From independence in 1980 until 1985, more children went to primary school, than during 90 years under the white minority rule of Southern Rhodesia.

Under ESAP, expenditures on health and education fell throughout the 1990s. Real per capita recurrent expenditure by the Ministry of Health and Child Welfare, from 1991-1995, of about 40 per cent, with recurrent expenditure on primary and secondary education declining by 30 per cent (Dhliwayo, 2001). By 1996, the health allocation of the budget was only 2.1 per cent of GDP, at a time when the HIV/AIDS pandemic was devastating the young productive workers. Where the majority of the people seek health care (80%), the rural clinics and district hospitals received less than 49 per cent of the public health budget. The total education allocation declined from 6.3 per cent of GDP in 1986-87 to 4.8 per cent in 1999. The drop-out rate for girls is higher than for boys.

What is not so well documented is that ESAP encouraged the Large Scale Commercial Farmers (LSCF) to grow export crops for the global market and less food crops for the regional market. Perhaps in macro-economic terms, the trade-off worked. The LSCF grew export crops (tobacco, cotton, paprika, flowers and game meat) for export earnings while the smaller farmers increased their production of maize, sorghum and groundnuts. Yet droughts and floods (1999) hit the small scale farmers the worst, reducing food security (Chattopadhyay, 2000). Further, seeing good pasture go for game meat for overseas consumption or Government preserves being sold to private (often foreign) tourist firms did not endear poor peasants with the ranchers and tourist operators. UNCTAD has found that SAPs can hurt small scale farmers: "Sub-Saharan Africa suffers from structural handicaps that are impossible to remove or reduce through the standard policy reform programmes. There are indications that some ingredients of reforms have actually aggravated constraints on the growth of small-holder production" (UNCTAD, 2000).

For most Zimbabweans, their identities are still linked to their home villages. Historically families survived colonialism (and the 1992, 2002 droughts) by having some members remain in rural areas and others work in town. During drought, the city-based relatives sent cash to the rural family. During periods of less employment, rural relatives provided food or work for the unemployed family members. ESAP brought not just a period of unemployment but a decade of misery. Relatives did not have enough land to sustain a household. The historical land hunger, and very real actual hunger, became worse as people tried to survive by selling commodities in informal markets (Kinsey, 2000). Even urban Zimbabweans still know how to grow food, as a quick glance in any township will demonstrate[7].

As is predicted by the theory, ESAP benefited the wealthy first, with the goal they would invest in growth in Zimbabwe. ESAP encourages production for the global market, not the regional or national, even for food security. Yet these two goals of structural adjustment do not take into consideration a post-conflict society, where factors of production are highly inequitably distributed. Benefiting the very few, who have already been historically advantaged, may not be conducive to political stability. 'Structurally adjusting' an economy in the post (political) apartheid era should probably begin with adjusting (transforming) the apartheid economic structures and relationships, not only as an issue of justice but as one of economic development. The market privileges the privileged, who can take advantage of new market 'opportunities[8].'

A major threat to food security, therefore, is loss of sovereignty over food production. By allowing the global market to determine production, an agriculturally rich country like Zimbabwe will produce flowers and fruit for Europe during its winter. Reducing subsidies for small scale farmers growing food (and raising interest rates) renders them vulnerable to the global market[9].

Contrary to the principles of SAPs, the State will have to play a major role both in land reform and in food security for the foreseeable future. In addition to questioning the internationally accepted approach to land reform and the internationally advocated total market liberalization, Southern Africans challenge the policy that food security will be provided by trading a few commodities on the global market (Kinsey, 1999). One pillar of Southern African food security is the production of grains for the regional market, stored for ready availability in times of crisis. Another pillar, most often ignored by the North, is the production of biodiverse food crops by small scale farmers, including urban agriculture in countries like Zimbabwe and Tanzania. Time and again, when the first pillar has buckled, as in the drought of 1991-92 and in Zimbabwe today because of political oppression, it is the second one which keeps people alive.

Addressing the international context for the current Zimbabwe crisis does not minimize the importance of the domestic causes of the crisis. An international perspective does turn the focus to continuing constraints on change in Zimbabwe, even after internal political transformation. As discussed above, these constraints are severe and antithetical to the interests of the majority of the Zimbabwean people. As the international community engages to assist Zimbabweans in transforming their political and economic relations, that community is also responsible for addressing international exigencies which will impede any Zimbabwean political leaders in pursuing national interests for transfers of land, for multiple regional markets, and for regional food security. By ignoring the global constraints, international actors set up a situation in which it will be difficult for any elected Government to rule. Alternative policies exist in the region, but they conflict with dominant international agendas. This source of crisis is as important to address as internal ones. The stakes are high, nothing less than the long-term viability of the political economies of Zimbabwe and Southern Africa.

11.6 MOUNTING INFLATION

According CCZ's bread basket for June 2007, a family of six now requires Z$8.2 million to live an average life. Families that live below this amount are regarded as poor. The figure shows an increase of 13,445 per cent in year-on-year inflation from $61097 (revalued) which was required by the same size of family in June 2006. The basic salaries have however failed to keep up with inflation. The CCZ attributed the rising breadline to increase in non-food items such as rent and household maintenance and a rise in basic commodities such as cooking oil, sugar, mealie-meal, rice and bread.

A packet of 2 kg rice recorded the highest jump of 34.714 per cent, while fresh milk (500 ml) went up by 32643 per cent. Transport cost was up 27.172 per cent while bread weighed in with 20.226 per cent (The Economist, 2007). Prices of important grocery commodities are given in Table 11.3.

The minimum wage is now about Z$130,000 a month but the tax threshold is only Z$15000 and most people now pay the top rate on their incomes of 40 to 45 per cent PLUS a series of levies (NSSA, Aids, Manddata, Standards) which raises the top tax rate to over 50 per cent. If NEC rates and pensions are taken out, most low income employees get less than Z$60,000 a month.

Table 11.3: Prices of Important Grocery Commodities in Zimbabwe

	Commodities	*Prices (Z$)*
1.	1 loaf bread	• $2,800
2.	1 dozen eggs	• $3,500
3.	2kg sugar	• $2,000
4.	500g powdered milk	• $18,000
5.	1kg mince	• $25,000
6.	2kg chicken portions	• $20,000
7.	750ml cooking oil	• $7,500
8.	1 packet cerevita cereal	• $8,000
9.	2 litres mazoe orange	• $10,000
10.	4 pack toilet rolls	• $3,500
11.	1 packet of 5 tomatoes	• $1,000
12.	1 packet onions	• $1,000
13.	1 banana	• $500
14.	1 orange	• $500
15.	1 apple	• $800
16.	1 packet 8 sanitary pads	• $8,000
17.	1kg of dried kapenta	• $5,000
18.	1 can heinz baked beans	• $4,017
19.	1kg margerine	• $10,000
20.	2kg rice	• $8,000
21.	1 litre coke	• $2,500
22.	1 bottle cane/vodka	• $9,700
23.	1 carton cigarettes	• $13,000
24.	500g pork sauages	• $12,000
25.	250g bacon	• $8,000

Source: Michael Wines (2007).

The average and the majority of Zimbabwean folk earn from a paltry $200,000 to $800,000. Few lower middle class earn $800,000 to $1-million. The middle class and above $1-million to infinity. International Monetary Fund warned that hyper inflation in Zimbabwe could reach a year-on-year rate of 100,000 per cent by the end of 2007, while the country's central bank announced the issuance of a Z$200,000 bank note[10] (Michael Wines, 2007). Economists blame inflation on massive Government money printing to pay Government expenses—but President Robert Mugabe was saying he wants to print more money to fund municipal projects.

11.7 ANTI-INFLATION CAMPAIGNS: CHAOS TO ECONOMY

Zimbabwe's campaign to quell its rampant inflation by physically forcing merchants to lower prices is edging the nation close to chaos. As the police and a pro-government youth militia swept into shops and factories, threatening arrest and worse unless prices were rolled back, staple foods vanished from store shelves and some merchants reported huge losses. News reports stated that some shopkeepers who refused to lower prices were beaten by the youth militia, known as the "Green Bombers" (Michael Wines, 2007). Crowds of ordinary citizens were following the police and militia from shop to shop, descending on the stores to buy goods at the Government-ordered prices. Because the Government has threatened to seize any business that does not sell goods at the advertised price, the merchants are keeping their shop open, but with virtually nothing on its shelves.

Economists warned that the price rollbacks were unsustainable and that shops and manufacturers would shut down and layoff their workers rather than produce goods at a loss. The economic collapse would quickly lead to social unrest if Zimbabwe's already shrunken workforce were hit by extensive layoffs and if foods like corn meal, cooking oil and sugar became unavailable.

President Robert Mugabe, who faced a controversial election in 2008, has often threatened to impose price controls over the eight-year course of Zimbabwe's economic decline, but the controls generally were short-lived and loosely enforced (Michael Wines, 2007). In contrast, the latest crackdown appears to be gathering momentum, as enforcers moved over the weekend to halt price increases by wholesalers and manufacturers as well as retailers. The Government's Ministry of Industry and International Trade ordered companies to roll back their prices to the levels of June 18, 2007, a reduction of roughly 50 per cent. Many initially ignored the command, but after Mugabe delivered a caustic nationally broadcast speech pledging to seize the assets of industries and businesses that evaded controls, the Government has more strictly enforced the order.

The Government intends to cope with the shortages by subsidizing producers of basic goods. Flour, which is controlled entirely by the State, will be sold to bakers for 10 million dollars a ton, half the market price. Similarly, many suppliers of basic goods have been insisted by the Government that they will be allowed to buy gasoline at one tenth the going price. The Government apparently plans to make up those losses by printing more money. Zimbabwe's dollar is loosing its value in every month because the Government has constantly issueing new bills to pay its mounting debts.

It is difficult to predict that inflation will come down without addressing the fundamental problems affecting the economy. Many a times authorities have tended to address symptoms and whether wittingly or unwittingly ignoring the actual disease. And indeed, basic figures kept by the Government itself indicate that the economy continues to point on a downward spiral unless foreign donors provide a drip for resuscitation. The last economic growth ever recorded was during the implementation of the western backed Economic Structural Adjustment Programme (ESAP) before the Government dumped it over disagreements with major donors (Chattopadhyay, 2000). As a consequence, the Government continues to borrow heavily from the domestic money market and recent figures show the debt at $46.1 trillion, up from $15.9 trillion the previous year. Basic commodities are very expensive and most families cannot afford the luxury of three-square meals a day and let alone transport and rent.

11.8. CONCLUSION

Zimbabwe, once the Southern Africa's second largest economy after South Africa, has become a laughing stock with its currency trading in thousands of dollars against regional currencies. The Zimbabwe dollar trading at 0.91 against the United States dollar in 1981 has been free falling even against the Zambian Kwacha to trade at well over $100 000, compared to a reverse exchange rate in January of 1997.

The economy of Zimbabwe is collapsing under the weight of international sanctions, almost total unemployment, and the highest rate of inflation in the world. The economy poorly transitioned from white-minority rule to majority rule in 1979, deteriorating from one of Africa's strongest economies to the world's worst. Inflation has surpassed that of all other nations at 11,000 per cent, with the next highest in Burma at 40 per cent.

Properly managed, Zimbabwe's wide range of resources should enable it to support continuing economic growth. The country has an important percentage of the world's known reserves of metallurgical-grade chromite. Other commercial mineral deposits include coal, asbestos, copper, nickel, gold, platinum and iron ore. However, its ongoing political turmoil and the world's highest rate of AIDS infection have greatly hampered its progress. Robert Mugabe's policies towards land reform have led to internal upheaval and population displacement, high inflation, and an inability of the country to feed itself.

(Note: This chapter was written when the Zimbabwean crisis was at its peak)

NOTES

1. Zimbabwe's inflation is hardly history's worst—in Weimar Germany in 1923, prices quadrupled each month, compared with doubling about once every three or four months in Zimbabwe.
2. 100 megawatts from the Democratic Republic of Congo, 200 megawatts from Mozambique and upto 450 from South Africa, and 300 megawatts from Zambia.
3. But Jesse Jackson commented during a visit to South Africa in June 2006, "Land reform has long been a noble goal to achieve but it has to be done in a way that minimises trauma. The process has to attract investors rather than scare them away. What is required in Zimbabwe is democratic rule, democracy is lacking in the country and that is the major cause of this economic melt down".
4. On November 1, 1989 a former Government Minister in Rhodesia, Denis Walker, produced a paper in London for the Conservative Monday Club's Foreign Affairs Committee on *Land Reform in Zimbabwe*. In his last paragraph he stated that "once the land has been redistributed, the commercial farms will be broken up, the remaining white farmers reduced by exile or imprisonment; Zimbabwe's Government, already morally bankrupt, will decline towards economic collapse."
5. However, the only sanctions in place are personal sanctions against

about 130 senior Zanu-PF figures; there are no sanctions against trade or investment with Zimbabwe.

6. As the US Secretary of State, in 1976 Henry Kissinger promised ZANU (Zimbabwe African National Union) and ZAPU (Zimbabwe African People's Union) US$ 1-1.5 billion to facilitate economic transition, including land transfers, as part of the agreement to end guerrilla warfare. To date, the United States Government has delivered zero for land reform. The United Kingdom's role is almost the same, making promises and delivering very little.
7. The Director of Seed Co-estimated the maize production on minuscule urban plots would be about 50 tonnes/ha if the same labour intensity (constant vigilance) and inputs were used on a hectare plot. It is only in recent times that people in "born townships" (established in early 1920s) refuse to go home to the rural areas. Many Zimbabweans are genuinely land-hungry — they know how to farm and desire small plots of land. Urbanization in Zimbabwe has not followed the US pattern of cutting all links with the rural community.
8. The WTO and the USA Trade and Development Act (the old AGOA) further assist the privileged, by requiring "national treatment" of foreign firms. If a foreign corporation wants to buy land in Zimbabwe, the Government is supposed to treat it equally to any Zimbabwean request. If a foreign corporation wants to sell seed or access the national gene bank, it is supposed to be treated equally to Seed Co.
9. Worse still, such decisions about agricultural production are ones neither the US nor the EU has been willing to relinquish to the global market. Before the WTO in 1989, for example, the US rate of farm subsidies stood at 25 per cent, yet by 1999, it remained 24 per cent. During the same period, EU supports were 44 per cent of gross farm receipts in 1989 and 49 per cent in 1999.
10. It has become harder to estimate actual inflation in the absence of any official data releases.

REFERENCES

Adams, Martin and John, Howell (2001). "Redistributive Land Reform in Southern Africa," *Natural Resource Perspectives*, No. 64, January, Overseas Development Institute.

Blessing, Zulu (2007). 'IMF Officials Warns Zimbabwe Consumer Inflation Headed for 100,000 per cent, *Interview with IMF Officials*, July 31, Washington.

Chattopadhyay, Rupak (2000). "Zimbabwe: Structural Adjustment,

Destitution, and Food Insecurity," *Review of African Political Economy*, No. 84, 307-316.

Dhliwayo, Rogers (2001). *The Impact of Public Expenditure Management under ESAP on Social Services: Health and Education*, Paper presented at the Structural Adjustment Participatory Review Initiative (SAPRI) Poverty Reduction Forum, Harare, Zimbabwe, 9-10 April.

Kinsey, B.H. (2000). "The Implications of Land Reform for Rural Welfare," *Land Reform in Zimbabwe—Constraints and Prospects*, ed. T.A.S Bowyer-Bower and Colin Stoneman, Aldershot: Ashgate.

Kinsey, B.H. (1999). "Land Reform, Growth and Equity: Emerging Evidence from Zimbabwe's Resettlement Programme," *Journal of Southern African Studies* 25, No. 2, 169-192.

Michael, Wines (2006). 'How Bad is Inflation in Zimbabwe?', *The New York* Times, May 2.

Michael, Wines (2007). 'Zimbabwe's Anti-inflation Campaign brings Chaos to Economy,' *Internet Source*, July 5.

Moyo, Sam (2000a). *The Interaction of Market and Compulsory Land Acquisition Processes with Social Action in Zimbabwe's Land Reform*, Paper presented at Sapes Trust Annual Colloquium, Harare, Zimbabwe, 24-27 September.

Moyo, Sam (2000b). *Land Reform under Structural Adjustments in Zimbabwe—Land Use in the Mashonaland Provinces*. Uppsala: Nordiska Afrikainstitutet.

Paul, Nyakazeya (2007). 'Zimbabwe: June Inflation 13000 per cent', *Zimbabwe Independent*, July 27.

Potts, Debby (2000). "Zimbabwean People's Perceptions of the Land Resettlement Programme: The Case of Rural-Urban Migrants," *Land Reform in Zimbabwe—Constraints and Prospects*, ed. T.A.S Bowyer-Bower and Colin Stoneman, Aldershot: Ashgate.

Poverty Reduction Forum and Institute for Development Studies (PRFIDS) (1999). *Human Development Report*, Zimbabwe, Harare: UNDP.

The Economist, (2007). *How to Stay Alive when it all run out*, July 12.

UNCTAD, (2000). *African Development in Comparative Perspective*, World Press, Trenton, NJ.

Van Zyl, Johann; Nick Vink, Johann Kirsten, Danswan Poonyth, (2001). "South African Agriculture in Transition: the 1990s," *Journal of International Development* 13, No. 6, 725-739.

12

Role of NGOs in Rural Development in Africa

A Case of Oromo Self-Help Organization (OSHO) in Ethiopia

12.1 INTRODUCTION

The Oromo Self-Help Organization is a non-profit, non-political, and non-religious humanitarian organization with the aim of contributing to relief, rehabilitation and development of Oromia Region in Ethiopia. It was implementing projects with different funding sources since 2003 in the field of integrated food security and rural infrastructure (However, OSHO is implementing projects in Oromia region in various fields since 1995).

OSHO's Development Oriented Emergency Food Aid Project's contributions can be analyzed in terms of its role in poverty reduction, employment generation, reduction of unemployment, and food aid and the like activities. The objective of this chapter is to address and to analyse the socio-economic results of OSHO's above said project in the field of food security and to know its effectiveness in rural development in Ziway Dugda Woreda (Panchayat).

The specific objectives of this chapter include:

(i) To investigate the socio-economic contributions of OSHO's Development Oriented Emergency Food Aid Project in the project area; and
(ii) To know the structural changes that have taken place by using result-based project evaluation.

Secondary data obtained from the Woreda Office and from the organization are used in this chapter.

12.2 ROLE OF NGOs IN ETHIOPIA

Ethiopia is characterized by efforts of the Government to establish structural stability as per the constitution of 1994 and the general principle of good governance; the legal and constitutional framework provides a federal system with democratic and decentralized decision making. However, the political and administrative culture is rooted and influenced by periods of strong centralization in feudalistic and socialistic system. New norms of cooperation and development of effective coordination platform at the interfaces between all level (from national to local, State and civil society) have to be developed. Important success emerged in the form of inclusion of non governmental or no party actors in political decision-making processes; unique dialogue between the Government and civil society (FDRE, 2005). The key development problems of Ethiopia is linked to this transformation processes. Wars and famines have had set backs for development efforts. Government structures at all levels have limited capacity in applying the still fragile structure of the federal system and to provide basic service for the population and to fight poverty.

In the framework of local development effort, local NGOs have become increasingly important and are gaining acceptance on the part of State representatives. These local development efforts provide platform for new forms of cooperation between State and civil society as both are involved in this programmes and to widen the space of the civil society to assure their role in decision-making processes which affects their development needs and aspirations.

In Ethiopia the NGO sector has been playing a prominent role since the Derg Regime. During the crisis in the Eighties international emergency aid was channeled almost entirely through the NGOs. Today, there are around 270 NGOs registered in Ethiopia of which about 125 are international (HRD, 2005). Many of the Ethiopian NGOs are closely linked to the Government and operate in relief, rehabilitation and charity with rather conservative approaches. A small group is even active in the fields of promoting democratization;

however advocacy, civil and legal education, networking and cooperation have never been a characteristic of the NGO sector in Ethiopia.

National NGOs have often been the artificial product of the international need for tools for the delivery of the relief assistance, and indigenous consolidation of civil society. NGOs emerged in the Nineties tend to be more aware of their privileges (For instance, duty free import of equipment) than their responsibilities. The Government has been by and large, suspicious of the NGO sector, concerned by what it sees as the undesirable "inefficiency and competition for hearts and minds" engendered by the establishment of a parallel or plural resource provision system (Christine, M., 2004). These attitudes have led to the establishment of a regulatory environment which some NGOs regard as "in-conductive and obstructive to their operations".

The current administrative procedure as part of the legalization for NGOs refers the registration of NGOs at the federal level. This has to be renewed every year based on the results of an external auditing. NGOs, which do not fulfill this requirement, might not be able to reconfirm their legal status. For a first time registration of an NGO considerable number of pre-conditions have to be met, which could prevent or atleast delay registration. On the other hand, those stipulations could also be seen as an advantage for a sustainable institutional set up of actors as they prevent ad-hoc groups with firm structure and clear vision themselves as NGOs (FDRE, 2005). However, in the framework of local development effort, local NGOs become slowly more important and gained acceptance on the part of State representatives. There are also voices from the Government encouraging all civil society organizations to engage in development activities within the overall objective to empower grassroot organizations. There was no hindrance in the cooperation of registered NGOs with non-registered grassroot initiatives such as community based organizations and self-help groups.

Recently the Government of Ethiopia is encouraging and supporting the establishment of various NGOs for their socio-economic contributions and for their developmental role. As a result NGOs movement is expanding and growing at a rapid race. Accordingly many NGOs with different aims and objectives are spreading in the country. It may be for charity and development purpose, profit purpose, religious purpose, trade purpose, and so on.

12.3 BACKGROUND OF THE DEVELOPMENT ORIENTED EMERGENCY FOOD AID PROJECT

The German Development Cooperation plays an important role in supporting the efforts of the Government to establish federal system processes to develop the culture of cooperation and consultation according to the intention of the legal and constitutional framework. One of the three priority areas of Ethio-German Cooperation is capacity-building in governance including strengthening of federalism, decentralized governance and the democratic system in Ethiopia. The programme has also experience in open-self-help fund and with regional and development planning projects which aimed at strengthening policy advice capabilities of agencies of the Ethiopian federal system at Central and regional levels.

Another important evidence of the German Co-operation in this area is provided by the present project at the local level which is implemented by the OSHO with the support of the German Agro Action (DWHH/GAA). Emergency aid is combined with rural development and capacity development for the State actors as well as the beneficiaries. Its main goals are to ensure the survival of drought victims (OSHO, 2004). This programme got benefits from the experiences of previous successful projects in the same region. For a detailed account see the Appendix Table of this Chapter. Major elements of its strategy are participation, coordination, transparency and emphasis on the selection of the beneficiary.

The Project "Developmental Oriented Emergency Food Aid in Ziway Dugda" is implemented by Oromo Self-Help Organization (OSHO) with the financial and technical support of DWHH/GAA founded by BMZ. The visit to this project was suggested by DWHH/ GAA (Deutsch Welt hunger hilfe/German Agro Action) as an example of a participatory project under difficult framework condition. The main project goal is to help the target groups to overcome the acute deficiency in food staples by reducing their structural susceptibility to drought consequences. The development orientation of this relief project is expressed in particular by the rehabilitation and construction of rural infrastructure and the protection of natural resources mainly through Food-For-Work (FFW) and Cash-For Work (CFW) programmes (OSHO, 2004). In addition, it also targeted the development of self help capacities of rural households and the capacity of the local administration.

The project in 2002 and 2003 focused on 27 Kebeles (Wards) in three different Woredas (Panchayats) of Arsi zone in Oromiya Region. The project area in 2004 comprised only 6 Kebeles in Ziway Dugda Woreda. The project was integrated into the emergency planning of DPPC (Disaster Prevention and Preparedness Commission) which has the mandate of coordinating all international donors in the field of relief aid (FAO, 2004). The core elements of its implementation approach are sustainability, participation in planning, result-based monitoring and evaluation, gender sensitivity, introduction and institutionalization of innovations, empowerments and capacity building of stockholders. OSHO targeted resource poor and economically weaker peasants association of the Woredas with more emphasis on poorest households and most deprived and marginalized sections in the society.

12.4 PROJECT SITE AND THE TARGET GROUPS

Ziway Dugda Woreda is a highly drought prone area with total population of 102,142. People are primarily agrarian; income they generate from their occupation are very low and even it is not sufficient to feed their family for a whole year. The population was by and large under-nourished and deprived, especially vulnerable during drought years.

(i) Agro-climatic Conditions

Arsi Zone is part of Oromiyo Region and is located in the south-east of Central Ethiopia. Administratively, it comprises of 20 Woredas. Due to the climatic conditions and structural problems, majority of the area is affected by chronic and repeatedly acute food security problems, including that of 2004. Ziway Dugda Woreda is facing drought and environmental degradation from time to time due to its location and around 97 per cent of the inhabitants live in rural areas

(OSHO, 2004). Survival of these subsistence farmers depends on the cultivation of wheat, maize, teff, barley, sorghum, and beans as well as animal husbandry. The average land holding per family is about 1.7 ha. With elevation between 1550 m and 1800 m, the area is divided in medium altitude and that is particularly drought affected.

The agro-ecological climate is semi-arid. Administratively, Ziway Dugda Woreda is divided into 34 rural and one urban Kebele (Ogolcho). The structural cause of the low productivity of the agricultural sectors is due to its complete dependence on rain, land scarcity relative to the population growth, uncertainty for the farmers due to the landholding system, irregular, delayed and insufficient rainfall, lack of inputs and ploughs, lack of grazing land and overgrazing, weakly elaborated traditions in agriculture as a result of the traditional emphasis on cattle breeding, inadequate Government advisory/extension service systems in agriculture and mobilization of the workforce for Government initiated mass campaign (For instance, the unsuccessful water harvesting pond campaign).

The chronic food-insecurity of Ziway-Dugda is also caused by the weakness of the district structure and administration. Malaria and other water-born diseases are rampant. At present about 65 per cent (earlier 10%) of the population have access to safe potable water due to the intervention by OSHO in the past years (mainly flat wells with handpumps).

(ii) Socio-Cultural Backwardness

Social taboos and traditional practices, particularly with respect to women and girls are widespread; genital mutilation, forced marriage, abduction for the purpose of marriage, rape, polygamy, and the compulsory take over of a widow by the next male relative of the deceased husband. Means methods of family planning are largely unknown as well as not accessible. The participation of women in decision-making processes within the family, at a village and district level are very low. Although, the legal situation for women in Ethiopia has improved in many aspects under the present Government (right of inheritance, divorce, ownership of land, protection against HTP and other violent physical action), traditional practices in rural areas such as that in Ziway Dugda have to date remained largely unchanged.

(iii) Healthcare and Demography

Healthcare services in the project area are limited to 5 clinics, 5 healthcare centres and 5 rural pharmacies/drug stores. About 24 per cent of the children die before reaching the age of 5 years (OSHO, 2004). More than 50,000 of the population (around 48%) in Ziway Dugda are lesser than 15 years of age. The Woreda has 25 elementary schools and one high school. Teacher student ratio is on an average 84 and 67 at elementary and high schools respectively (OSHO, 2004). About 15-25 per cent of the students are females. During the past years, the number of female students has steadily increased. School attendance decreases sharply during periods of drought and food deficiency, because the students have to work in order to assist the survival of families. During these periods, they are involved in collection of edible plants and also firewoods for the production of charcoal as additional income.

(iv) Infrastructural Facilities

The asphalt road from Addis to Awasa connects the project site to the Capital and an all weather gravel road connects Meki district and Assella district. Despite this road connectivity and the vicinity to the capital, the area is extremely marginalized; electric power is not available, telecommunication services are intermittently available through one telephone line in the district town Ogolcho. Major markets in the project area are located in the neighbouring district, Meki and Ziway. OSHO, through the support of earlier donors have constructed project building (offices and small warehouses) in Ogolcho. The water supply in Ogolcho is depended on local wells.

12.5 DEVELOPMENT ORIENTED EMERGENCY FOOD AID PROJECT

The present project involved all 35 Kebeles of the Ziway Dugda Woreda, located in Arsi Zone, which was recurrently hit by droughts and environmental damages. The project location is in the low lands of the Rift Valley, some 200 km South-east of the Ethiopian capital of Addis Ababa. The main sources of income in the project area are from rainfed agricultural and cattle breeding.

The target group of the project is resource poor drought affected subsistence farmers (agro-pastoralists), whose food security is structurally endangered and their survival during the past ten years have been acutely threatened as a result of recurrent droughts. The target group is ethnically a homogenous group, of whom more than 95 per cent are Arsi Oromo. The method of "participatory public community targeting," which has been successfully employed by OSHO since 2003, involves the whole village community, which undertakes the selection according to the criteria of need and potential.

The project of OSHO is categorized in the area of development oriented emergency and transition assistance, and its aim is to ensure the survival of drought victims and at the same time to reduce the structural causes of chronic vulnerability of food insecurity (OSHO, 2004). Promotion of self-help capacity of the affected people in the area was given priority in order to contribute towards better susceptibility of drought effects.

In the project area (1,044 km^2), about 300 km of rural roads have been constructed by the inhabitants of the Woredas (mainly by the BMZ financed intervention in the preceding years) and this road construction activities will continue in the coming years. The possibilities for the generation of non-agricultural income in the project area are very limited and offer mainly the production and sales of charcoals. In the past ten years, the situation in Ziway Dugda is characterized by food deficiency, as a result of the aforementioned facts and irregular rainfalls and extremely high population growth. The agricultural produce was not sufficient, even in "good years" to feed the population, which in turn led to famines and food deficiency in many parts of the Woreda.

Since 1995, OSHO has been implementing projects in Ziway Dugda in the areas of rural potable water supply, healthcare, emergency relief and integrated food security (OSHO, 2004). In the past twelve years 14 projects with an estimated cost of \$ 7,775,046 has been implemented by OSHO, which benefited 864,497 people (See Appendix Table of this chapter).

12.6 RESULT-BASED MONITORING AND EVALUATION

Result-Based Monitoring and Evaluation (RMBE) is an exercise to assess the performance of an institution and/or a programme or a project, on the basis of impacts and benefits that the institution and/ or the programme/project is expected to produce. Traditional monitoring and evaluation method measures and reports status of results, which is in the form of a reactive tool. On the other hand RBME measures and reports results to produce results, which is a pro-active tool (Christine, M., 2004). RMBE is often seen as a dynamic tool of planning and budgeting for improving substantive performance and achieving results.

For the application of RBME we have to identify important indicators. Indicators are signs that show changes or progress that have been induced by an activity or a set of activities. On the basis of indicators performance or results of a project can be identified. Indicators are classified as follows:

(i) Performance levels of indicators; which includes—

- Institutional/Agency level indicators, and
- 'Developmental' or Programme/Project level indicators.

(ii) 'Thematic' indicators.

All these levels of indicators must be inter-linked with one another in a complementary manner to contribute to a Strategic Results Framework (SRF) for the entire development management process.

Institutional level indicators attached to every institution (Ministry, Department or an agency) are established to perform a particular function or to deliver a package of quality services, both current as well as future. It should also make contributions to the sector to which the institution belongs as well as to the economy as a whole (HRD, 2005). These roles and responsibilities of an institution are expressed through its vision and mission statements. Results of 'vision' and 'mission' outcomes are the institutional indicators.

On the other hand the project level indicator, which is used in the present paper, depends on the project. A project is an activity or a set of activities that are undertaken either to overcome a problem and/or to develop an opportunity. Under RBME before implementing the project we should know answers to the following questions.

- ❖ What will be the impacts?
- ❖ What will it achieve?
- ❖ What will it produce?
- ❖ What are the activities and resources needed? and
- ❖ What are the external factors?

Successful implementation of a project should be based on the solid steps such as statement of problems, articulation of long-term development objectives/impact indicators, immediate objectives/effect indicators, expected outputs/output indicators, activities/inputs/ financial resources, and understanding of threats, risks, complementarities etc. Development objective is the main overall objective of the project that is meant to contribute to in the long-run, as impacts. It should be used as the main point of reference and should be clearly defined. At the same time it should not be too ambitious and too broad. It should be stated in a manner that the immediate objective will significantly contribute to achieving the development objectives (FAO, 2004). It represents sufficient justification for the project and should be expressed as a desired end and not as a mean (or a process). Development objectives should be expressed in verifiable terms.

The immediate objective sets out the operational purpose of the project and it gives the anticipated achievement of the project but it is outside the project's direct control. It will determine the magnitude of the project both in terms of resources and strategy. Immediate objectives should not be too ambitious, unclear or complex. It is likely to occur once the project outputs have been produced. A project should have only one immediate objective and should be formulated as a desired state, not a process. It should be precisely and verifiably defined. The outputs are the results that can be guaranteed by the project as a consequence of its activities (HRD, 2005). It is to be ensured that all essential outputs for achieving the project objective should be included. It is also to be ensured that only the outputs that can be guaranteed by the project management are included. We should ensure that all outputs are feasible within the available resources, outputs are precisely and verifiably defined, and each output can be seen as a necessary mean to achieve the immediate objective.

An activity is an action, which is necessary to transform given inputs into planned outputs within a specified period of time. Regarding the activities we should ensure that all essential activities necessary to produce the anticipated outputs are included, all activities contribute directly to the output level above, only those activities to be performed by the project are included, activities are stated in terms of actions being undertaken rather than completed outputs, the time available for each activity is realistic, and activities are acceptable in terms of economic, social, and moral grounds.

12.7 APPLYING RBME IN DEVELOPMENT ORIENTED EMERGENCY FOOD AID PROJECT

The main objective of the present project was improvement of the living standard of the targeted population through income generation in the form of social asset creation (infrastructures including roads, water supply, irrigation schemes, schools/hospital construction, etc.) to ensure food security, initiation of micro-enterprises in agriculture and non-agriculture sectors in the villages through micro-financing facilities and modernizing the society through social awareness campaigns and trainings by giving special focus on women.

Major results to be achieved through the project are categorized into three:

(i) Ensure food security through income generation;
(ii) Development of micro-enterprises; and
(iii) Modernization of the society.

Beneficiaries were identified through the participatory public community targeting, which has been successfully applied by the OSHO for the last five years and ensures a high quality with respect to take over of responsibility, transparency, justice and targeted considerations of disadvantaged groups without lobby. The project has undertaken Cash For Work (CFW) activities in support of the livelihood security of the targeted population, especially during the months of highest food deficiency (August–November) by undertaking other agricultural works (OSHO, 2007). These measures also support the target groups to acquire productive and suitable assets with which they can even overcome the preceding emergency situations. The project generated 38 working days of employment per target population at a rate of 35 rupees (7 Ethiopian Birr).

Table 12.1: Infrastructure Created through FFW and CFW by OSHO, 2007

No.	*Infrastructure*	*Completed*	*Ongoing*	*Total*	*Beneficiaries*
1.	Pump Irrigation	8 pumps, 48 ha	2 pumps, 91.5 ha	10 pumps, 139 ha	558 households, 2790 people
2.	Gravity Irrigation	1 scheme, 25 ha	—	25 ha	100 households, 500 people
3.	Elementary School Construction	10	1	11	4,480 students
4.	School Expansion	2	—	—	1,280 students
5.	Clinic, new Construction	5	1	6	18,000 people
6.	Clinic Maintenance	2	—	2	3,000 people
7.	Water Supply, Shallow Well	10	—	10	726 households, 3630 people
8.	Water Supply, Roof Water, Harvesting Reservoirs	9	6	15	7,500 students
9.	Veterinary Clinic Construction	2	1	3	9,000 households
10.	New Road Construction	281.5 km	-	281.5 km	
11.	Road Maintenance	227 km	30 km	257 km	
12.	Bridge Construction	2	—	2	
13.	Community Managed Seed Bank Construction	26 seed stores	—	26 seed stores	

Source: OSHO's Programme Implementation Report, 2007.

The planned implementation through the Productive Safety Net Programme (PSNP) activities was combined with the CFW activities. The number of man-days for each activity is set in such a way that on the average about 20 per cent additional work output has to be delivered by the target groups through own contribution (OSHO, 2007). Alongwith CFW, Food For Work (FFW) programme was also implemented by OSHO. Thirteen projects were implemented by OSHO under FFW and CFW in the study area. It includes construction of irrigation projects, school/hospital, veterinary hospitals, water supply/rainwater harvesting, road/bridges and community managed seed banks. Details of the projects are given in Table 12.1.

The project generated both direct and indirect benefits in the study area; directly the society is assisted with either cash or food for their daily work and indirectly the infrastructure they constructed have improved their own socio-economic welfare.

Along with income generation activities OSHO also promoted thrift habit among the target groups through micro-finance activities mainly for women as part of the Development Oriented Emergency Food Aid Project. It was based on saving, guarantee groups and free selection of business activity, where small credit was invested. The groups opened their account at Oromia Credit and Saving Share Company (OCSSC), which has a branch in the district town Ogolocho. They established themselves a credit and saving cooperative and to this end the groups were given training in operation and management of saving, credit and cooperatives. After the completion of the project extension services and further training were given by OSHO and the Department of Cooperative Development in the district. The major achievements in this area are given in Table 12.2.

Table 12.2: Micro Financing and Credit Provision by OSHO, 2007

No.	*Activity*	*Completed*	*Ongoing*	*Total*	*Beneficiaries*
1.	Women credit and saving/ cooperatives establishment	3 WCS/ primary cooperatives with 138 women members	3 primary cooperatives with 120 volunteer women for saving	6 WCS/ primary cooperatives, with 258 women members	1,290 family members and neighboured community
2.	Transformation of Community Managed Seed Bank (CMSB) to Grain Banks	5, Community Managed Grain Banks with 1,250 Members	Secure the legal entity for cooperatives	5 community managed grain Banks with 1,250 members	6,250 family members and neighboured community

Source: OSHO's Pogramme Implementation Report, 2007.

The selection of beneficiaries was through a synchronized criteria having equal weightage to economic backwardness and educational levels. Selected members were given training in micro-finance related areas such as capacity-building in entrepreneurship in micro-enterprises and credit management.

The third main objective of the OSHO's project is modernizing the society by ensuring gender development, eradication of HIV/AIDS through public awareness and education, family planning and eradication of social taboos which is strongly rooted in the rural societies. Emphasis was also given to development of agriculture and related sectors and alternative technology training. OSHO initiated massive public awareness campaign in this regard through popular training programmes. In each Kebele a committee was set up dedicated to the handling of the themes within the community and it also drawn up a working plan (OSHO, 2007). OSHO gave special emphasis to women in these training/public awareness programmes (by ensuring atleast 75 per cent of the trained). Trainers were from among both international and national gender experts of OSHO. All the Government employees of the district administration actively participated in the co-ordination activities of the programme. Both trainers and trainees were given per-diem for attending the training workshops. Details of the training programme are given in Table 12.3.

Table 12.3: Training and Capacity-Building

No.	*Activity*	*Completed*	*Ongoing*	*Total Beneficiarie*
1.	Agricultural Techniques, Irrigation and Animal Husbandry Training	1,496 Households	440 Households	1,936 Households
2.	Gender, HIV/AIDS, Family Planning, HTP	14,055 Households	6,000 Households	20,055 Householo
3.	Alternative Technology Training	66 Households as Community Trainers	330 Households Community Members	About 396 Households and Community Members
4.	Micro Finance Saving and Credit Management	138 Women	120 Women	258 Women
5.	Financial and Cooperative Management	130 Committee Members	14 Committee Members	144 Committee Members became Beneficiary

Source: OSHOs Report on Capacity-Building.

12.8 CONCLUSION

Under the action of OSHO by the year 2000 about 39,717 people in 23 Kebeles had received food aid for a period of nine months. In the year 2003 about 76,000 and in 2004 about 9,000 were supported through food rationing within the framework of two BMZ financed emergency programmes that have been implemented by OSHO/BMZ. Under the action of OSHO and its overall goals, the food security of the population of Ziway Dugda Woreda has insured to a great extent and their susceptibility to the consequences of drought has reduced. During the project duration the targeted groups could overcome their acute deficiency in food staples and have reduced their structural susceptibility to drought consequences.

The major achievements of the project, which can be quantified through results in Ziway Dugda are the following:

(i) *Securing immediate survival/food security*: Diversification of agricultural production and introduction of non-agricultural activities and income generation have directly promoted the food security atleast by enhancing the villagers' entitlement to food.

(ii) *Mobilization of self-help and food security through self-help*: The measures and interventions for building infrastructure, resource conservation and securing farm production bases had important components which contributed towards the promotion of self-help potentials in achieving sustainable food production. Training programmes and systematic follow ups with a view to strengthen the self-help capacity promoted the independent management of production and marketing.

(iii) *Strengthening agricultural extensions*: Innovative interventions in areas such as irrigation, introduction and expansion of drought-resistant seeds had direct results in food production. These measures enabled the beneficiary farmers to replenish productive and secured properties. These had direct effect on the vulnerability to food insecurity. Marketing of seeds, cattles, and construction materials promoted the development of local markets and transportation.

(iv) *Overcoming emergency situations such as droughts, and long-term developments including the modernization of the society from the socio-cultural structural backwardness*: The project was mainly aimed at equipping the local communities in overcoming the drought triggered food insecurity. Through this intervention the project helped in the strategic improvement at the household level by promoting the livelihood security.

REFERENCES

Christine, Magistretti (2004). *NGO's Contribution to the Deliberation of the European Population Forum,* Genewa.

Eric, Tollens (1998). *Food Security in ACP Countries*, Leuven, Belgium.

Federal Democratic Republic of Ethiopia (FDRE), (2005). *Equality between National, State, Local to Civil Society*, Report of the Ministry of Finance.

Food and Agriculture Organization (FAO), (2004). *Crop and Food Supply Assessment*, Crop and Food Supply Assessment Mission to Ethiopia, Addis Ababa.

Human Resource Department (HRD), (2005). *NGO Agency Material Management Training for NGOs Promotion,* Federal Democratic Republic, Addis Ababa, December.

OSHO, (2004). *Proposal on Rural Development in Ziway Dugda*, Addis Ababa.

OSHO, (2007). *Programme Implementation Report, 2007*, Addis Ababa.

APPENDIX

Table 12.A.1: Projects/programmes implemented by OSHO in Ziway Dugda, 1997-2004

Year	*Donor*	*Beneficiaries*	*Location*	*Project Content*	*Budget in US Dollar*
1997-1999	OCAA	24,000	Ziway-Dugda	Water supply	157,400
1998-1999	Ethio-Italian Cooperation	5,000	Ziway-Dugda	Water supply Ogolcho	88,500
1999-2001	EU	32,980	Ziway-Dugda	Integrated food security	349,300
2000-2001	EU, OCAA, DWHH	146,987	Ziway-Dugda and others	Emergency food relief	2,025,388
2001	UNOPS/ICU	2,000	Z-D, Arata	Water supply	122,356
2002-2003	OFSO	9,550	Z-D, Merti	Integrated food security	516,000
2002-2003	EU	364,563	Gololcha	Emergency food relief	1,519,040
2003-2003	CRDA	15,000	Z-D	Water supply	19,075
2003-2003	BMZ, DWHH	39,785	Z-D	Devt. Oriented, emergency relief food	441,823
2003	OCAA	28,222	Adama, Dugda, Z-D	Emergency food relief	247,464
2003	BMZ, USAID, OFA, DWHH	76,000	Z-D	Devt. Oriented emergency food relief	1,300,000
2003	USAID/OFA	57,500	Z-D	Emergency relief, seeds	278,700
2003-2004	USAID/OFDA	13,000	Z-D	Water supply	85,000
2003-2004	BMZ	50,000	Z-D	Devt. Oriented emergency relief	625,000
TOTAL		864,497			7,775,046

Source: OSHO's Programme Implementation Report, 2007.

13

Non-Western Ideologies of Economic Development

Quest for an Indigenous Sub-Saharan African Model

13.1 INTRODUCTION

During the latter decades of the Twentieth Century the Third World saw the emergence of indigenous and domestically grown theories of economic development. Much of the development literature, which originated in the Western World failed in the developing countries due to the socio-economic and political institutional differences and it resulted in the realization that the Third World need not imitate the development experience of the West. After failures of west-led developmentalism and the resultant socio-economic repercussions in Africa, Asia, and Latin America in Twentieth century, the idea of indigenous grown theories of development become more attractive among the intellectuals. These models of development were more closely attuned to local conditions than the imported and often ill-fitting western ones. Accordingly a Sub-Saharan African theory of development, an East Asian theory (Confucian Theory), an Indian theory (Hindu Model), a Latin American theory, and an Islamic theory of development were emerged. The present Chapter discusses the need, opportunity and practical difficulties of the Sub-Saharan African Model. It also reviews the emergence of indigenous models of development in the region and the influence of the West including colonization.

13.2 SPACE FOR NON-WESTERN MODELS OF ECONOMIC DEVELOPMENT

Middle of the Twentieth Century witnessed independence of many countries in Asia, Africa and Lain America from their Western colonial powers. During the colonial period these countries' social, political, and economic institutions were restructured by the ruling powers on the Western lines. Accordingly just after independence these colonial regions were forced to follow the same development models that existed in the West. One of the most influential development models was that of W.W. Rostow. As per this model all countries should pass through different stages in their path to development from underdevelopment to take off, to drive to maturity and to modernity (For a detailed discussion read Rostow W.W, 1960). The inevitable and universal movement through different stages of development was propagated by the Western Universities and policy-makers in the developing regions. Rostow's analysis with its antiseptic processes and happy ending had a major impact on the reorganization of U.S foreign assistance programmes, of which he was the chief.

Major criticisms raised against the Western models of development include (Wiarda H.J, 1983):

- Ethnocentric, based on American or European models that often had little relevance to the Third World;
- Combined all developing regions together regardless of socio-economic and institutional differences between Africa, Asia and Latin America;
- Suggested all socio-economic and political developments go together, but what really experienced in the developing regions is that socio-economic modernization has disrupted political stability;
- Ignored class conflicts during the transitional stages of development;
- Ignored international factors and influences such as transnational religious bodies, global market forces and international lending agencies;
- Misinterpretation of traditional institutions by giving way to the new ones, however, what we witnessed is adaptation to the changes. In many cases it even destroyed traditional institutions; and

- Tied to the U.S and Western foreign policy goals of creating stable, friendly, middle class societies.

The idea of building a development model based on local institutions and practices reflected not only dissatisfaction with existing models but also nationalistic, cultural, and ethnic pride in utilizing 'third world' institutions and practices. Indigenous models of development flowered and flourished during the last, waning decades of the Cold War when the two major superpowers and the rival systems they represented, capitalism and socialism, both seemed to be in trouble. However, during the Cold War period almost all developing regions were divided on developmental lines by following either the U.S-led capitalist path or the Soviet-led Socialist path.

The emergence of Non-Alignment Movement (NAM) is the Third World's quest for an independent World, where they can enjoy socio-economic and political justice. These group of countries refused to align themselves with either Cold War bloc—and asserted their own foreign policies and development models—was at the same time an expression of greater nationalism and independence[1].

After the disintegration of the Soviet Union and the Eastern Europe and the resultant end of the Cold war the developing regions started strengthening and practicing their own and indigenous grown development models. It is the period when free market or neo-liberal economic policies acquired the cachet of a new orthodoxy and is known as the culture of consumerism.

13.3 MODERNIZATION THEORY *VS* DEPENDENCY THEORY: A NON-WESTERN VIEW

The multi-faceted field of modernization theory has three dimensions. Firstly, the process since the industrial revolution and the political revolutions at the end of the 18th century when the small group of today's modern societies developed in Western Europe and North America; Secondly, the many successful and unsuccessful efforts to catch up and reduce the gap to the leading societies by poorer and less developed countries; Finally, the efforts of the modern societies to cope—via innovation and reform—with new internal problems and, more importantly, with the changing international and globalizing environment (Zapf, 1991).

Based on the main features of modern societies the modernization can be defined as the mechanisms of inclusion, value pluralism, differentiation and status upgrading (*i.e.* welfare development). It also includes the basic institutions, which mean basic societal inventions, namely, competitive democracy, the market economy, mass consumption, and the welfare state (Zapf, 1991). A more dynamic definition is given by Johannes Berger: "Modernization is the internal achievement of a society; the particular processes of modernization support each other in combination; the leading nations do not impede the followers; the processes of modernization are converging in a common goal" (modern society, modernity) (Berger, 1996). This means that development cannot be explained by exploitation nor can it be accomplished by simply copying institutions. Despite the basic fact of rising differentiation there is the parallel process of rising interdependence. Despite visible trends of globalization the indigenous forces are decisive (*See* Figure 13.1).

Figure 13.1: Modernization Process (Modernization: I)

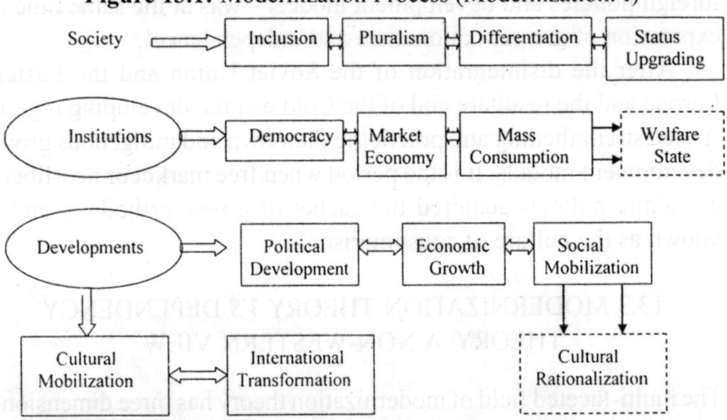

Jeffrey Alexander (1994) distinguishes four stages of the modernization, which coincide roughly with the last four decades of the 20th century: the 1960s, 1970s, 1980s and the 1990s. Early modernization theory reconstructed Western development and, in its liberal belief of granted progress and the universalization of American values, projected them world-wide, especially on the developing countries. One popular model combines political development (state- and nation-building, participation, redistribution), economic growth, and social mobilization with cultural rationalization, psychic mobilization and international transformation (Zapf, 1969).

Against this doctrine a radical Marxist criticism of capitalism arose in dependency theory and in world-systems theory. Both explained underdevelopment at the periphery by exploitation through the capitalist centre. The dependency school believes that dependency is an external condition, that the centre nations get all the benefits from unequal exchange, and that the peripheral countries should sever their ties with the core countries (*See* Figure 13.2). The world system school adds the concept of semi-peripheries with an economic emphasis on import-substitution; this school shifts its focus from the nation-state to the whole world; long-term historical trends are its units of analysis (So, A, 1990).

Figure 13.2: Dependency Argument

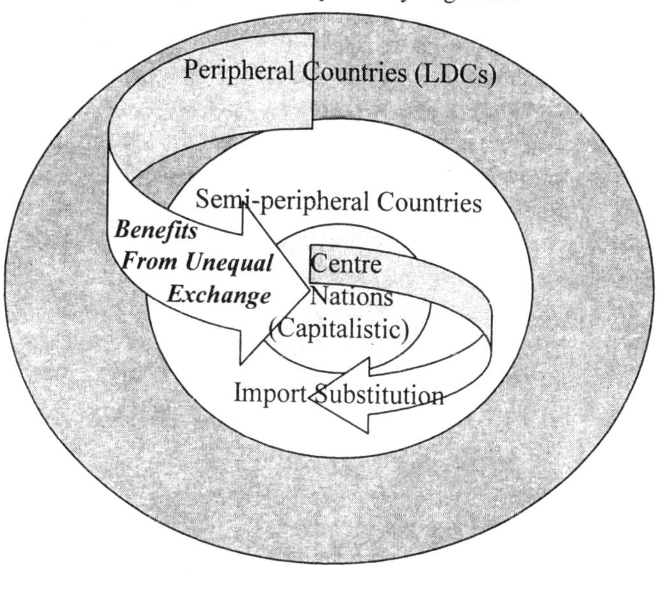

Both theories predicted the transition, already underway, of late capitalism into socialism. However, when this transition failed to occur and when some developing countries, especially in East Asia, made spectacular progress, the controversy lost its momentum. Several theories of post-modernism tried to "deconstruct" liberal modernization theory as well as the Marxist alternatives. Post-modernists ridiculed these approaches as out-dated "great narratives" and tried to substitute them with multiple cultural and constructivist contingency theories.

But with the breakdown of Communism and with the success of some Asian and South American countries attention again turned toward the pre-conditions and achievements of democracy and the market economy. Since 1987-88 the number of democratic regimes has increased from 66 to 121 States (Freedom House, 2002). This stage is called as "neo-modernism" or "modernization II" which indeed relies on democracy and free economic development, this time however without the concept of convergence to Western cultural patterns and without underestimating nationalist and fundamentalist counter-movements (*See* Figure 13.3). The neo-modernization analysis focused on the following issues (Tiryakian, 1998).

- Modernization is the result of actions by individuals and collectives, not an automatic development of systems;
- It seek new ways to achieve the goals and fulfil the values; but whether these aims can be accomplished, will depend on the resources;
- Modernization is not a consensual process, but a competition between modernizers, conservatives and by-standers;
- Science is a major driving force, but religion and tradition must not be underestimated;
- The general criterion for the success of modernization is the welfare development of the whole population;
- Centers of modernization may change and move; and
- Modernization is not continuous-linear; it has also cycles and regressive crises.

Earlier in West neo-modernism was treated as the state of the art but, in the meantime, it has already entered a new stage; fundamentalist and/or terrorist threats in several parts of the world would seem to be as "clash of civilizations" as the most relevant conflict at the beginning of 21st century (Huntington, 1993). The fundamental source of conflict is shifting from ideological or economic to cultural. Lines between cultures are defined as 'fault lines', and the Velvet Curtain of culture is equivalent of the divisive and provocative iron curtain of old (Hartmann, 1995).

Figure 13.3: Modernization Process-II (Since 1987-88)

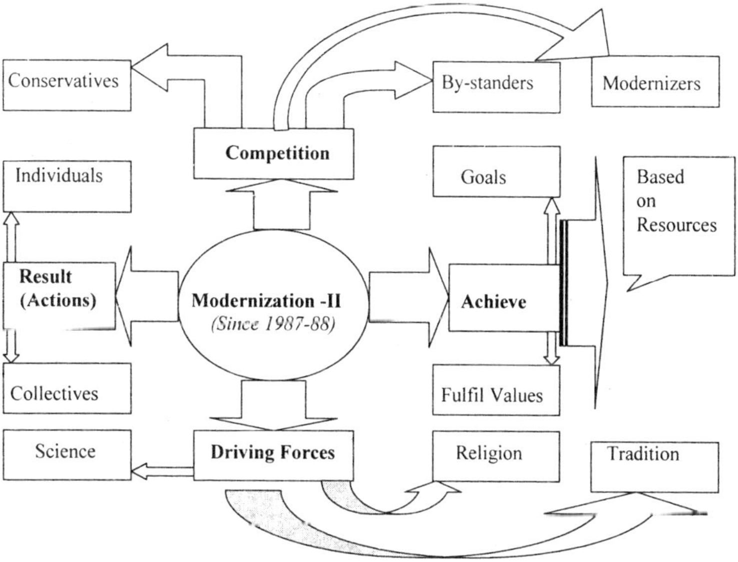

As we know, the modernization of the West was already the subject of discussion around the turn of the 20th century: industrialization of the modernization theory and the growth of productive forces in dependency theory as specialization.

As to the early modernization theory of the 1950-60s one must remember that this theory was designed as a programme explicitly directed to the non-Western world, that is, it was devoted to the "export" of Western institutions and values.

Dependency and world-systems theories by definition concentrate on the non-Western world, as the periphery of a capitalist centre which, according to proponents of these theories, gained its leading position by exploitation, that is, by "the development of underdevelopment". During the stage of culturalism and constructivism, which still has influence today, the non-Western world was considered to have committed the same fallacies as the West by not being aware that there is no reality outside our interpretations of it. As an aside, the merit of the cultural or constructivist view is the distinction of modernization qua process and modernity qua civilization, and the discussion of the "dark side", namely, the violence, social cost and alienation produced in this civilization (Mergel, 1997). The neo-modernism stage was also challenged, for example, by theories of globalization, even "cosmopolitization", on the one hand, and by non-Western resistance/opposition, in the form of "clash of civilizations", or even shorter as the "West against the rest".

13.4 INFLUENCE OF THE WEST IN AFRICA

In the modern era of Globalization epitomizing global communications and transportation the people of different continents are vastly getting closer. The Western ideologies and way of life are fastly spreading to the African and Asian societies through features movies, radio, television, VCRs, satellites, cell phones, internet, home fax machines, electronic mail, and teleconferencing (Black, C.E, 1968). It has helped even the remote societies in the developing countries to get the fruits of development. However, it has influenced and transformed the indigenous socio-cultural institutions in these regions. In some cases the result is a virtual onslaught of global cultural trends of dress, styles, music, behaviour, and even beliefs—including democracy, human rights and consumerism.

While parts of Africa were influenced by Europeans prior to the colonial period, impact became widespread only in the Nineteenth century. By 1900 the African continent had been divided primarily among the British, Italian, German, French, Spanish and Portuguese Governments. Two types of colonial control measures the imperialist powers used in Africa: one, attempted to eliminate the traditional structures and institutions and in its place implant the Western institutions. Second method used was an approach to integrate the Western systems with the indigenous institutions. These differing approaches of the European colonizers to their African territories affected the persistence of traditional structures. Even though colonialism had serious repercussions, various factors influenced the degree of European domination on indigenous institutions. Traditional ways of governance and indigenous economic structures suffered under all colonizers; one of the most serious consequences was the division of same ethnic groups into different regions/countries[2].

Borders drawn by colonial powers did not correspond to the realities of ethnic groups.

European conquest also generated new hostilities among the Africans themselves; while disputes between different ethnic groups were not uncommon in pre-colonial Africa, colonialism has often been blamed for exacerbating these tensions. Western penetrations also created tribal, linguistic and ethnic divisiveness. Some studies show that tribalism is also a product of colonialism; the colonial legacy has been blamed for apartheid in Southern Africa and the war of liberation in Southern Rhodesia (Davidson, B., 1992). The belief among the younger generations that African ways and economic institutions are backward and consequently modernization of institutions is urgently warranted gets more support. Instead of improving the efficiency of traditional mode of agricultural systems, industries and services the African elites totally thrown out their economic institutions and heritages for the sake of implanting the Western ones. Traditional mode of fishing based on dug-out canoes suffered due to Western style of fishing. The nomadic style of live-stocking affected due to agricultural developments on the Western lines. Pervasive famines became a common feature and millions suffered due to food insecurity. Traditional industries were also suffered in the similar fashion.

The rise of money economy affected the traditional economic structures in Africa. Demand for labour force expanded, export crops developed, trade expanded and new development centers emerged in the form urban centers. In the mineral rich Central and Southern Africa large numbers of indigenous people were forced to work in mines, which distorted the traditional social and economic systems (Ayittey, G., 1991). The introduction and emphasis given by the European powers to cash crops also influenced the indigenous economic balance; however cash crops attracted men, while women continued to farm food crops. This lead to emergence of dualistic economies in villages and affected the balance in the rural societies.

Western foreign aid brought relief in many parts of the continent and alongwith this it deepened the Africa's reliance on the West. It encouraged large scale import of western technology and luxury goods. Huge foreign aid was utilized for purchasing the costly machines like modern tractors, air-conditioners, etc. without proper training for the use of these machines or without spareparts for maintenance (Huntington, Samuel, 1996). These tied aid packages created large scale demonstration effect among the elite classes in Africa on the Western lines. Accordingly many of the African countries started specializing in the production of those primary goods, which was initiated by the imperialists through dependent on industrialized technologies (*See* Figure 13.4).

After independence many western ideas and institutions remained in Africa and newer ones also developed. African elites also sought to modernize their economies and consequently damaged many of the indigenous institutions in the process. Westernism was equated with modernity and consequently significant areas of Africa became firmly enmeshed in the western dominated capitalist system and after experience experimented with western style socio-economic and political institutions.

13.5 AFRICA'S REDISCOVERY OF ITS TRADITIONS AND RESISTANCE TO THE WEST

Over the years many African intellectuals have learned that Western institutions and practices cannot be easily transplanted into their societies. Cultural, historical, institutional, economical and social differences make Africa unique and different from the West. Search for solutions to manifold problems finally point towards the rediscovery of home-grown institutions and their strength. These indigenous institutions are presumably being more viable and functional than the artificially imposed Western ones. The importance of institutions such as kinship in the rural societies can not be neglected for Africa's development.

As early as in 19th and 20th Century itself the African society expressed its resistance to the Westernization. Marxism got renewed support in the 1970s and dependency theory gained prominence throughout colonial territories[3]. A new sense of political and economic nationalism permeated the continent alongwith nationalism. Africa's frustration to West was demonstrated through the Non-Aligned Movement (NAM) and the Group of 77. OPEC's ability to exert pressure on the industrialized world through the creation of an oil oligopoly gave the NAM countries hope that they could similarly influence the West through collective action.

Figure 13.4: Colonial Influence in Africa

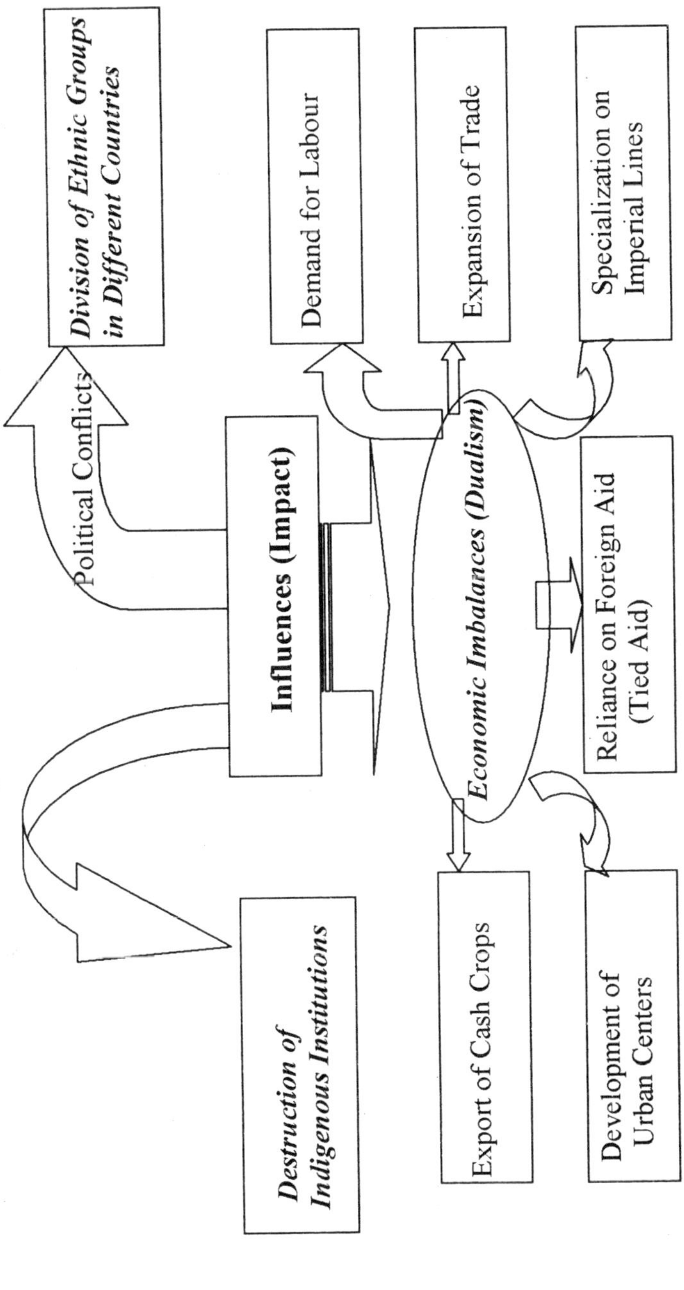

The formation of Organization of African Union (OAU) was also an expression of the continent through collective action against the West. The effort to force the industrialized world to reverse Africa's negative position in the world economy through the NIEO was similarly a showcase of the African resistance. However, most of these attempts could not gain the anticipated gains due to many internal and external influences resulting in continued reliance on the West. Loans and grants from the World Bank and the International Monetary Fund strengthened the West's influence over the continent. These Western backed monetary giants in the name of structural adjustment and stabilization policies still controlling the African economies and societies. Curtailment of the role of Government, wage freezing, trade liberalization and enforcement of market solutions, all weakened the already weak African societies. The economic reforms further ensured the western dominance in the continent. Rising debts in the African States further amplified their dependence.

The Western emphasis on economic and political liberalization in Africa is reminiscent of the earlier modernization approach. The latest version emphasizes civil society, creation of accountable states, democratization and market economies; all these echo 1960s modernization theory. Parallel political and economic transitions are billed as necessary rather than inevitable, and retrogression is characterized as unacceptable rather than implausible (Harbeson, J. and D. Rothchild, 1995). While the recent version of modernization theory is less ethno-centric than its predecessor, it also fails to take account of the economic, political, social, and cultural realities of Africa.

These failures raise doubts about the future success of ongoing economic and political changes in Africa. The West's great champion, South Africa also started signalling socio-economic shocks in recent years[4]; representing skid down the slippery African slope, one which has oiled the failure of so many other countries to build a prosperous democracy after winning political liberation. Although the African model remain unclear and would likely vary in different countries, African societies have demonstrated many Western practices and institutions to their particular context.

13.6 QUEST FOR A SUB-SAHARAN AFRICAN DEVELOPMENT MODEL

Sub-Saharan Africa is home to more than 600 million people who are distributed unevenly among the fifty-one States of the region. Natural resources are also unevenly distributed due to the wide variety of endowments, climates and terrains. Just as diverse as topography are Sub-Saharan Africa's social, economic and cultural conditions. Hundreds of different languages and ethnic groups are indigenous to Africa; many peoples speak even different languages in small localities. Despite the diversity, African countries have much in common; Colonialism was experienced throughout the continent.

Immediately after independence, most of the new States of Africa tried to adopt the Western path of development by modeling and restructuring the indigenous socio-economic and political institutions. This approach assumed that Africa would progress through stages of development similar to the stages experienced by Western 'developed' countries. Eventually, the economies, societies and polities of Africa would resemble their Western counterparts (Mazrui, 1986). The proponents of modernization theory presumed that traditional African practices and institutions were dysfunctional. However, Western institutions were seldom adapted to African culture and traditions, and rarely worked as well as anticipated; which lead to the awakening among the African scholars for a regeneration of the indigenous and home grown path of development. Moreover, much of Sub-Saharan Africa has been and continues to be in political and economic turmoil.

Economic situation in Africa has worsened since 1980s. Population continued to grow while GNP remains stagnant, which made the demographic figures at bottom. Today nearly 40 per cent of Africans are under sixteen years old, whereas the continent captures a paltry three per cent of foreign direct investment (Davidson, B., 1992). Africa's political statistics have also remained grim; since independence more than twenty countries in Sub-Saharan Africa have undergone more than one violent transfer of leadership. During the early 1990s elected democratic leaders come to power in many Sub-Saharan African countries, however, it failed due to military coups in many countries by the end of the Twentieth century. From colonial to the present day, power in Africa has largely remained in the hands of those adopting a Western approach. However, Westernism has not completely penetrated the continent, in that many indigenous institutions and practices continue to survive. While not all native institutions are beneficial, many have persisted because they are effective.

Figure 13.5: A SSA Development Model

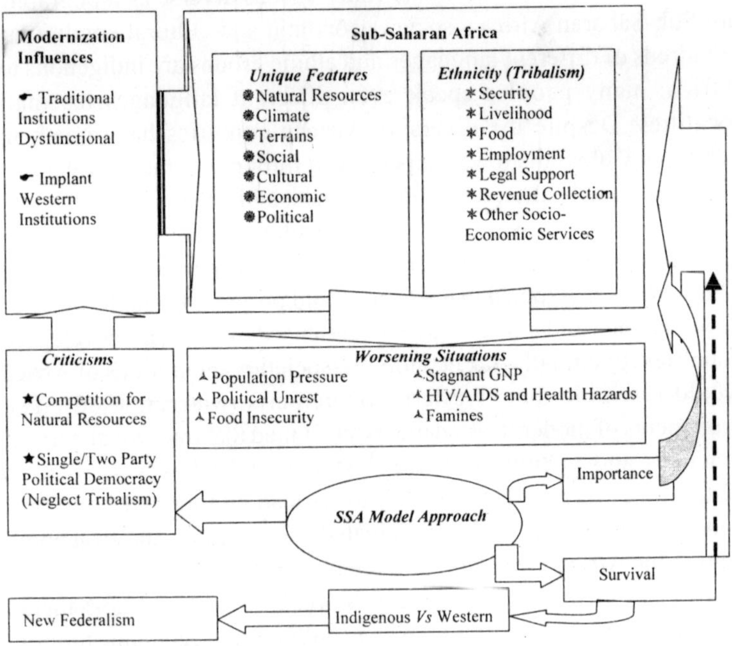

African socio-economic fabric is based on the traditional institution of tribalism or ethnicity. In Africa neither the Marxian nor the developmentalist approach provided adequate answers; instead they suggested to get rid of tribalism as the only hope for socio-economic progress. However, the tribe or the ethnic group provided one of the few institutions that helped hold African society and economy together by providing security, means of living, education and other essential socio-economic services including food and employment (Wiarda H.J., 2000). By the end of the Twentieth century African intelligentsia started questioning the Western backed dysfunctional centralized regimes and argued for a more decentralized or even federal regime in which localized ethnic organizations would be given the right place rather than snuffed out. The question raised among the young thinkers in Africa is modernization versus tribalism (See Figure 13.5).

Forced to live together in one State/Country or region forced the tribal communities compete for meagre natural resources; which lead to large scale ethnic tensions and fights in the continent. The conflicts in Sudan and Somalia are not exceptions. The Western style of democratic systems based on single or two party political systems completely neglected the multitude of ethnic and tribal communities and it aggravated the political tensions[5]. In Africa chiefs, paramount chiefs or the traditional office-holders still control much land and have access to communal labour. These institutions allocate shares of jointly owned lands and to kin groups and define community holdings (Chazan, N., 1992). They are still levying taxes, collect other forms of revenue and serve as judges and arbiters of local disputes. The Westerners completely neglected the power of these institutions.

13.6.1 Integration of Indigenous Vs the West

Despite the influence of the West in the urban areas, it could not penetrate much in the society especially in villages, where 70 per cent of Africans live. Accordingly the indigenous socio-economic and political institutions survived by accommodating the Western ones. Indigenous elements are combined with the western institutions to produce a modern and truly African alternative[6]. Tribal or ethnic chiefs and consensus political and economic ideologies have been incorporated in many African country's systems. The traditional leaders are also involved with development efforts and meet regularly with Cabinet ministers.

Scholars and political leaders have rediscovered that the institutions of the tribe or ethnic groups often perform many useful services. It provides police and justice functions, offer economic and social services, and serves as a means of conveying ethnic interests to Central Governments and to implement public policies. In some countries the institution of the chief is being incorporated into constitutions and the Governmental system. Reassessing the roles of tribalism and chiefs has also stimulated a re-examination of State and economic structure, leading to considerations of different forms of federalism as distinct from unitary centralism. The new and more positive view of traditional institutions has also been used to stimulate pride in native cultures and practices.

African people started valuing their indigenous institutions in the same way that their own intellectuals do or that there is any agreement in which institutions can be preserved than imported Western ones.

13.7 CONCLUSION

The quest for an indigenous model of development in Africa should start from the historical influences during the colonial period. Western influence during the colonial period was concentrated in those areas brought into the international economy by Europeans. In ports and mineral or export crop areas European political, economic, social or cultural practices were dominant. Post-independence Africa under African, albeit often Westernized, leaders continued the spread of Western practices usually to the detriment of indigenous ways. The post-independence African elite attempted to protect Africa from the West in the Group of 77, NAM and OAU.

Much of traditional African polity, economics, culture and society have withstood the Western onslaught. African practices managed to survive by blocking out or else adapting to Western institutions. Many African countries have taken Western institutions and altered them to fit the African context. The major question we discussed is will Western-style democracy and economic reforms be pushed forward, further challenging the social, political and economic realities of indigenous Africa? Africa's future lies in its ability to restructure its indigenous institutions and to reform the Western ones to the needs of the African societies.

The concept of liberalism makes little sense in Africa; latter is based on individualism, but there is little individualism in Africa; however it assumes the abstract universalism in socio-economic fabrics. Any developmental concept which will not consider the African realities can not sustain in this diverse Continent.

NOTES

1. Some Western scholars are of the opinion that indigenous models was related to the Cold War, then once the Cold War ended, presumably the context and opportunities to put forward home grown models of development would change as well. And that is what actually happened.
2. In the initial European scramble for territory, African kinship groups were broken up. For instance, Somalis were among those who suffered most from this colonial effect; colonizers divided them between present-day Somalia, Ethiopia, Djibouti and Kenya.
3. Regimes such as those in Mozambique, Zimbabwe and Ethiopia voiced Marxist or Leninist opposition to capitalism.
4. Rising unemployment, collapsing and growing lawlessness, and a political opposition divided by ethnic tensions have raised doubts about the future of South Africa.
5. Traditional political structure continued to decay after independence; new leaders removed authority from traditional chiefs and kings who were seen as relics of backward Africa and were even accused of collaborating with colonial leaders.
6. For instance an indigenous language in Eastern Africa, *Kiswahili*, adopted the Roman alphabet but has since remained the primary language. It is used by the people and Government of Tanzania. At the same time the percentage of educated people fluent in English has declined. The use of *Kiswahili* is also strong in neighbouring Kenya.

REFERENCES

Ayittey, George (1991). *Indigenous African Institutions*, New York: Transnational Publishers.

Berger, Johannes (1996). "Was bedeutet die Modernisierungstheorie wirklich—und was wird ihr bloß unterstellt?, *Leviathan* (24), pp. 45-62.

Black, C.E. (1968). *The Dynamics of Modernization*, New York: Harper and Row.

Chazan, N. (1992). *Politics and Society in Contemporary Africa*, Boulder, CO: Lynn Rienner Publishers.

Davidson, B. (1992). *The Black Man's Burden: Africa and the Curse of the Nation-State*, New York: Times Books.

Freedom House, (2002). *Freedom in the World*, New York: Freedom House.

Harbeson, J. and D., Rothchild (1995). *Africa in World Politics: Post Cold War Challenges*, Boulder, CO: Westview Press.

Hartmann, Heinz (1995). "Clash of Cultures, When and Where?", *International Sociology* (10), pp. 115-125.

Huntington, Samuel (1996). *The Clash of Civilizations and the Remaking of World Order*, New York: Simon and Schuster.

Mazrui, A.A. (1986). *The Africans: A Triple Heritage*, London: BBC Publications.

Mergel, Thomas (1997). "Geht es weiter voran? Die Modernisierungstheorie auf dem Weg zu einer Theorie der Moderne", pp. 203-32 in: Th. Mergel/Th. Welskopp (eds.), *Geschichte zwischen Kultur und Gesellschaft*, München: Beck.

Rostow, W.W. (1960). *The Stages of Economic Growth: A Non-Communist Manifesto*, New York: Cambridge University Press.

So, Alvin Y. (1990). *Social Change and Development. Modernization, Dependency, and World System Theories*, Newbury Park: Sage.

Tiryakian, Edward, A. (1998). "Neo-Modernisierung: Lehren für die und aus der postsozialistischen Transformation", pp. 31-52, in: Klaus Müller (ed.), *Postsozialistische Krisen*, Opladen: Leske and Budrich.

Wiarda, H.J. (1983). *Ethnocentrism in Foreign Policy: Can We Understand the Third World*? Washington: American Enterprise Institute for Public Policy Research.

Wiarda, H.J. (2000). *Non-Western Theories of Development: Regional Norms versus Global Trends*, Belmont CA: Wadsworth/Thomson Learning.

Zapf, Wolfgang (1969). *Theorien des sozialen Wandels*, Köln: Kiepenheuer.

Zapf, Wolfgang (1991). "Modernisierung und Modernisierungstheorien", pp. 23-39 in: W. Zapf (ed.), *Die Modernisierung Moderner Gesellschaften*, Frankfurt: Campus.

Bibliography

Abate, Groum (2004). 'African Parks Strikes $1 Million Decide to Manage Nech Sar,' *Capital Ethiopia.com*, February, 24.

Adams, Martin and John, Howell (2001). "Redistributive Land Reform in Southern Africa," *Natural Resource Perspectives*, No. 64, January, Overseas Development Institute.

Adebo, A. and Akindele, S.T. (1990). "The Political Economy of Neo-colonial State and Under-Development in Nigeria" in Bamisaye, O.A. and Egbuwalo, M.O., (Eds), *Readings on the Political Economy of Nigeria since Independence*, Venture Ltd, Lagos.

African Development Bank (ADB), (2003). *Sudan Country Dialogue Paper 2003-2004.*

African Parks Foundation (APF), (2006). *Nech Sar National Park: Annual Report 2006*, Arba Minch.

African Parks Foundation (APFs), (2005a). *Joint Liaison Committee for Nech Sar National Park Projects—APs (Ethiopia) PLC*, Proposal, Arba Minch.

African Parks Foundation (APF), (2005b). *Nech Sar National Park: Illegal Fishing*, October 23, Arba Minch.

Aisha, Abdalla Hommaida (2006). *Poverty in Sudan*, Institute of African and Asian Studies, University of Khartoum, Sudan.

Ake, C. (1996). *Democracy and Development in Africa*, Brookings Institution, New York.

Akindele, S.T. (1990). "Colonialism and Economic Dependence: The Case of Nigeria" in Bamisaye, O.A. and Egbuwalo, M.O. (Eds), (1990). *Readings on the Political Economy of Nigeria since Independence*, Venture Ltd, Lagos.

Ali, Abdel Gader Ali, (2006). *Can the Sudan Reduce Poverty by Half by the Year 2015*, Working Paper Series, Arab Planning Institute, Kuwait.

Alison, M. Jones (2005). "A Proposed Management Plan for Ethiopia's Nech Sar National Park," *Forest, Ecology and People: Principles and Practices*, Columbia University.

Ariyabandu, R. de D. (1999). "Water Security through Rainwater Harvesting", *Integrated Development for Water Supply and Sanitation*, WEDC, Loughborough University, pp. 366 Ð 368.

Ashton-Jones Nick; Arnott, Susi and Douglas Oronto, (1998). *The Human Ecosystems of the Niger Delta: An Era Handbook*, Environmental Rights Action, London.

Ayittey, George (1991). *Indigenous African Institutions*, New York: Transnational Publishers.

Bailey, Douglass (2000). *Balkan Prehistory: Exclusions, Incorporation and Identity.* Routledge.

Bailey, Douglass (2005). *Prehistoric Figurines: Representation and Corporeality in the Neolithic.* Routledge.

Ban, Ki-moon (2007). *Washington Post.*

Barkan, *et al.,* (1998). 'Decentralization and Democratization in Sub-Saharan Africa,' *Occasional Papers: 45-49*, International Programmes, University of IOWA.

Bbc.co.uk, (2005). *Malawi issues food crisis appeal*, October.

Beadle, G. (1980). 'The Ancestry of Corn,' *Scientific American*, 242:113.

Beintema, N. and G.J. Stads, (2004). *Investing in Sub-Saharan African Agricultural Research: Recent Trends,* 2020 Africa Conference Brief 8, Washington, DC: International Food Policy Research Institute.

Bellwood, Peter (2004). *First Farmers: The Origins of Agricultural Societies,* Blackwell Publishers.

Bender, B. (1978). 'Gatherer-hunter to Farmer: A Social Perspective,' *World Archaeology*, 10 : 204-222.

Benson, T. (2004). *Africa's Food and Nutrition Security Situation: Where are We and How did We Get Here?* 2020 Discussion Paper No. 37, Washington, DC: International Food Policy Research Institute.

Berger, Johannes (1996). "Was bedeutet die Modernisierungstheorie wirklich—und was wird ihr bloß unterstellt?, *Leviathan* (24), pp. 45-62.

Binford, L.R. and S.R. Binford (1966). "A Preliminary Analysis of Functional Variability in the Monsterian of Levallois Facial," *Recent Studies in paleo-anthropology*, ed, J.D Clark and F.C Howell, American Anthropologist, Special Issue, 68 (2,2), 238-295.

Binford, L.R. (1983). *In Pursuit of the Past*, Thames and Hudson, New York.

Black, C.E. (1968). *The Dynamics of Modernization*, New York: Harper and Row.

Blessing, Zulu (2007). 'IMF Officials Warns Zimbabwe Consumer Inflation Headed for 100,000 per cent, *Interview with IMF Officials*, July 31, Washington.

Boler T. and Jellema A. (2005). *Deadly Inertia: A Cross Country Study of Educational Responses to HIV/AIDS.*

Bradford, B. July (1992). "Focus on Thailand" *Raindrop, Rainwater Harvesting Bulletin*, Volume 7, pp. 1 Ð 11.

Braidwood, R.J. (1960). 'The Agricultural Revolution,' *Scientific American*, 203 (3), 130-148.

Breman, H. and S. K., Debrah, (2003). *Improving African Food Security*, SAS Review 23 (1): 153–170.

Brian, D. Pellot (2007). *Report on Sudan's Environment Degradation*, UN Environment Programme, United Nations.

Brown, L.R. H., Feldstein, L. Haddad, C. Peña, and A., Quisumbing (2001). *Generating Food Security in the Year 2020: Women as Producers, Gatekeepers, and Shock Absorbers*. In The Unfinished Agenda, ed. P. Pinstrup-Andersen and R. Pandya-Lorch, Washington, DC: International Food Policy Research Institute.

Bureau for Economic Research (BER), (2006). *The Macro-economic impact of HIV/Aids under Alternative Intervention Scenarios (with specific reference to ART) on the South African Economy*, Stellenbosch University.

Business Day, (2006). *Sub-Saharan Lifespan Down by Five Years*, June.

Byerlee, D., Eicher, C., Liedholm, C. and Spencer, D.S.C., (1977). 'Rural Employment in Tropical Africa: Summary of Findings,' *Africa Rural Economy Working Paper No. 20*, Michigan State University, East Lansing

Cairncross, S. and Feacham, R., (1993). *Environmental Health Engineering in the Tropics*, Wiley.

Chattopadhyay, Rupak, (2000). "Zimbabwe: Structural Adjustment, Destitution, and Food Insecurity," *Review of African Political Economy*, No. 84, 307-316.

Chazan, N. (1992). *Politics and Society in Contemporary Africa*, Boulder, CO: Lynn Rienner Publishers.

Cheng, T. (1966). *Archaeology in China: New Light on Prehistoric China*, W. Heffer and Sons, Cambridge.

Childe, V.G. (1952). *Man Makes Himself*, New American Library, New York.

Chossudovsky, Michel (1997). *The Globalization of Poverty: Impacts of IMF and World Bank Reforms*, 2nd Edition Book Ltd, London.

Christine, Magistretti. (2004). *NGO's Contribution to the Deliberation of the European Population Forum*, Geneva.

Clutton, Brock J. (1999). *A Natural History of Domesticated Animals*, Cambridge University Press, Cambridge.

Cohen, M. (1977). 'Population Pressure and the Origins of Agriculture: An Archaeological Example from the Coast of Peru,' *Origins of Agriculture,* ed, C. Reed Mouton, The Hague.

Cohen, M. (1977). *The Food Crisis in Prehistory*, Yale University Press, New Haven, CT.

Davidson, B. (1992). *The Black Man's Burden: Africa and the Curse of the Nation-State*, New York: Times Books.

Deborah Fahy Bryceson, *et al.*, "Maize Marketing Policies in Tanzania, 1938-1998," *Agricultural Marketing in Tropical Africa*, African Studies Centre, Leiden. 1999.

Department for International Development of the United Kingdom (DFID). (2006). *Country Engagement Plan.*

Development Technology Unit (DTU), University of Warwick, http:/../ www.eng.warwick.ac.uk/DTU/Rainwater harvesting.

Dhliwayo, Rogers. (2001). *The Impact of Public Expenditure Management under ESAP on Social Services: Health and Education*, Paper presented at the Structural Adjustment Participatory Review Initiative (SAPRI) Poverty Reduction Forum, Harare, Zimbabwe, 9-10 April.

Diagne, S.B. and Ossebi. (1996). "The Cultural Question in Africa: Issues, Politics and Research Prospects", *Codestria Working Paper Series 3/98.*

Diamond, Jared. (2002). *Evolution, Consequences and Future of Plant and Animal Domestication,* Nature Magazine, Vol. 418.

Dreze, J and A. Sen. (1989). *Hunger and Public Action*, Clarendon Press, Oxford.

Economic Commission for Africa (ECA). (1984). *Women in the Artisanal Fishing Industry in Senegal and Ghana*, Research Centre for Women, Addis Ababa.

Eric, Tollens. (1998). *Food Security in ACP Countries*, Leuven, Belgium.

ESSWA (Ethiopian Society of Sociologist, Social Workers and Anthropologists) (1998). *The Role of Indigenous Associations and Institutions in Development*-Abstracts, Workshop Organized by ESSWA, Addis Ababa, June 25-26.

European Commission (EC). (2005). *Country Strategy Paper and National Indicative Programme 2005-2007*

Fage, J.D. (2001). *A History of Africa*, 4th edition, Routledge.

FAKT and Kenya Rainwater Association (KRA). (1997). *Mvua ni maji Ð Rainwater Harvesting by Women's Groups in Kenya*, Video, FAKT, Stuttgart.

FAO, (1987). *Africa: Mean Annual Rainfall Map*, (Scale 1:1,000,000), Rome.

FDRE (Federal Democratic Republic of Ethiopia), (1995). 'Proclamation of the Constitution of the Federal Democratic Republic of Ethiopia,' *Negarit Gazetta*, No. 1, Addis Ababa.

Federal Democratic Republic of Ethiopia (FDRE), (2005). *Equality between National, State, Local to Civil Society*, Report of the Ministry of Finance.

Fishbein, R. (2003). *The State of Food Insecurity in the World 2003: Monitoring Progress Towards the World Food Summit and Millennium Development Goals*, Rome.

Flannery, K.V. ed. (1986). *Guila Naquitz: Archaic Foraging and Early Agriculture in Oaxaca Mexico*, Academic Press, New York.

Food and Agriculture Organization (FAO), (2004) *Crop and Food Supply Assessment*, Crop and Food Supply Assessment Mission to Ethiopia, Addis Ababa.

Food and Agricultural Organization of the United Nations (FAO), (2005) *Rural Women Carry Family Burdens: Focus, AIDS—A Threat to Rural Africa.*

Food and Agriculture Organization, Sustainable Development Department (FAO–SDD). (1996). World Food Summit, *Technical Background Documents*.

Freedom House, 2002. *Freedom in the World*, New York: Freedom House.

GCE, (2004). *Learning to Survive.*

Gebauer, A.B. and T. Douglas Price, *Transition in Agriculture in Prehistory*, New York.

Ghai, D. (1987). 'Economic Growth, Structural Change and Labour Absorption in Africa: 1960–85', *UNRISD Discussion Paper No. 1*, Geneva.

Global Fund to Fight AIDS, Tuberculosis and Malaria (GFFA), (2005). *Grants to Countries in Africa, Rounds 1-5 Funding*, September.

Gootu, S. (1993). "Portfolio Investment Flows to Emerging Markets" in: Claossens and Gooptu (eds.) *Portfolio Investment in Developing Countries*, World Bank Discussion Paper 228, Washington D.C.

Gould J and Nissen-Petersen E. (1999). *Rainwater Catchment Systems for Domestic Supply*, IT Pubs.

Gould, J. and A.Von Oppen. (1994). 'Of Rhetoric and Market: The Liberalization of Food Trade in East Africa,' *Socilogia Ruralis*, Vol. 34, No. 1.

Haggblade, S. Hazell, P. and Brown, J. (1987). 'Farm-Non-farm Linkages in Rural Sub-Saharan Africa: Empirical Evidence and Policy

Implications,' *Discussion Paper*, Agriculture and Rural Development Department, The World Bank, Washington, DC.

Hanmer, L. *et al.*, (1996). *Poverty in Sub-Saharan Africa—What can we learn from the World Bank's Poverty Assessments?* Institute of Social Studies, The Hague.

Hans, Ruthenberg. (1971). *Farming Systems in the Tropics*, Clarendon Press, Oxford.

Harbeson, J. and D. Rothchild. (1995). *Africa in World Politics: Post Cold War Challenges*, Boulder, CO: Westview Press.

Harlan, Jack R. (1992). *Crops and Man: Views on Agricultural Origins* ASA, CSA, Madison.

Harris, D.R. and G.C. Hilman, eds. (1989). *Foraging and Farming: The Evolution of Plant Exploitation*, Unwin Hyman, London.

Hartmann, Heinz. (1995). "Clash of Cultures, When and Where?", *International Sociology* (10), pp. 115-125.

Henry J. Kaiser Family Foundation (HJKFF), (2002). *Hitting Home: How Households Cope with the Impact of the HIV/AIDS Epidemic*, October.

Hosegood V. McGrath N, *et al.* (2004). 'The impact of adult mortality on household dissolution and migration in Rural South Africa', *AIDS*, July 23rd, Vol. 18, issue 11.

Human Resource Department (HRD), (2005). *NGO Agency Material Management Training for NGOs Promotion,* Federal Democratic Republic, Addis Ababa, December.

Huntington, Samuel. (1996). *The Clash of Civilizations and the Remaking of World Order*, New York: Simon and Schuster.

ILO (GET). *Global Employment Trends (2003*). Geneva

ILO (KILM), (2003). *Key Indicators of the Labour Market*, 3rd Edition, CD-ROM, Geneva

Inter Academy Council, (2004). *Realizing the Promise and Potential of African Agriculture*, Amsterdam.

International Food Policy Research Institute (IFPRI), (2000). *Women: The Key to Food Security*, Washington, DC.

International Fund for Agricultural Development (IFAD), (2002). *Country Strategic Opportunities Paper-2002.*

International Rainwater Catchment Systems Association (IRCSA), http://www.ircsa.org.

Jarriage, J.F and R.H, Meadow. (1980). 'The Antecedents of Civilization in the Indus Valley,' *Scientific American*, 243: (2).

Jayne, T. and S. Jones. (1997). 'Food Marketing and Pricing Policy in Eastern and Southern Africa,' *World Development*, Vol. 25, No. 9.

Jeffrey Sachs. (2006). *Scientific American Website.*

John H. Cleave. (1974). *African Farmers: Labour Use in the Development of Small-Holder Agriculture*, Praeger, New York.

Kaisernetwork.org. (2005). *US has Increased Global Condom Distribution in Recent Years, Targeting Mostly High-Risk Groups*, September.

Kayizzi, Mugerwa Steve. (1999). *The African Economy: Policy, Institutions and the Future*, Routledge.

Kherallah, M.C. Delgado, E. Gabre-Madhin, N. Minot, and M., Johnson. (2000). *The Road Half Travelled: Agricultural Market Reform in Sub-Saharan Africa,* Food Policy Report 10, Washington, DC: International Food Policy Research Institute.

King. (1984). 'Science, Technology and Education in the Development of Indigenous Technological Capability,' in M. Fransman and K. King (eds), *Technological Capability in the Third World*, Macmillan, London.

Kinsey, B.H. (1999). "Land Reform, Growth and Equity: Emerging Evidence from Zimbabwe's Resettlement Programme," *Journal of Southern African Studies* 25, No. 2, 169-192.

Kinsey, B.H. (2000). "The Implications of Land Reform for Rural Welfare," *Land Reform in Zimbabwe—Constraints and Prospects*, ed. T.A.S Bowyer-Bower and Colin Stoneman, Aldershot: Ashgate.

Krugman, P. and Verables, A.J. (1995). "Globalization and the Inequality of Nations" *Quarterly Journal of Economics*, Vol. 110.

Lall, S. (1989). 'Human Resource Development and Industrialization with Special Reference to Sub-Saharan Africa,' *Journal of Development Planning*, No. 19

Lechevallier, M and G. Quivron. (1985). 'Results of the Recent Excavations at the Neolithic Site (Mehrgarh, Pakistan),' *South Asian Archaeology*.

Legge, A.J and Peter A. Rowley. (1967). 'Gazelle Drives in the Ancient Near East,' *Scientific American.*

Leipziger, D., M. Fay, Q. Wodon, and T. Yepes. (2003). Achieving the Millennium Development Goals: The Role of Infrastructure, Policy Research Working Paper 3163. World Bank.

Lele, Uma. (1975). *The Design of Rural Development: Lessons from Africa*, World Bank Research Publication, The Johns Hopkins University Press, Baltimore and London.

MacNeish, R. (1964). 'The Origins of New World Civilization,' *Scientific American*.

Madunagu, E. (1999). "Globalization and its Victims," *Guardian,* July 26.

Mandefro. (1998). *Ethiopia: Anatomy of a Traditional Polity*, Clarendon Press, Oxford.

Maxwell. S. (1996). "Food Security: A Post-Modern Perspective,' *Food Policy*, Vol. 21, No. 2, pp. 155-170.

Mazrui, A.A. (1986). *The Africans: A Triple Heritage*, London: BBC Publications.

MEDAC (Ministry of Development and Co-operation). (1998). *Regional Development in Ethiopia: An Overview*, Department of Regional Planning and Development, Addis Ababa.

Mergel, Thomas. (1997). "Geht es weiter voran? Die Modernisierungstheorie auf dem Weg zu einer Theorie der Moderne", pp. 203-32 in: Th. Mergel/Th. Welskopp (eds.), *Geschichte zwischen Kultur und Gesellschaft*, München: Beck.

Messer, E, and M. J. Cohen. (2004). *Breaking the Links Between Conflict and Hunger in Africa,* 2020 Africa Conference Brief No. 10, Washington, DC: International Food Policy Research Institute.

Michael, Wines. (2006). 'How Bad is Inflation in Zimbabwe?', *The New York* Times, May 2.

Michael, Wines. (2007). 'Zimbabwe's Anti-inflation Campaign brings Chaos to Economy,' *Internet Source*, July 5.

Milimo, J. and Fisseha Y. (1986). 'Rural Small-Scale Enterprises in Zambia: Results of a Country-wide Study,' *MSU International Development Working Paper 28*, Michigan State University, East Lansing.

Ministry of Foreign Affairs of Ethiopia (MFAE). (2002). *Tourism, Investment and Banking System,* Addis Ababa.

Moshomba, Richard E. (2000). *Africa in the Global Economy*, Lynne Rienner.

Moyo, Sam. (2000a). *The Interaction of Market and Compulsory Land Acquisition Processes with Social Action in Zimbabwe's Land Reform*, Paper presented at Sapes Trust Annual Colloquium, Harare, Zimbabwe, 24-27 September.

Moyo, Sam. (2000b). *Land Reform under Structural Adjustments in Zimbabwe—Land Use in the Mashonaland Provinces*. Uppsala: Nordiska Afrikainstitutet.

Mule, H. (2000). "Challenges to African Governance and Civil Society", *Africa Notes*, May.

New Partnership for Africa's Development (NEPAD). (2002). *Comprehensive Africa Agriculture Development Programme*, Rome: Food and Agriculture Organization of the United Nations.

Norman, D.W. (1974). *The Organizational Consequences of Social and Economic Constraints and Policies in Dry Land Areas*, Paper presented to the Second International Seminar on Change in Agriculture, September 9-19, Reading UK.

Obadina, T. (1998). "Globalisation, Human Rights and Development", *Africa Today*, October.

OECD. (2007). *African Economic Outlook 2006-2007.*

Ohuabunwa, Mazi S.I. (1999). "The Challenges of Globalization to the Nigerian Industrial Sector", *Nigerian Tribune*, December 14.

Olowu Delele. (1993). *African Local Governments as Instruments of Economic and Social Development*, International Union of Local Authorities, Hague.

OSHO. (2004). *Proposal on Rural Development in Ziway Dugda*, Addis Ababa.

OSHO. (2007). *Programme Implementation Report, 2007*, Addis Ababa.

Oxfam International and Save the Children. (2002). *HIV/AIDS and Food Insecurity in Southern Africa.*

Oxfam. (2002). *Rigged Rules and Double Standards: Trade, Globalization, and the Fight against Poverty*, Oxfam International.

Oyejide, T.A. (1998). "African Trade Prospects in a Globalizing Era", *Cooperation South*, No. 2.

Paarlberg, R. L. (2002). *Governance and Food Security in an Age of Globalization*, 2020 Discussion Paper 36, Washington, DC: International Food Policy Research Institute.

Paul Nyakazeya. (2007). 'Zimbabwe: June Inflation 13,000 per cent', *Zimbabwe Independent*, July 27.

Pausewang, *et al.* (2002). *Ethiopia Since the Derg: A Decade of Democratic Pretension and Performance*, ZED Books, London.

Pearce EA and Smith CG. (1998). The Hutchinson World Weather Guide, 4th Ed, Helicon.

PEPFAR. (2006). *Action Today, A Foundation For Tomorrow: Second Annual Report to Congress on the President's Emergency Plan for AIDS Relief*, February.

Plant, Martin. (2005). *People Problems for Ethiopian Game Park*, BBC News-Ethiopia, September, 26.

Potts, Debby. (2000). "Zimbabwean People's Perceptions of the Land Resettlement Programme: The Case of Rural-Urban Migrants," *Land*

Reform in Zimbabwe—Constraints and Prospects, ed. T.A.S Bowyer-Bower and Colin Stoneman, Aldershot: Ashgate.

Poverty Reduction Forum and Institute for Development Studies (PRFIDS) (1999). *Human Development Report,* Zimbabwe, Harare: UNDP.

Price and Feinman. (1997). *Images of the Past*, Mayfield Publishing Company, California.

Price, T.D and A.B. Gebauer. (1995). *Last Hunters-First Farmers: New Perspective on the Transition to Agriculture*, School of American Research, Santa Fe, NM.

Pyne, Stephen J. (1997). *Vestal Fire: An Environmental History Told Through Fire, of Europe and Europe's Encounter with the World*; University of Washington Press, Seattle.

Reardon, T., E. Crawford, V. Kelly, and B. Diagana. (1995). *Promoting Farm Investment for Sustainable Intensification of African Agriculture,* Policy Synthesis No. 3, East Lansing, MI, USA.

Redman, C. (1978). The Rise of Civilization: *From Early Farmers to Urban Society in the Ancient Near East*, W.H Freeman and Company, New York.

Rees D.G and Thomas T.H. (1999). "Low-cost Roofwater Harvesting in the Humid Tropics" *Integrated Development for Water Supply and Sanitation,* WEDC, Loughborough University, pp. 418-421.

Refugees International (RI). (2005). Evictions from Nech Sar National Parks, Addis Ababa.

Renfrew, C and Paul Bahn. (1996). *From Archaeology: Theories, Methods and Practice*, Thames and Hudson, New York.

Rindos. (1984). *The Origins of Agriculture: An Evolutionary Perspective*, Academic Press, New York.

Rodney, Walter. (1982). *How Europe Underdeveloped Africa,* Howard UP, Washington.

Rodrik, Dani. (1994). "The rush to free trade in the developing world: Why so late? Why now? Will it last? In S. Haggard and S. Webb (eds), *Voting for Reform*, Oxford University Press and the World Bank, New York.

Rosegrant, *et al*. (2005). *Looking Ahead: Long-term prospects for Africa's Agricultural Development and Food Security*, Washington D.C: IFPRI.

Rosen, S. *et al.*, (2004). 'The cost of HIV/AIDS to businesses in Southern Africa', *AIDS,* 18:317-324.

Rostow, W.W. (1960). *The Stages of Economic Growth: A Non-Communist Manifesto*, New York: Cambridge University Press.

Rugasira, J., *Rakai Women Groups involved in Rainwater Harvesting Activities (Women leading the development process in the new millennium)*, Uganda Rainwater Harvesting Association and SIDA.

Ruthenberg, H. (1980). *Farming Systems in the Tropics*, Clarendon Press, Oxford

Sachs, Jeffrey and Andrew, Warner. (1995). *Economic Reform and the Process of Global Integration*, Brookings Papers on Economic Activity, Vol. 1.

Sahn, David E, Paul A. Dorosh and Stephen D. (1997). Younger *Structural Adjustment Reconsidered: Economic Policy and Poverty in Africa*, Cambridge University Press.

Sauer, C.O. (1952). *Agricultural Origins and Dispersals*, American Geographical Society, New York.

Sen. A. (1981). *Poverty and Famines—An Essay on Entitlements and Deprivation*, Clarendon Press, Oxford.

Seppala, P. (1998). 'Liberalized and Neglected? Food Marketing in Eastern Africa', *World Development Studies No. 12*, WIDER, United Nations University.

Shelton J.D. and Johnston, B. (2001). *Condom Gap in Africa: Evidence From Donor Agencies and Key Informants*.

Sijm, J. (1997). *Food Security and Policy Interventions in Sub-Saharan Africa: Lessons from the Past Two Decades*, Erasmus University, Rotterdam.

Singh, Shamsher. (1983). 'Sub-Saharan Agriculture: Synthesis and Trade Prospects,' *World Bank Staff Working Paper No. 608*, Washington D.C.

Smith, B.D. (1998). *The Emergence of Agriculture*, Scientific American Library, New York.

So, Alvin Y. (1990). *Social Change and Development. Modernization, Dependency, and World System Theories*, Newbury Park: Sage.

Steinberg, M. *et al.* (2002). *Hitting Home: How Households Cope with the Impact of the HIV/AIDS Epidemic*, The Henry J Kaiser Foundation, October.

Tagwiregi, J. (1991). 'Zimbabwe: Food Access and Nutrition Linkages,' in M. Rukuni and J. Wyckoff (eds), *Market Reforms Research Policies and SADCC Food Security*, UZ/MSU Food Security Research in Southern Africa Project, Harare.

Tandon, Y. (1998). "Globalization and Africa Options", *AAPS Newsletter*, African Association of Political Science, Vol. 3, No. 1 January-April, Harare.

Teshome, Teshale. (1994). *The Making of Modern Ethiopia: 1896-(1974)*. Red Sea Press, Lawrenceville, N.J.

The Economist, (2007). *How to Stay Alive when it all run out*, July 12.

Thorbecke, E. (1992). *The Anatomy of Agricultural Product Markets and Transactions in Developing Countries*, Institute for Policy Reform, Washington DC.

Thorbecke, E. (1997). 'Whither Africa?' *Africa Notes*, April.

Tiryakian, Edward A. (1998). "Neo-Modernisierung: Lehren für die und aus der postsozialistischen Transformation", pp. 31-52, in: Klaus Müller (ed.), *Postsozialistische Krisen*, Opladen: Leske & Budrich.

Toyo, Eskor. (2000). *Background to Globalisation*, A Mimeograph Published by the Academic Staff Union of Universities (ASUU), Nigeria.

Tussie, D. (1994). "Globalization and Word Trade from Multilateralism to Regionalism" *Oxford Development Studies* 26 (1): 32-46.

UN Economic Commission for Africa (ERA), (2003). *Economic Report on Africa (2003)*. Addis Ababa.

UNAIDS, (2006). *Report on the Global AIDS Epidemic*.

UNCTAD, (2000). *African Development in Comparative Perspective*, World Press, Trenton, NJ.

UNEP, (2007). Sudan: *Post-Conflict Environmental Assessment-2007*.

United Nations Development Group (UNDG), (1999). *Common Country Assessment* 1999.

United Nations Development Programme (UNDP), (2002). *Common Country Assessment and United Nations Development Assistance Framework 2002-2006*.

United Nations Development Programme (UNDP), (2003). Human Development Report (2003). *Millennium Development Goals: A Compact Among Nations to End Human Poverty*, New York.

United Nations Development Programme (UNDP), (2005). *Human Development Report (2005)*. Overview.

United Nations Population Fund (UNFPA), (2002). *Proposed Projects and Programmes 2002-2006*.

United Nations Refugee Agency (UNHCR), (2006). *Country Operations Plan -2006*.

United Nations System in Sudan (UNSS), (2005). *Work Plan for Sudan—2005*.

United Nations University, Institute for Natural Resources in Africa, and World Bank (UNU–INRA/World Bank). (1999). *Africa can Feed Just 40 per cent of its Population in (2025).* Press Release for World Food Day, Legon, Ghana, and Washington, DC.

United State Agency for International Development USAID, (2004). *Interim Strategic Plan for Sudan, 2004-2006.*

USDA, (1981). 'Food Problems and Prospects in Sub-Saharan Africa: The Decade of the 1980s,' *Foreign Agricultural Research Report No. 166*, Washington.

Van Zyl, Johann; Nick Vink, Johann Kirsten, Danswan Poonyth. (2001). "South African Agriculture in Transition: The 1990s," *Journal of International Development* 13, No. 6, 725-739.

Vestal, Theodore M. (1999). *Ethiopia: A Post Cold War African State*, Pracger, London.

Weber. M.T. *et al.*, (1988). 'Informing Food Security Decisions in Africa: Empirical Analysis and Policy Dialogue,' *American Journal of Agricultural Economics*, Vol.70, No. 5, pp. 1044-1052.

White, J. (1982). *Discovery of a Lost Bronze Age*, University Museum, University of Pennsylvania. Wright, Gary A. (1971). 'Origins of Food Production in Southwestern Asia: A Survey of Ideas' *Current Anthr*opology, Vol. 12, No. 4/5 (October-December, 1971), pp. 447-477.

WHO, (2007). *Towards Universal Access: Scaling up Priority HIV/AIDS Interventions in the Health Sector*, April.

WHO/UNICEF, (2000). *Water Supply and Sanitation Sector Monitoring Report (2000)*. Publication WHO/EOS/96.15; see also www.africanwater.org/csscoverage.htm#Africa.

Wiarda, H.J. (1983). *Ethnocentrism in Foreign Policy: Can We Understand the Third World*? Washington: American Enterprise Institute for Public Policy Research.

Wiarda, H.J. (2000). *Non-Western Theories of Development: Regional Norms* versus *Global Trends*, Belmont CA: Wadsworth/Thomson Learning.

Wohicke, M. (1993). "The Causes of Continuing Underdevelopment", *Law and the State*. (Volume 47) Institute for Scientific Co-operation, Tubingen.

Woodhouse, P. (1988). 'The Green Revolution and Food Security in Africa: Issue in Research and Technology Development,' *Development Policy and Practice Research Group Working Paper No. 10*, Open University, Milton Keynes.

World Bank, (1981). Accelerated Development in Sub-Saharan Africa: An Agenda for Action, Washington, D.C.

World Bank, (2002). *Education and HIV/AIDS: A Window of Hope.*

World Bank, (2004). *Targets and Indicators for MDGs and PRSPs: What Countries have Chosen to Monitor,* Washington, DC: World Bank.

World Food Programme (WFP), (2002). *Country Programme 2002-2006.*

World Health Organization (WHO), (2003). *Country Cooperation Strategy for WHO and Sudan 2003-2007.*

WTO (ITS), (2003). *International Trade Statistics*, New York

Zapf, Wolfgang. (1969). *Theorien des sozialen Wandels*, Köln: Kiepenheuer.

Zapf, Wolfgang. (1991). "Modernisierung und Modernisierungstheorien", pp. 23-39 in: W. Zapf (ed.), *Die Modernisierung moderner Gesellschaften*, Frankfurt: Campus.

Zeller, M.G. *et al.* (1999). 'Rural Financing for Food Security for the Poor: Implications for Research and Policy,' *Food Policy Review*, No. 4, IF PRI, Washington.

Index

Absenteeism, 167-68
Abstract universalism, 228
Abuja Food Security Summit, 53
Adult mortality, 60
African agricultural system, 59
African-American activists, 180
African civil society organizations, 10
African Development Bank, 54
African Federal System, 151
African Growth and Opportunity Act, 17
African intelligentsia, 226
Agrarian crisis, 36
Agrarian Structure, 128
Agricultural commodities, 42
Agricultural expansion, 122
Agricultural plots, 119
Agricultural price policy, 34
Agricultural stagnation, 56
Agricultural techniques, 79
Agro-climatic Condition, 200
Agro-food system, 47
AIDS crisis, 13, 19-20, 138, 162-65, 171-73, 187
AIDS pandemic, 20, 138, 172, 187
Alexander, Jeffrey, 11, 216
Amaro Mountains, 111
Amazon Basin, 73
American Senate, 17
Anglo-American Corporation, 186
Animal husbandry, 80, 201
Animal-rearing, 124
Anti-desertification action plan, 131
Anti-inflation campaigns, 191
Antiretroviral
    drugs, 163, 169-70
    therapy, 163
Apartheid commando raids, 186
APF, 112-14
Arab traders, 80
Aral Sea, 120
Archaeological
    perceptions, 69
    record, 69-71, 80, 82
Arid-land dwellers, 131
Armed conflicts, 58

BAU projects, 55-56
Blue Nile, 121-22

Capitalism, 24, 215, 217
Capitalist centre, 217, 219
Cash crops, 4, 113, 128, 165, 221
Central statistics office, 178
Centralized regimes, 226
Cereal demand, 50-51
Clash of civilizations, 218, 220
Climate change, 16-17, 118, 123
Coax countries, 9
Cold war, 8-10, 19, 215
Colonial
    influence, 223
    periods, 7, 214, 220, 228
Colonialism, 7, 81, 220-21, 225
Commercial farms, 181
Consumer subsidies, 35
Crisis of African economies, 18

Debt crisis, 2, 19
Debt relief, 18-19, 145
    unconditional, 19
Decentralization process, 151-52

Deforestation, 1, 117, 123, 125
Dependency theories, 24, 215, 217, 219, 222
Developing countries, 22, 25, 42, 45, 49-50, 59-61, 91, 101-02, 129-32, 186, 213, 216-17, 220
Development oriented emergency food aid project, 199, 202, 206, 208
Development projects, 6, 125
    social, 155
    socio-economic, 155
Developmentalist approach, 226
Dietary diversification, 62
Domestication, 70, 72, 74-78, 82, 84
    animal, 70
Donor countries, 9, 14, 52, 134
Droughts, 1, 3, 31, 33, 62, 65, 117-18, 123-24, 127, 132, 178-80, 187, 189, 200-03, 210
Dry seasons, 96

Early farming villages, 74-75
Ecological crisis, 118
Economic agendas, 65
Economic apartheid, 185
Economic crisis, 20, 61, 181, 185
Economic hardships, 183
Economic indicators, 13, 142
Economic liberalization, 61
Economic policies, 14, 20
Economic shocks, 31, 34
Economies
    global, 2, 15, 17, 25
    industrialized, 140
    informal, 139
    market, 216, 218, 224
Environmental refugees, 117-20, 129-32
Epidemic, 60, 142, 162-64, 166-71, 173
Export crops, 4, 187, 221
External determinants, 36

Farmers, 1, 35, 64, 70, 76, 124, 128-29, 179, 187, 201
    small-holder, 42, 48-49, 129
    small scale, 187-88
    white, 180-81
Farming, 41, 70, 75, 77, 80-81, 127
Federal systems, 153-54, 197, 199
Fertile Crescent, 76, 79
Fishing, 221
Food aid, 25, 33, 53, 126, 183, 196
Food and Agricultural Organisation, 46, 50, 59-60, 93, 96, 200, 205
Food and Agricultural Policy, 34
Food chain, 48
Food crisis, 37, 50
Food deficiency, 202-03
Food emergencies, 31, 50
Food insecurity, 13, 33, 45, 49-50, 52, 55, 58, 62, 64-65, 126, 165, 203, 210, 221
    chronic, 46
    transitory, 46
Food production, 33, 37, 39, 45-46, 48, 59-60, 77, 82, 84, 165, 188, 210
    domestic, 36, 39
    neglected, 37
    policies, 32
    preceded, 82
    sustainable, 210
    trends, 32
Food security, 1, 45-46, 48-50, 54, 57-62, 65-66, 177, 188, 196, 203, 206, 210
    integrated, 196, 203
    long-term household, 54
    regional, 189
Food storage, 72, 77
Food-surplus continent, 17
Foreign investment, 5, 20, 170
Fuel shortages, 180-81

G-7 richest countries, 14
German Agro Action, 199
Global fund, 171

HIV, 7, 13, 19-20, 60, 138, 141, 147, 162-74, 187, 208 *see also* AIDS
Homelands, 117, 131

Hyperinflation, 177-78

ILO, 139, 141-42, 148
Individualism, 228
Industrial centre, 179
Inflation, 1, 176-78, 181, 183, 189-90, 192-93
Institutional capacity, 21, 26, 145, 154
Inter-Academy Council, 58-59
International Federation of Red Cross and Red Crescent Societies, 122
International Fund for Agricultural Development, 54
International lending agencies, 214
International Monetary Fund, 177, 181, 183, 190, 224
Intra-African trade, 53

Jerrycans, 99-100

Kalahari desert, 75

Labour availability, 38-39, 41
Labour markets, 138, 140-42, 145, 148
Land reform, 177, 185-86, 188, 193
Least developed countries, 17

Malnourished people, 46, 58
Malnutrition, 46, 48, 58, 60, 62, 66, 120, 127
Micro-enterprises, 206, 208
Micro-finance activities, 208
Millennium Development Goals, 14, 50, 65, 133, 138, 140
Modernization theory, 215, 218-19, 224-25

NAM countries, 222
NEPAD, 10, 53
Nile River Valley, 79
Non-agricultural activities, 143, 210
Nutritious kernels, 71-72

Organisation for Economic Co-operation and Developments, 6, 12-13, 17, 19
Organization of African Union, 224
Oromo Self-Help Organization, 196, 199
OSHO, 196, 199-203, 206-10

Pastoralists, 123-24
Plantation systems, 81
Policy reform agendas, 32, 34-36
Political apartheid, 185
Potable water, 101
Poverty
chronic, 25, 58
extreme, 14, 126, 164
rural, 41, 133
severity of, 126-27
vicious circles of, 133, 148
Pre-colonial Africa, 221
Press freedom, 10
Primary centres of domestication, 72
Project level indicators, 204
Promotional agencies, 88

Rain-fed agricultural land, 124-25
Rainwater harvesting, 88-89, 207
relevance of, 88
Red Sea, 80, 120
Refugees, 120, 125, 129-31, 133-34
Regional economic communities, 53
Regional economic growth, 141
Regional nutrition strategy, 54
Regional planning and development, 153
Rift Valley, 111, 202
River Nile, 121
Road construction activities, 203
Rural Africa, 88-89
Rural clinics, 186-87

Sedentism, 78, 84
Self-sufficiency, 24, 32-33
Sen, Amartya, 25
Slaughter, 71-72
Social indicators, 56
Socialism, 23, 215, 217
Socialist approach, 24

Socio-economic fabric, 226
Strategic commodities, 53
Structural adjustment, 34, 188, 224
Structural adjustment programmes, 20, 34, 36, 61, 177
Subsistence farmers, 4, 201, 203
Survivalist-oriented activities, 142
Sustainable development, 1, 13, 113, 132, 134

Third World, 213-15
Tractorization, 40-41
Trading partner countries, 22
Transmitted disease, 169
Tribalism, 221, 226-27
Tropical climate, 6
Tropical countries, 6

UNAIDS, 162-63, 167-68
UNEP, 118, 121, 124-25, 132
UNHCR, 125, 130, 134

Volcanic activities, 111
Vulnerability, 16, 25, 210

Water quality, 94, 96, 103
Water resources management, 65
Water sources, 88-90, 92-93, 98, 100, 103, 108
  back-up, 91
  limited, 75
  nearest, 90
  safe, 13
  traditional, 93-94
Water table, 89, 123
Weeding, 40, 71
Wet seasons, 6, 94, 96, 108-09
World Bank, 19, 34, 36, 58, 168, 224
World Development Report, 26
World Food Programme, 183
World Food Summit, 53
World Trade Organization, 2
World's refugees, 36

Zimbabwean Crisis, 177, 185, 193
Zonal administrations, 155-56